MICROSOFT
Windows 2000
Introductory Concepts and Techniques

Gary B. Shelly
Thomas J. Cashman
Steven G. Forsythe

COURSE TECHNOLOGY
ONE MAIN STREET
CAMBRIDGE MA 02142

Thomson Learning™

SHELLY
CASHMAN
SERIES®

Australia • Canada • Denmark • Japan • Mexico • New Zealand • Philippines
Puerto Rico • Singapore • South Africa • Spain • United Kingdom • United States

Asia (excluding Japan)
Thomson Learning
60 Albert Street, #15-01
Albert Complex
Singapore 189969

Japan
Thomson Learning
Palaceside Building 5F
1-1-1 Hitotsubashi, Chiyoda-ku
Tokyo 100 0003 Japan

Australia/New Zealand
Nelson/Thomson Learning
102 Dodds Street
South Melbourne, Victoria 3205
Australia

Latin America
Thomson Learning
Seneca, 53
Colonia Polanco
11560 Mexico D.F. Mexico

South Africa
Thomson Learning
Zonnebloem Building,
Constantia Square
526 Sixteenth Road
P.O. Box 2459
Halfway House, 1685
South Africa

Canada
Nelson/Thomson Learning
1120 Birchmount Road
Scarborough, Ontario
Canada M1K 5G4

UK/Europe/Middle East
Thomson Learning
Berkshire House
168-173 High Holborn
London, WC1V 7AA United Kingdom

Spain
Thomson Learning
Calle Magallanes, 25
28015-MADRID
ESPANA

TRADEMARKS
Course Technology and the Open Book logo are registered trademarks and CourseKits is a trademark of Course Technology.

SHELLY CASHMAN SERIES® and **Custom Edition**® are trademarks of Thomson Learning. Some of the product names and company names used in this book have been used for identification purposes only and may be trademarks or registered trademarks of their respective manufacturers and sellers. Thomson Learning and Course Technology disclaim any affiliation, association, or connection with, or sponsorship or endorsement by, such owners.

DISCLAIMER
Course Technology reserves the right to revise this publication and make changes from time to time in its content without notice.

PHOTO CREDITS: *Project 1, pages WIN 1.4-5* Mainframe, man, Bill Gates, and computer, Courtesy of Image Club; *Project 2, pages WIN 2.2-3* Background circuit board, Courtesy of PhotoDisc, Inc.; Bill Gates, Courtesy of Microsoft Corporation; *Project 3, pages WIN 3.2-3* Moon, Earth, man on the Moon with flag, the Space Shuttle launch, Mars, Mars terrain, Courtesy of NASA; compass, Courtesy of PhotoDisc, Inc.; background map, Courtesy of Map Art by Cartesia Software.

ISBN 0-7895-4468-7

1 2 3 4 5 6 7 8 9 10   BC   04 03 02 01 00

MICROSOFT
Windows 2000
Introductory Concepts and Techniques

C O N T E N T S

Preface

The Shelly Cashman Series® offers the finest textbooks in computer education. The *Microsoft Windows 2000* books continue with the innovation, quality, and reliability consistent with this series. We are proud that our *Microsoft Windows 3.1*, *Microsoft Windows 95*, and *Microsoft Windows 98* books were used by more schools and more students than any other series in textbook publishing.

In our *Microsoft Windows 2000* books, you will find an educationally sound and easy-to-follow pedagogy that combines a step-by-step approach with corresponding screens. The Other Ways and More About features offer in-depth knowledge of Windows 2000. The project openers provide a fascinating perspective on the subject covered in the project. The Shelly Cashman Series *Microsoft Windows 2000* textbooks will make your computer applications class exciting and dynamic and one that your students will remember as one of their better educational experiences.

Objectives of This Textbook

Microsoft Windows 2000: Introductory Concepts and Techniques is intended for a one-unit course that covers Windows 2000. No computer experience is assumed. The objectives of this book are:

- To teach the fundamentals and skills necessary to adequately use Windows 2000
- To provide a knowledge base for Windows 2000 upon which students can build
- To expose students to real-world examples and procedures that will prepare them to be skilled users of Windows 2000
- To encourage independent study and help those who are working alone in a distance education environment

When students complete the course using this textbook, they will have a basic knowledge and understanding of Windows 2000.

The Shelly Cashman Approach

Features of the Shelly Cashman Series *Microsoft Windows 2000* books include:

- **Project Orientation:** Related topics are presented using a project orientation that establishes a strong foundation on which students can confidently learn more advanced topics.
- **Screen-by-Screen, Step-by-Step Instructions:** Each task required to complete a project is identified throughout the development of the project. Then, steps to accomplish the task are specified and are accompanied by screens.
- **Thoroughly Tested Projects:** Every screen in the textbook is correct because it is produced by the author only after performing a step, which results in unprecedented quality.
- **Two-Page Project Openers:** Each project begins with a two-page opener that sets the tone for the project by describing an interesting aspect of Windows 2000.
- **Other Ways Boxes for Reference:** Microsoft Windows 2000 provides a variety of ways to carry out a given task. The Other Ways boxes displayed at the end of most of the step-by-step sequences specify the other ways to do the task completed in the steps. Thus, the steps and the Other Ways box make a comprehensive reference unit.
- **More About Feature:** These marginal annotations provide background information about the topics covered, adding interest and depth to learning.

Other Ways

1. Double-click My Computer icon, right-drag folder icon to 3½ Floppy (A:) icon in My Computer window, click Copy Here
2. Double-click My Computer icon, drag folder icon to 3½ Floppy (A:) icon
3. Right-click the folder icon, click Copy, double-click My Computer icon, right-click 3½ Floppy (A:) icon, click Paste

More About

The Windows 2000 Desktop

The Windows 98 and Windows 2000 desktops are similar. Two features introduced in Windows 98, the Active Desktop and Quick Launch toolbar, remain part of the Windows 2000 desktop. The much-lauded Channel bar, designed to allow quick access to the Internet from the Windows 98 desktop, was a bomb and has been eliminated.

v

Organization of This Textbook

Microsoft Windows 2000: Introductory Concepts and Techniques provides detailed instruction on how to use Windows 2000. The material is divided into three projects:

Project 1 – Fundamentals of Using Microsoft Windows 2000 Professional In Project 1, students learn about user interfaces and Microsoft Windows 2000. Topics include launching Microsoft Windows 2000; mouse operations; maximizing and minimizing windows; moving, sizing, and scrolling windows; launching an application program; using Windows Help; and shutting down Windows 2000.

Project 2 – Working on the Windows 2000 Desktop In Project 2, students work on the Windows 2000 desktop. Topics include creating a document on the desktop by launching an application; creating and naming a document on the desktop; opening, saving, printing, and closing a document on the desktop; storing documents in a folder on the desktop; opening, modifying, and printing documents within a folder; copying a folder onto a disk; creating shortcuts on the Start menu and desktop; sharing a folder; deleting documents, shortcuts, and folders; turning on the Active Desktop™; adding active content; and using Web Help to obtain online Help.

Project 3 – File, Document, and Folder Management and Windows 2000 Explorer In Project 3, students manage windows and files on the desktop and learn to use Windows 2000 Explorer. Topics include using the My Computer window; displaying drive and folder contents; opening a document and launching an application program from a window; cascading and tiling open windows; Windows 2000 Explorer; displaying files, folders, and drive and folder contents in Explorer; expanding a drive or folder; launching an application from Explorer; copying, moving, renaming, and deleting files and folders in Explorer; displaying object properties; finding files and folders; using the Run command; viewing and searching for computers and shared resources on a network; and mapping a drive letter to a computer resource.

End-of-Project Student Activities

A notable strength of the Shelly Cashman Series *Microsoft Windows 2000* textbooks is the extensive student activities at the end of each project. Well-structured student activities can make the difference between students merely participating in a class and students retaining the information they learn. These activities include:

- **What You Should Know** A listing of the tasks completed within a project together with the pages where the step-by-step, screen-by-screen explanations appear. This section provides a perfect study review for students.

- **Test Your Knowledge** Four activities designed to determine students' understanding of the material in the project. Included are true/false questions, multiple-choice questions, and two other unique activities.

- **Use Help** Users of Windows 2000 must know how to use Help. This book contains extensive Help activities. These exercises alone distinguish the Shelly Cashman Series from any other set of Windows 2000 instructional materials.

- **In the Lab** These assignments require students to make use of the knowledge gained in the project to solve problems on a computer.

- **Cases and Places** Unique case studies allow students to apply their knowledge to real-world situations. These case studies provide subjects for research papers based on information gained from a resource such as the Internet.

Shelly Cashman Series Teaching Tools

A comprehensive set of Teaching Tools accompanies this textbook in the form of a CD-ROM. The CD-ROM includes the Instructor's Manual and other teaching and testing aids. The CD-ROM (ISBN 0-7895-4469-5) is available through your Course Technology representative or by calling one of the following telephone numbers: Colleges and Universities, 1-800-648-7450; High Schools, 1-800-824-5179; Career Colleges, 1-800-477-3692; Canada, 1-800-268-2222; and Corporations and Government Agencies, 1-800-340-7450. The contents of the CD-ROM follow.

- **Instructor's Manual** The Instructor's Manual is made up of Microsoft Word files that include lecture notes, solutions to laboratory assignments, and a large test bank. The files allow you to modify the lecture notes or generate quizzes and exams from the test bank using your own word processing software. Where appropriate, solutions to laboratory assignments are embedded as icons.

- **Figures in the Book** Illustrations for every screen in the textbook are available. Use this ancillary to create a slide show from the illustrations for lecture or to print transparencies for use in lecture with an overhead projector.

- **Course Test Manager** Course Test Manager is a powerful testing and assessment package that enables instructors to create and print tests from the large test bank. Instructors with access to a networked computer lab (LAN) can administer, grade, and track tests online.

- **Interactive Labs** Eighteen hands-on interactive labs solidify and reinforce computer concepts.

- **WebCT Content** This ancillary includes book-related content that can be uploaded to your institution's WebCT site. The content includes a sample syllabus, practice tests, a bank of test questions, and more.

Acknowledgments

The Shelly Cashman Series would not be the leading computer education series without the contributions of outstanding publishing professionals. First, and foremost, among them is Becky Herrington, director of production and designer. She is the heart and soul of the Shelly Cashman Series, and it is only through her leadership, dedication, and tireless efforts that superior products are made possible. Becky created and produced the award-winning Windows series of books.

Under Becky's direction, the following individuals made significant contributions to these books: Doug Cowley, production manager; Ginny Harvey, series specialist and developmental editor; Ken Russo, senior Web designer; Mike Bodnar, associate production manager; Stephanie Nance, graphic artist and cover designer; Mark Norton, Web designer; Meena Mohtadi, production editor; Chris Schneider, Hector Arvizu, and Kathy Mayers, graphic artists; Jeanne Black and Betty Hopkins, Quark experts; Nancy Lamm, copyeditor; and Marilyn Martin proofreader.

Special thanks go to Richard Keaveny, managing editor; Jim Quasney, series consulting editor; Lora Wade, product manager; Erin Bennett, associate product manager; Francis Schurgot, Web product manager; Marc Ouellette, associate Web product manager; Rajika Gupta, marketing manager; and Erin Runyon, editorial assistant.

Gary B. Shelly
Thomas J. Cashman
Steven G. Forsythe

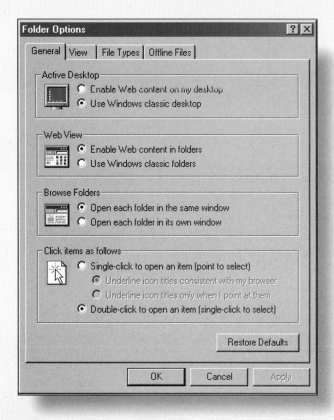

FIGURE 1

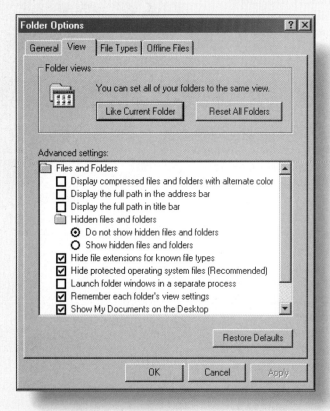

FIGURE 2

Instructions for Restoring the Default Folder Options Settings

The projects and assignments in this textbook are presented using the default folder options settings, as chosen by Microsoft Corporation. To ensure your success in completing the projects and assignments, you must install the Windows 2000 Professional operating system on your computer system and restore the folder options settings. The following steps illustrate how to restore the default folder options settings.

1. Double-click the My Computer icon on the desktop.
2. Click Tools on the My Computer menu bar.
3. Click the Folder Options command on the Tools menu to display the Folder Options dialog box (Figure 1).
4. If necessary, click the General tab in the Folder Options dialog box to display the General sheet.
5. On a piece of paper, write down the name of each folder option that is selected in the General sheet in the Folder Options dialog box.
6. Click the Restore Defaults button in the General sheet.
7. Click the View tab to display the View sheet (Figure 2).
8. On a piece of paper, write down the name of each advanced setting that is selected in the View sheet in the Folder Options dialog box.
9. Click the Restore Defaults button in the View sheet.
10. Click the OK button in the Folder Options dialog box.

As a result of restoring the default folder option settings, you can perform the steps and assignments in each project of this book. If, after finishing the steps and assignments, you must restore the folder options to their original settings, perform steps 1 through 4 above, click the option button of each setting you wrote down in step 5, perform step 7 above, click the check box and option button of each setting you wrote down in step 8, and then perform step 10.

Microsoft Windows 2000

PROJECT 1

Fundamentals of Using Microsoft Windows 2000 Professional

You will have mastered the material in this project when you can:

OBJECTIVES

- Describe the Microsoft Windows 2000 operating system family
- Explain operating system, server, workstation, and user interface
- Identify the objects on the Microsoft Windows 2000 desktop
- Perform the basic mouse operations: point, click, right-click, double-click, drag, and right-drag
- Open, minimize, maximize, restore, and close a Windows 2000 window
- Move and size a window on the Windows 2000 desktop
- Scroll in a window
- Understand keyboard shortcut notation
- Launch an application program
- Use Windows 2000 Help
- Shut down Windows 2000

Windows 2000

Leads the Way in the New Millennium

In the twenty-first century, the Microsoft Windows 2000 operating system leads the way with its advanced and improved software technology, making it easier, more cost-effective, and enjoyable for people and businesses to use computers. Microsoft Corporation under the leadership of Bill Gates has been a continuous source of innovative products.

Bill Gates's computing efforts began when he was in grade school, when he and classmate, Paul Allen, learned the BASIC programming language from a manual and programmed a mainframe computer using a Teletype terminal they purchased with the proceeds from a rummage sale. In high school, Gates and Allen had a thirst for more computing power. They wrote custom programs for local businesses during the summer and split their $5,000 salaries between cash and computer time. They also debugged software problems at local businesses in return for computer use.

In Gates's sophomore year, one of his teachers asked him to teach his computer skills to his classmates. In 1972, Gates and Allen read an article in *Electronics* magazine about Intel's first microprocessor chip. They requested a manual from Intel, developed a device that experimented with pushing the chip to its limits, and formed the Traf-O-Data company; an endeavor that ultimately would lead to the formation of something much larger.

In 1973, Gates entered Harvard and Allen landed a programming job with Honeywell.

They continued to communicate and scheme about the power of computers when, in 1975, the Altair 8800 computer showed up on the cover of *Popular Electronics*. This computer was about the size of the Traf-O-Data device and contained a new Intel computer chip. At that point, they knew they were going into business. Gates left Harvard and Allen left Honeywell

When they formed Microsoft in 1975, the company had three programmers, one product, and revenues of $16,000. The founders had no business plan, no capital, and no financial backing, but they did have a product – a form of the BASIC programming language tailored for the first microcomputer.

In 1980, IBM approached Microsoft and asked the company to provide an operating system for its new IBM personal computer. The deadline? Three months. Gates purchased the core of a suitable operating system, dubbed Q-DOS (Quick and Dirty Operating System). Microsoft's version, MS-DOS, would become the international standard for IBM and IBM-compatible personal computers. Riding the meteoric rise in sales of IBM-compatible computers and attendant sales of MS-DOS, Microsoft continued to improve its software stream of revisions. At a significant branch of the family tree, Windows made it debut, providing an intuitive graphical user interface (GUI). Similarly, Windows 95, Windows 98, and Windows NT provided further advances.

The Microsoft Windows 2000 operating system family expands the possibilities even further with the Windows 2000 Server, Windows 2000 Advanced Server, and Windows 2000 Data Center designed for use on a server in a computer network. The Windows 2000 Professional can be used on computer workstations and portable computers. As you will learn as you complete the projects in this book, you can control the computer and communicate with other computers on a network. In the networked society of the new millennium, Windows 2000 leads the way.

Microsoft Windows 2000

Fundamentals of Using Microsoft Windows 2000 Professional

PROJECT 1

C A S E   P E R S P E C T I V E

After weeks of planning, your organization finally installed Microsoft Windows 2000 Advanced Server edition on their server and Microsoft Windows 2000 Professional on all workstations. As the computer trainer for the upcoming in-house seminar, you realize you should know more about Microsoft Windows 2000 Professional but have had little time to learn about it. Since installing Windows 2000 Professional, many employees have come to you with questions. You have taken the time to answer their questions by sitting down with them at their computers and searching for the answers using the Microsoft Help feature.

From their questions, you determine that you should customize the seminar to cover the basics of Windows 2000 Professional, including basic mouse operations, working with windows, launching an application, and searching for answers to their questions using Windows 2000 Help. Your goal is to become familiar with Microsoft Windows 2000 Professional in order to teach the seminar effectively to participants.

Introduction

An **operating system** is the set of computer instructions, called a computer program, that controls the allocation of computer hardware such as memory, disk devices, printers, and CD-ROM and DVD drives, and provides the capability for you to communicate with the computer. The most popular and widely used operating system for personal computers is **Microsoft Windows**. The most powerful of the Microsoft Windows operating systems, **Microsoft Windows 2000**, is designed for business users.

Microsoft Windows 2000 Operating System Family

The Microsoft Windows 2000 family of operating systems consists of the Microsoft Windows 2000 Server, Microsoft Windows 2000 Advanced Server, Microsoft Windows 2000 Data Center, and Microsoft Windows 2000 Professional.

The Microsoft Windows 2000 Server, Microsoft Windows 2000 Advanced Server, and Microsoft Windows 2000 Data Center operating systems are designed for use on a server in a computer network. A **server** is a computer that controls access to the hardware and software on a network and provides a centralized storage area for programs, data, and information. The complexity of the network determines which operating system runs on the server. Figure 1-1 illustrates a simple computer network consisting of a server, three computers (called workstations), and a laser printer connected to the server (Figure 1-1).

The choice of which operating system to use on a server depends on the requirements of an organization and the complexity of its computer network. The **Microsoft Windows 2000 Server edition** is an operating system ideal for small to

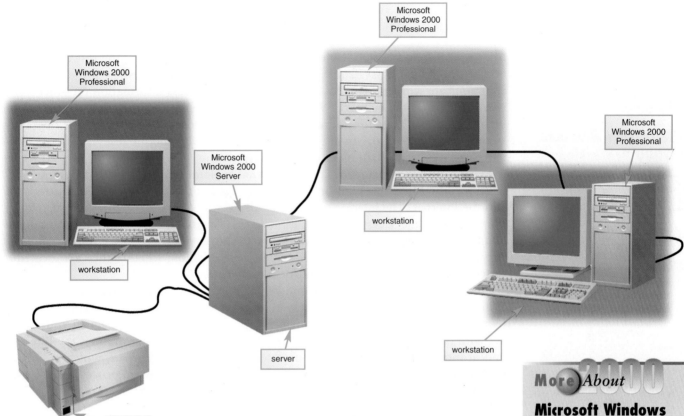

Microsoft Windows 2000 Professional

Microsoft Windows 2000 Professional

Microsoft Windows 2000 Professional

Microsoft Windows 2000 Server

workstation

workstation

workstation

server

laser printer

FIGURE 1-1

medium-sized organizations with numerous workgroups and branch offices. The **Microsoft Windows 2000 Advanced Server edition** is a more powerful mid-range operating system for use with larger organizations that run demanding applications such as e-commerce, have corporate Internet and intranet sites, and perform database-intensive work. Microsoft Windows 2000 Advanced Server edition improves the performance of the network by allowing the server to run up to four processors and use larger amounts of memory than the Microsoft Windows 2000 Server edition.

The **Microsoft Windows 2000 Data Center edition** is the most powerful operating system produced by Microsoft and meets the needs of businesses and Internet Service Provider (ISP) organizations with large scale Internet and intranet operations. This edition allows the server to run up to 16 processors. Because the network illustrated in Figure 1-1 is relatively simple, the Microsoft Windows 2000 Server operating system is chosen to run on the server.

Microsoft Windows 2000 Professional is the operating system designed for use on computer workstations and portable computers. A **workstation** is a computer connected to a server. In Figure 1-1, the operating system installed on the three workstations is Microsoft Windows 2000 Professional.

This book demonstrates how to use Microsoft Windows 2000 Professional to control the computer and communicate with other computers on a network. In Project 1, you will learn about Windows 2000 and how to use the Windows 2000 user interface.

More About

Microsoft Windows 2000

Microsoft Windows 2000 combines the best business features of Windows 98 with the strengths of Windows NT 4.0. Windows 98, designed for use on personal computers, is the most popular operating system for personal computers. Windows NT 4.0, designed for use on a computer network, is the most widely used version of Windows NT.

More About

Microsoft Windows 2000

A vast amount of information about Microsoft Windows 2000 is available on the Internet. For additional information about Microsoft Windows 2000, launch the Internet Explorer browser (see pages WIN 1.35 thru WIN 1.37), type www.scsite.com/win2000/more.htm in the Address box in the Microsoft Internet Explorer window, and then press the enter key.

Microsoft Windows 2000 Professional

Microsoft Windows 2000 Professional (called **Windows 2000** for the rest of this book) is an operating system that performs every function necessary for you to communicate with and control your computer and access information on other workstations on the network. Windows 2000 is called a **32-bit operating system** because it uses 32 bits for addressing and other purposes, which means the operating system can address more than four gigabytes of RAM (random-access memory) and perform tasks faster than older operating systems.

Windows 2000 includes **Microsoft Internet Explorer (IE)**, a software program developed by Microsoft Corporation, that integrates the Windows 2000 desktop and the Internet. The **Internet** is a worldwide group of connected computer networks that allows public access to information on thousands of subjects and gives users the ability to send messages and obtain products and services. Internet Explorer allows you to work with programs and files in a similar fashion, whether they are located on your computer, a local network, or the Internet.

Windows 2000 is easy to use and can be customized to fit individual needs. Windows 2000 simplifies the process of working with documents and applications by transferring data between documents, organizing the manner in which you interact with the computer, and using the computer to access information on the Internet and/or intranet. Windows 2000 is used to run **application programs**, which are programs that perform an application-related function such as word processing. To use the application programs that can be executed under Windows 2000, you must know about the Windows 2000 user interface.

What Is a User Interface?

A **user interface** is the combination of hardware and software that you use to communicate with and control the computer. Through the user interface, you are able to make selections on the computer, request information from the computer, and respond to messages displayed by the computer. Thus, a user interface provides the means for dialogue between you and the computer.

Hardware and software together form the user interface. Among the hardware devices associated with a user interface are the monitor, keyboard, and mouse (Figure 1-2). The **monitor** displays messages and provides information. You respond by entering data in the form of a command or other response using the **keyboard** or **mouse**. Among the responses available to you are responses that specify which application program to run, what document to open, when to print, and where to store data for future use.

The computer software associated with the user interface consists of the programs that engage you in dialogue (Figure 1-2). The computer software determines the messages you receive, the manner in which you should respond, and the actions that occur based on your responses.

The goal of an effective user interface is to be **user friendly**, which means the software can be used easily by individuals with limited training. Research studies have indicated that the use of graphics can play an important role in aiding users to interact effectively with a computer. A **graphical user interface**, or **GUI** (pronounced gooey), is a user interface that displays graphics in addition to text when it communicates with the user.

Microsoft Windows 2000 Professional

For additional information about Windows 2000 Professional, launch the Internet Explorer browser (see pages WIN 1.35 thru WIN 1.37), type www.scsite.com/ win2000/more.htm in the Address box in the Microsoft Internet Explorer window, and then press the ENTER key.

The Windows 2000 Interface

Some older interfaces, called command-line interfaces, required that you type keywords (special words, phrases, or codes the computer understands) or press special keys on the keyboard to communicate with the interface. Today, graphical user interfaces incorporate colorful graphics, use of the mouse, and Web browser-like features, making today's interfaces user-friendly.

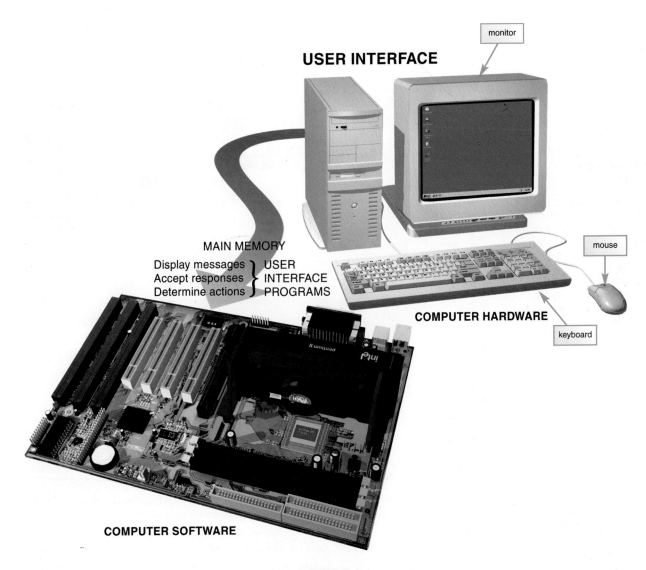

USER INTERFACE

monitor

MAIN MEMORY
Display messages } USER
Accept responses } INTERFACE
Determine actions } PROGRAMS

mouse

COMPUTER HARDWARE

keyboard

COMPUTER SOFTWARE

FIGURE 1-2

The Windows 2000 graphical user interface was designed carefully to be easier to set up, simpler to learn, faster and more powerful, and better integrated with the Internet than previous versions of Microsoft Windows.

Launching Microsoft Windows 2000

When you turn on the computer, an introductory screen containing the words, Microsoft Windows 2000 Professional, and the Please Wait... screen display momentarily followed by the Welcome to Windows dialog box (Figure 1-3 on the next page). A **dialog box** displays whenever Windows 2000 needs to supply information to you or wants you to enter information or select among several options. The **title bar**, which is at the top of the dialog box and blue in color, identifies the name of the dialog box (Welcome to Windows). The Welcome to Windows dialog box displays on a blue background and contains the Windows logo, title (Microsoft Windows 2000 Professional Built on NT Technology), keyboard icon, instructions (Press Ctrl-Alt-Delete to begin.), a message, and the Help link.

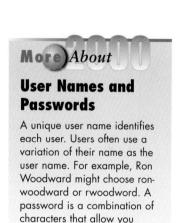

More About 2000

User Names and Passwords

A unique user name identifies each user. Users often use a variation of their name as the user name. For example, Ron Woodward might choose ron-woodward or rwoodword. A password is a combination of characters that allow you access to certain computer resources on the network. Passwords should be kept confidential.

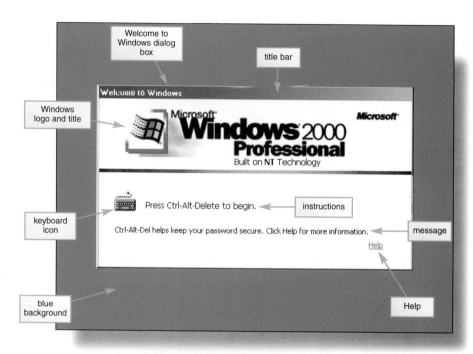

FIGURE 1-3

Holding down the CTRL key and pressing the ALT and DELETE keys simultaneously will remove the Welcome to Windows dialog box and display the Log On to Windows dialog box (Figure 1-4). The Log On to Windows dialog box contains the User name and Password text boxes, Log on to box, Log on using dial-up connection check box, and four command buttons (OK, Cancel, Shutdown, and Options). A **text box** is a rectangular area in which you can enter text. Currently, the user name (Brad Wilson) displays in the User name text box, a series of asterisks (*****) displays in the Password text box to hide the password entered by the user, and the

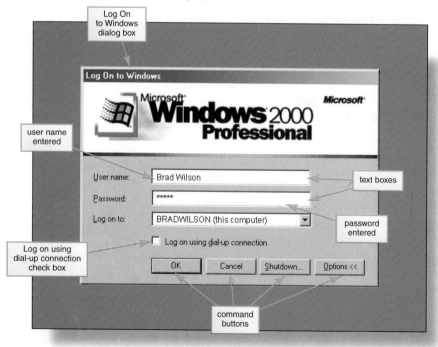

FIGURE 1-4

computer name, BRADWILSON (this computer), displays in the Log on to box. The **check box** represents an option to log on using an established dial-up Internet connection. The **command buttons** allow you to perform different operations, such as accepting the user name and password or displaying additional options. If you do not know your user name or password, ask your instructor.

Entering your user name in the User name text box and your password in the Password text box and then clicking the OK button will clear the screen and allow several items to display on a background called the **desktop**. The default color of the desktop background is green, but your computer may display a different color.

The items on the desktop in Figure 1-5 include five icons and their names on the left side of the desktop and the taskbar at the bottom of the desktop. Using the five **icons**, you can store documents in one location (**My Documents**), view the contents of the computer (**My Computer**), work with other computers connected to the computer (**My Network Places**), discard unneeded objects (**Recycle Bin**), and browse Web pages on the Internet (**Internet Explorer**). Your computer's desktop may contain more, fewer, or different icons because you can customize the desktop of the computer.

The **taskbar** shown at the bottom of the screen in Figure 1-5 contains the Start button, Quick Launch toolbar, taskbar button area, and status area. The **Start button** allows you to launch a program quickly, find or open a document, change the computer's settings, shut down the computer, and perform many more tasks. The **Quick Launch toolbar** contains three icons. The first icon allows you to view an uncluttered desktop at any time (**Show Desktop**). The second icon launches Internet Explorer (**Launch Internet Explorer Browser**). The third icon launches Outlook Express (**Launch Outlook Express**).

More About

The Windows 2000 Desktop

The Windows 98 and Windows 2000 desktops are similar. Two features introduced in Windows 98, the Active Desktop and Quick Launch toolbar, remain part of the Windows 2000 desktop. The much-lauded Channel bar, designed to allow quick access to the Internet from the Windows 98 desktop, was a bomb and has been eliminated.

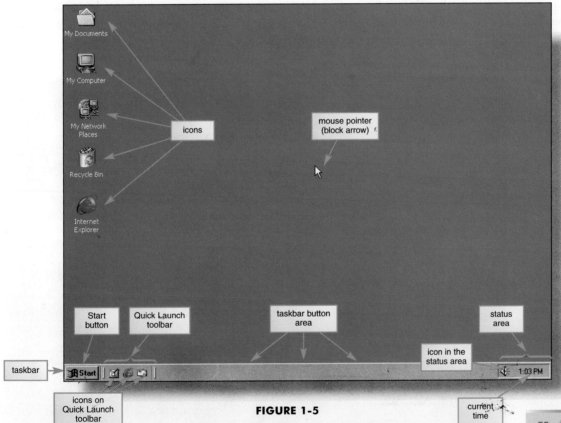

FIGURE 1-5

The **taskbar button area** contains buttons to indicate which windows are open on the desktop. In Figure 1-5, no windows display on the desktop and no buttons display in the taskbar button area. The **status area** contains a **speaker icon** to adjust the computer's volume level. The status area also displays the current time (1:03 PM). The status area on your desktop may contain more, fewer, or some different icons because the contents of the status area can change.

Nearly every item on the Windows 2000 desktop is considered an object. Even the desktop itself is an object. Every **object** has properties. The **properties** of an object are unique to that specific object and may affect what can be done to the object or

More About

The Contents of the Desktop

Because Windows 2000 can be easily customized, your desktop may not resemble the desktop in Figure 1-5. For example, the icon titles on the desktop may be underlined or objects not shown in Figure 1-5 may display on your desktop. If this is the case, contact your instructor to change the desktop.

what the object does. For example, the properties of an object may be the color of the object, such as the color of the desktop. You will learn more about properties in Project 3 of this book.

In the middle of the desktop is the mouse pointer. On the desktop, the **mouse pointer** is the shape of a block arrow. The mouse pointer allows you to point to objects on the desktop and may change shape when it points to different objects. A shadow may display behind the mouse pointer to make the mouse pointer display in a three-dimensional form.

The Getting Started with Windows 2000 Window

The Getting Started with Windows 2000 window that may display on the desktop when you launch Windows 2000 is shown in Figure 1-6. The title bar (dark blue) contains the Windows icon, identifies the name of the window (Getting Started with Windows 2000), and contains the Close button, which you can use to close the window. The **Getting Started with Windows 2000 button** in the taskbar button area indicates the Getting Started with Windows 2000 window displays on the desktop. The ellipsis on the button indicates the button name (Getting Started with Windows 2000) is abbreviated on the button.

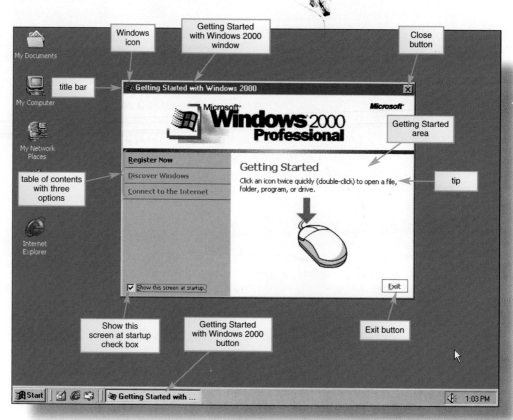

FIGURE 1-6

In the Getting Started with Windows 2000 window, a table of contents containing three options (Register Now, Discover Windows, and Connect to the Internet) and the Getting Started area containing constantly changing helpful tips about Windows 2000 display. The options in the table of contents allow you to perform different tasks such as registering the Windows 2000 operating system, learning Windows 2000 using the Discover Windows 2000 tour, and connecting to the

Internet. Pointing to an option in the table of contents replaces the contents of the Getting Started area with an explanation of the option. Clicking an option begins the task associated with the option.

A check box containing a check mark displays below the table of contents. The check mark in the check box represents an option to display the Getting Started with Windows 2000 window each time you launch Windows 2000. The **Exit button** at the bottom of the Getting Started area closes the window.

Closing the Getting Started with Windows 2000 Window

As noted, the Getting Started with Windows 2000 window may display when you launch Windows 2000. If the Getting Started with Windows 2000 window does display on the desktop, normally you should close it before beginning any other operations using Windows 2000. To close the window, complete the following step.

TO CLOSE THE GETTING STARTED WITH WINDOWS 2000 WINDOW

 Hold down the ALT key on the keyboard, press the F4 key on the keyboard, and then release the ALT key.

The Getting Started with Windows 2000 window closes and the desktop displays as shown in Figure 1-5 on page WIN 1.11.

The Desktop as a Work Area

The Windows 2000 desktop and the objects on the desktop emulate a work area in an office. You may think of the Windows desktop as an electronic version of the top of your desk. You can move objects around on the desktop, look at them and then put them aside, and so on. In Project 1, you will learn how to interact with and communicate with the Windows 2000 desktop.

Communicating with Windows 2000

The Windows 2000 interface provides the means for dialogue between you and the computer. Part of this dialogue involves your requesting information from the computer and responding to messages displayed by the computer. You can request information and respond to messages using either a mouse or a keyboard.

Mouse Operations

A **mouse** is a pointing device used with Windows 2000 that is attached to the computer by a cable. Although not required to use Windows 2000, Windows supports the use of the **Microsoft IntelliMouse** (Figure 1-7 on the next page). The IntelliMouse contains three buttons, the primary mouse button, the secondary mouse button, and the wheel button between the primary and secondary mouse buttons. Typically, the **primary mouse button** is the left mouse button and the **secondary mouse button** is the right mouse button although Windows 2000 allows you to switch them. In this book, the left mouse button is the primary mouse button and the right mouse button is the secondary mouse button. The functions the **wheel button** and wheel perform depend on the software application being used. If the mouse connected to the computer is not an IntelliMouse, it will not have a wheel button between the primary and secondary mouse buttons.

The Mouse

The mouse, though invented in the 1960s, was not used widely until the Apple Macintosh computer became available in 1984. Even then, some highbrows called mouse users "wimps." Today, the mouse is an indispensable tool for every computer user.

Microsoft Mice

For additional information about Microsoft mice, visit the Microsoft Mouse Web Site. To visit the site, launch the Internet Explorer browser (see pages WIN 1.35 thru WIN 1.37), type www.scsite.com/ win2000/more.htm in the Address box and press the ENTER key. To purchase a mouse, click the buy now button!!!

Buttons

Buttons are an integral part of Windows 2000. When you point to them, their functions display in ToolTips. When you click them, they appear to recess on the screen to mimic what would happen if you pushed an actual button. All buttons in Windows 2000 behave in the same manner.

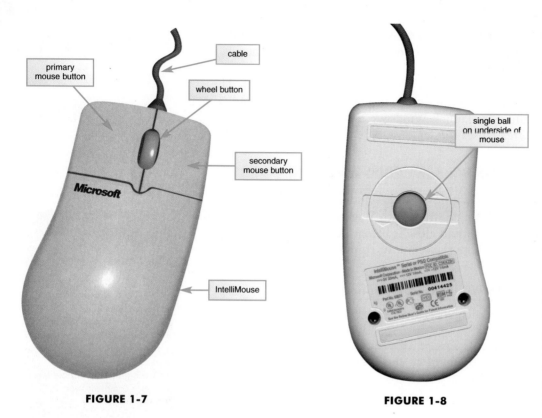

FIGURE 1-7

FIGURE 1-8

Using the mouse, you can perform the following operations: (1) point; (2) click; (3) right-click; (4) double-click; (5) drag; and (6) right-drag. These operations are demonstrated on the following pages.

Point and Click

Point means you move the mouse across a flat surface until the mouse pointer rests on the item of choice on the desktop. As you move the mouse across a flat surface, Windows 2000 senses the movement of a ball on the underside of the mouse (Figure 1-8), and the mouse pointer moves across the desktop in the same direction.

Click means you press and release the primary mouse button, which in this book is the left mouse button. In most cases, you must point to an item before you click. To become acquainted with the use of the mouse, perform the following steps to point to and click various objects on the desktop.

 To Point and Click

① **Point to the Start button on the taskbar by moving the mouse across a flat surface until the mouse pointer rests on the Start button.**

The mouse pointer on the Start button displays a ToolTip (Click here to begin) (Figure 1-9). The ToolTip, which provides instructions, displays on the desktop for approximately five seconds.

FIGURE 1-9

2 **Click the Start button by pressing and releasing the left mouse button.**

The *Start menu* displays and the Start button is recessed (Figure 1-10). A *menu* is a list of related commands. A *command* performs a specific action, such as obtaining help. Each command consists of an icon and a name. A *right arrow* follows some commands to indicate pointing to the command will display a submenu. An *ellipsis* (...) indicates more information is required to execute a command.

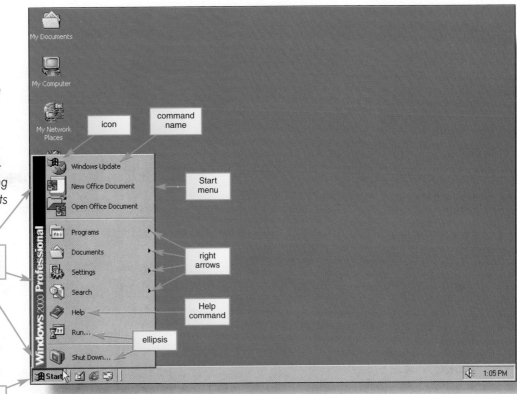

FIGURE 1-10

3 **Point to Programs on the Start menu.**

When you point to Programs, Windows 2000 highlights the Programs command on the Start menu and the *Programs submenu* displays (Figure 1-11). A *submenu* is a menu that displays when you point to a command followed by a right arrow. Whenever you point to a command on a menu, the command is highlighted.

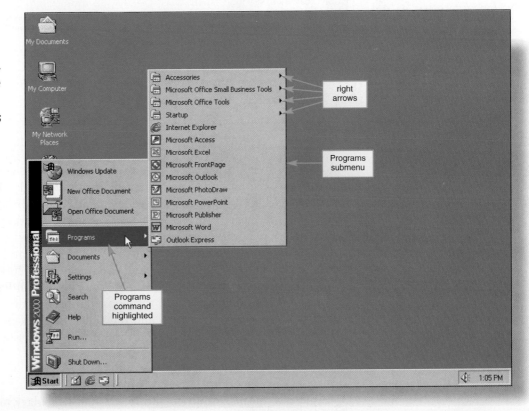

FIGURE 1-11

④ Point to an open area of the desktop (Figure 1-12).

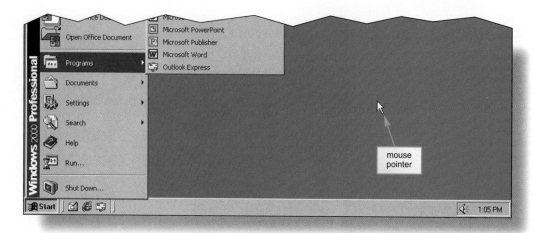

FIGURE 1-12

⑤ Click the open area of the desktop.

The Start menu and Programs submenu close (Figure 1-13). The mouse pointer points to the desktop. To close a menu anytime, click any open area of the desktop except on the menu itself. The Start button is no longer recessed.

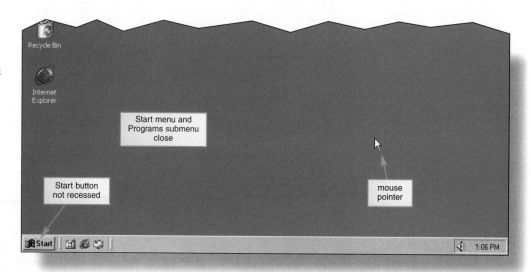

FIGURE 1-13

More About

The Right Mouse

The earliest versions of Microsoft Windows made little use of the right mouse button. In Windows 2000, the right mouse button makes it easy to display a list of commands for an object (called a shortcut menu) and to copy and move objects on the desktop.

The Start menu in Figure 1-10 on the previous page contains three sections. The top section contains commands to launch the Windows Update application (Windows Update), create or open a Microsoft Office document (New Office Document and Open Office Document); the middle section contains commands to launch an application, work with documents, customize options, and search for files or help (Programs, Documents, Settings, Search, Help, and Run); and the bottom section contains the command to shut down Windows 2000 (Shut Down).

When you click an object such as the Start button in Figure 1-10, you must point to the object before you click. In the steps that follow, the instruction that directs you to point to a particular item and then click is, Click the particular item. For example, Click the Start button means point to the Start button and then click.

Right-Click

Right-click means you press and release the secondary mouse button, which in this book is the right mouse button. As directed when using the primary mouse button for clicking an object, normally you will point to an object before you right-click it. Perform the following steps to right-click the desktop.

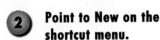 **To Right-Click**

1 **Point to an open area of the desktop and then press and release the right mouse button.**

A shortcut menu, consisting of nine commands, displays (Figure 1-14). Right-clicking an object, such as the desktop, displays a **shortcut menu** that contains commands specifically for use with that object. When a command on a menu appears dimmed, such as the Paste or Paste Shortcut commands, that command is unavailable.

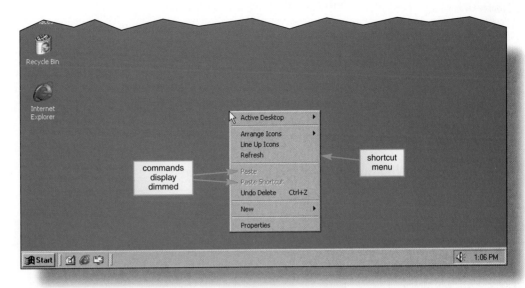

FIGURE 1-14

2 **Point to New on the shortcut menu.**

When you point to the New command, Windows 2000 highlights the New command and displays the New submenu (Figure 1-15). The number of commands on the New submenu and the actual commands that display on your computer may be different from those shown in Figure 1-15 because the New submenu lists some of the folders, application programs, and documents available on the computer.

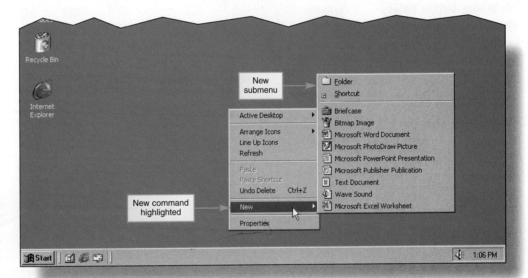

FIGURE 1-15

3 **Click an open area of the desktop to remove the shortcut menu and the New submenu.**

The shortcut menu and New submenu close (Figure 1-16). The mouse pointer remains on the desktop.

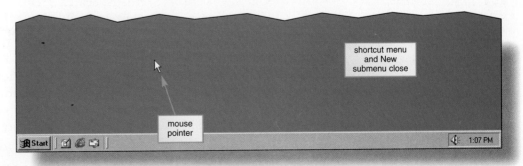

FIGURE 1-16

More About 2000

Double-Clicking

Double-clicking is the most difficult mouse skill to learn. Many people have a tendency to move the mouse before they click a second time, even when they do not want to move the mouse. You should find, however, that with a little practice, double-clicking becomes quite natural.

Whenever you right-click an object, a shortcut menu will display. As you will see, the use of shortcut menus speeds up your work and adds flexibility to your interaction with the computer.

Double-Click

Double-click means you quickly press and release the left mouse button twice without moving the mouse. In most cases, you must point to an item before you double-click. Perform the following step to open the My Computer window on the desktop by double-clicking the My Computer icon.

Steps To Open a Window by Double-Clicking

1 **Point to the My Computer icon on the desktop and then double-click by quickly pressing and releasing the left mouse button twice without moving the mouse.**

The My Computer window opens and the recessed My Computer button displays in the taskbar button area (Figure 1-17). The My Computer window allows you to view the contents of the computer.

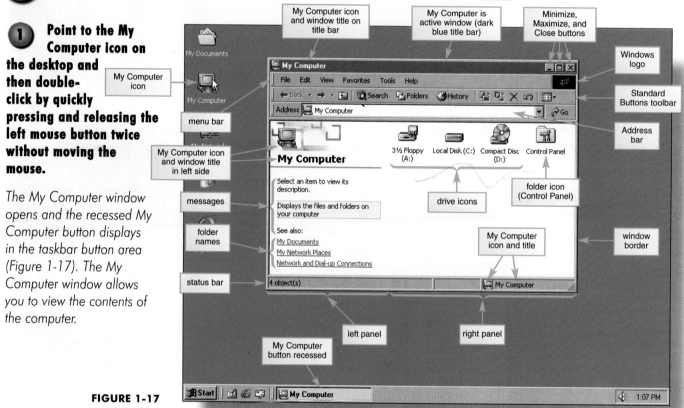

FIGURE 1-17

The My Computer window, the only open window, is the active window. The **active window** is the window you currently are using or that currently is selected. Whenever you click an object that can be opened, such as the My Computer icon, Windows 2000 will open the object; and a recessed button in the taskbar button area will identify the open object. The recessed button identifies the active window.

The contents of the My Computer window on your computer may be different from the contents of the My Computer window in Figure 1-17.

Double-Clicking Errors

While double-clicking an object, you easily can click once instead of twice. When you click an object such as the My Computer icon once, the icon becomes the active icon and Windows 2000 highlights the icon and its name. To open the My Computer window after clicking the My Computer icon once, double-click the My Computer icon as if you had not clicked the icon at all.

Another possible error is moving the mouse after you click the first time and before you click the second time. In most cases when you do this, the icon will be highlighted the same as if you click it just one time.

A third possible error is moving the mouse while you are pressing the mouse button. In this case, the icon might actually move on the screen because you have inadvertently dragged it. To open the My Computer window after dragging it accidentally, double-click the icon as if you had not clicked it at all.

The My Computer Window

The thin line, or **window border**, surrounding the My Computer window shown in Figure 1-17 determines its shape and size. The **title bar** at the top of the window contains a small icon that is the same as the icon on the desktop and the **window title** (My Computer) that identifies the window. The color of the title bar (dark blue) and the recessed My Computer button in the taskbar button area indicate the My Computer window is the active window. The color of the active window on your computer may be different from the dark blue color shown in Figure 1-17.

Clicking the icon at the left on the title bar will display the **System menu**, which contains commands to carry out the actions associated with the My Computer window. At the right on the title bar are three buttons, the Minimize button, the Maximize button, and the Close button, that can be used to specify the size of the window or close the window.

The **menu bar**, which is the horizontal bar below the title bar of a window (Figure 1-17), contains a list of menu names for the My Computer window: File, Edit, View, Favorites, Tools, and Help. At the right end of the menu bar is a button containing the Windows logo.

Below the menu bar, eleven buttons display on the **Standard Buttons toolbar**. The first six buttons allow you to navigate through an open window on the desktop (Back, Forward, and Up); search for and display files or folders (Search and Folders); and display a list of Web sites you previously have visited (History). Four of these buttons contain a **text label** (Back, Search, Folders, and History) that identify the function of the button. The last five buttons do not contain text labels. These buttons allow you to move and copy text within a window or between windows (Move To and Copy To); delete text within a window (Delete); undo a previous action (Undo); and display the icons in the window in different formats (Views). Pointing to a button without a text label displays the button name.

Below the Standard Buttons toolbar is the Address bar. The **Address bar** allows you to launch an application, display a document, open another window, and search for information on the Internet. The Address bar shown in Figure 1-17 contains the My Computer icon and window title.

The area below the Standard Buttons toolbar is divided into two panels. The My Computer icon and window title, My Computer, display in the left panel. Several messages and three folder names (My Documents, My Network Places, and Network and Dial-Up Connections) display below the icon and title in the left panel. The three folder names are underlined and display in blue font. Underlined text, such as the folder names, is referred to as a **hyperlink**, or simply a **link**. Pointing to a hyperlink changes the mouse pointer to a hand icon, and clicking a hyperlink displays the contents of the associated folder in the window. Because the My Computer window is divided into two panels and the left panel contains hyperlinks, the window is said to display in the **Web view**.

More About

My Computer

While the trade press and media once poked fun at the My Computer icon name, Microsoft continues to expand on the concept. Microsoft added the My Documents icon to the Windows 98 desktop and replaced the Network Neighborhood icon with the My Network Places icon. Microsoft still contends that beginners find these names easier to understand.

More About

The Contents of the My Computer Window

Because windows are easily customized, your My Computer window may not resemble the window in Figure 1-17. For example, different toolbars may display, icons may display smaller, or the panels may not display. If this is the case, contact your instructor to change the contents the My Computer window.

The right panel of the My Computer window contains four icons. A title below each icon identifies the icon. The first three icons, called **drive icons**, represent a 3½ Floppy (A:) drive, a Local Disk (C:) drive, and a Compact Disc (D:) drive. The fourth icon is the Control Panel folder. A **folder** is an object created to contain related documents, applications, and other folders. A folder in Windows 2000 contains items in much the same way a folder on your desk contains items. The **Control Panel folder** allows you to personalize the computer, such as specifying how you want the desktop to look.

Clicking a drive or folder icon selects the icon in the right panel and displays information about the drive or folder in the left panel. Double-clicking a drive or folder icon displays the contents of the corresponding drive or folder in the right panel and information about the drive or folder in the left panel. You may find more, fewer, or different drive and folder icons in the My Computer window on your computer.

A message at the left on the **status bar** located at the bottom of the window indicates the right panel contains four objects (see Figure 1-17 on page WIN 1.18). The My Computer icon and title display to the right of the message on the status bar.

Minimize Button

Two buttons on the title bar of a window, the Minimize button and the Maximize button, allow you to control the way a window displays or does not display on the desktop. When you click the **Minimize button** (see Figure 1-17 on page WIN 1.18), the My Computer window no longer displays on the desktop and the recessed My Computer button in the taskbar button area changes to a non-recessed button. A minimized window still is open but it does not display on the screen. To minimize and then redisplay the My Computer window, complete these steps.

More About

Minimizing Windows

Windows management on the Windows 2000 desktop is important in order to keep the desktop uncluttered. You will find yourself frequently minimizing windows and then later reopening them with a click of a button in the taskbar button area.

Steps   To Minimize and Redisplay a Window

1 **Point to the Minimize button on the title bar of the My Computer window.**

The mouse pointer points to the Minimize button on the My Computer window title bar (Figure 1-18). A ToolTip displays below the Minimize button and the My Computer button in the taskbar button area is recessed.

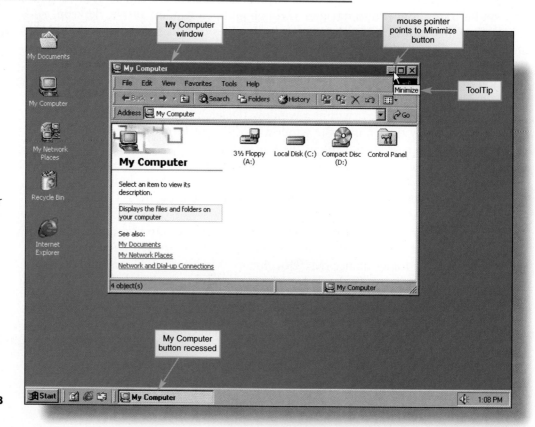

FIGURE 1-18

Click the Minimize button.

When you minimize the My Computer window, Windows 2000 removes the My Computer window from the desktop and the My Computer button changes to a non-recessed button (Figure 1-19).

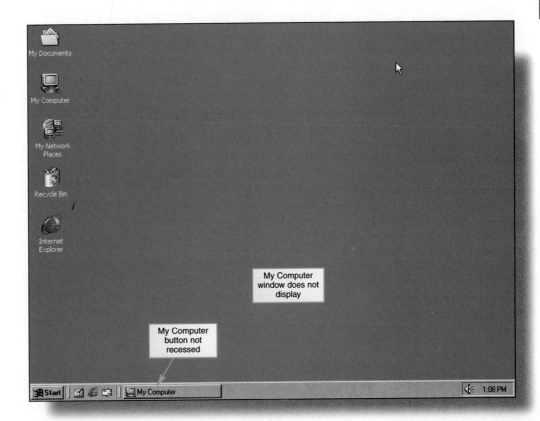

FIGURE 1-19

 Click the My Computer button in the taskbar button area.

The My Computer window displays on the desktop in the same place and size as it was before being minimized (Figure 1-20). In addition, the My Computer window is the active window because it contains the dark blue title bar, and the My Computer button in the taskbar button area is recessed.

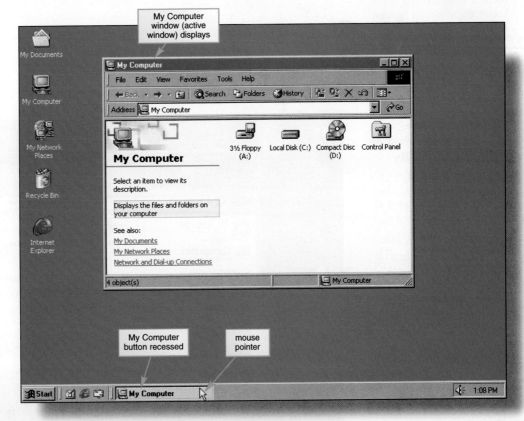

FIGURE 1-20

Maximizing Windows

Many application programs run in a maximized window by default. Often you will find that you want to work with maximized windows to better view the contents of the window. Did you know that double-clicking the title bar also maximizes a window?

The Restore Down Button

Hey – this is new in Windows 2000. The button on the title bar that restores the size of a window, which has always been referred to as the Restore button in previous versions of Windows, is now called the Restore Down button. Probably because when you click that button, the window is restored down to a smaller size.

Whenever a window is minimized, it does not display on the desktop but a non-recessed button for the window does display in the taskbar button area. Whenever you want a minimized window to display and be the active window, click its button in the taskbar button area.

Maximize and Restore Down Buttons

Sometimes when information displays in a window, the information is not completely visible. One method to display the entire contents of a window is to enlarge the window using the **Maximize button**. The Maximize button maximizes a window so the window fills the entire screen, making it easier to see the contents of the window. When a window is maximized, the **Restore Down button** replaces the Maximize button on the title bar. Clicking the Restore Down button will return the window to its size before maximizing. To maximize and restore the My Computer window, complete the following steps.

 To Maximize and Restore a Window

1 **Point to the Maximize button on the title bar of the My Computer window.**

The mouse pointer points to the Maximize button on the My Computer window title bar (Figure 1-21). A ToolTip displays below the Maximize button.

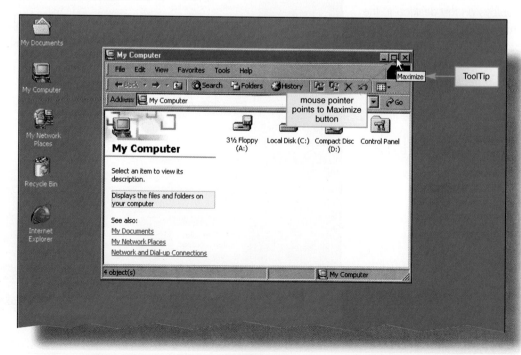

FIGURE 1-21

2 **Click the Maximize button.**

The My Computer window expands so it and the taskbar fill the desktop (Figure 1-22). The Restore Down button replaces the Maximize button, the My Computer button in the taskbar button area does not change, and the My Computer window still is the active window.

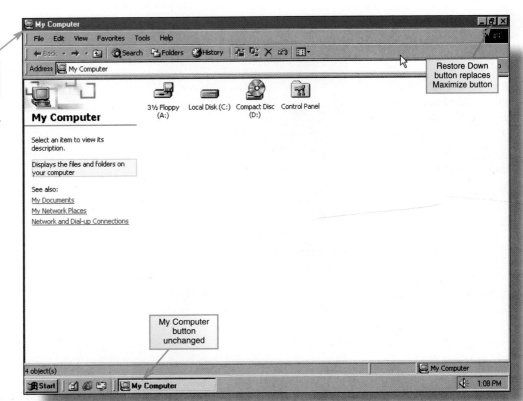

FIGURE 1-22

3 **Point to the Restore Down button on the title bar of the My Computer window.**

The mouse pointer points to the Restore Down button on the My Computer window title bar (Figure 1-23). A ToolTip displays below the Restore Down button.

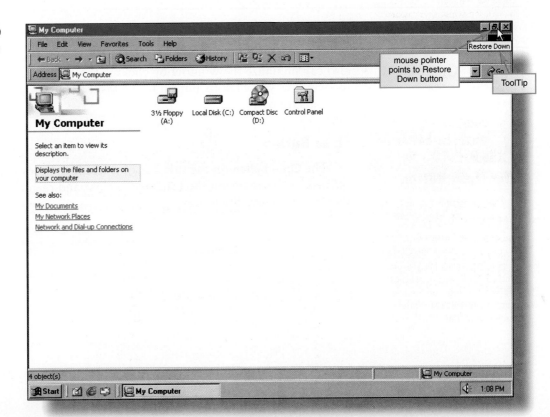

FIGURE 1-23

Click the Restore Down button.

The My Computer window returns to the size and position it occupied before being maximized (Figure 1-24). The My Computer button does not change. The Maximize button replaces the Restore Down button.

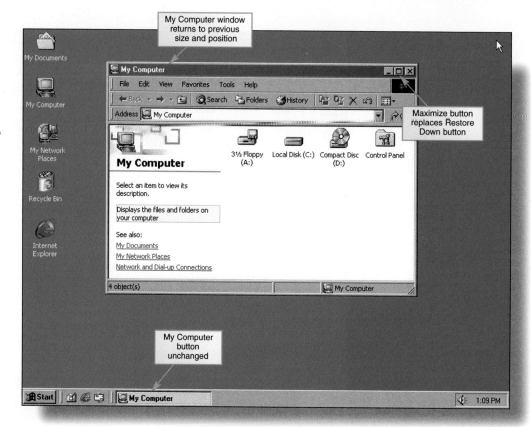

FIGURE 1-24

When a window is maximized, such as in Figure 1-22 on the previous page, you also can minimize the window by clicking the Minimize button. If, after minimizing the window, you click its button in the taskbar button area, the window will return to its maximized size.

The Close Button

In earlier versions of Windows, you had to double-click a button or click a command to close a window. Now you can click the Close button, right-click the title bar and click Close, double-click the window logo on the title bar, or press ALT+F4. Variety is the spice of life!

Close Button

The **Close button** on the title bar of a window closes the window and removes the taskbar button from the taskbar. To close and then reopen the My Computer window, complete the following steps.

To Close and Reopen a Window

1 Point to the Close button on the title bar of the My Computer window (Figure 1-25).

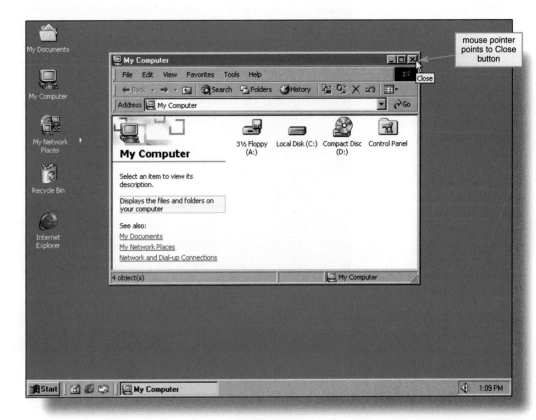

FIGURE 1-25

2 Click the Close button.

The My Computer window closes and the My Computer button no longer displays in the taskbar button area (Figure 1-26).

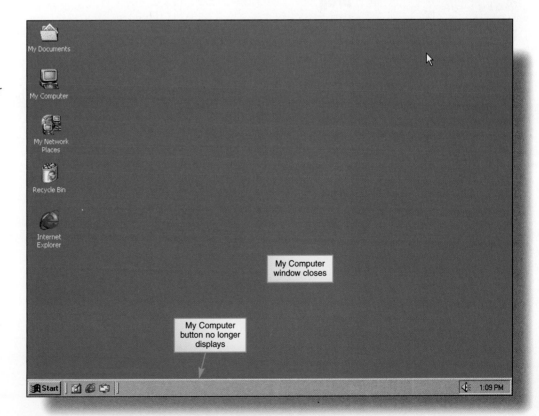

FIGURE 1-26

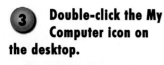

3 **Double-click the My Computer icon on the desktop.**

The My Computer window opens and displays on the desktop (Figure 1-27). The My Computer button displays in the taskbar button area.

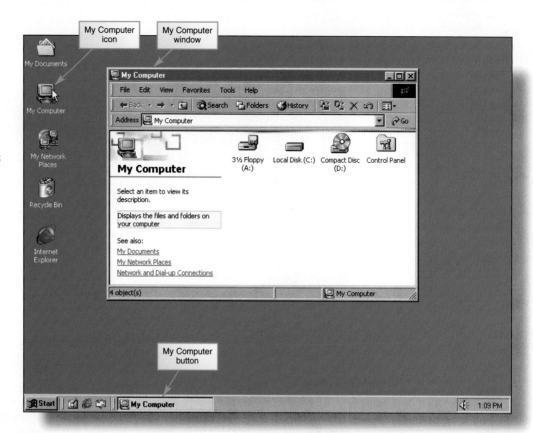

FIGURE 1-27

Dragging

Dragging is the second-most difficult skill to learn with a mouse. You may want to practice dragging a few times so you are comfortable with it. Do not let dragging become a drag – PRACTICE!!

Drag

Drag means you point to an item, hold down the left mouse button, move the item to the desired location, and then release the left mouse button. You can move any open window to another location on the desktop by pointing to the title bar of the window and then dragging the window. To drag the My Computer window to another location on the desktop, perform the steps on the next page.

To Move an Object by Dragging

① **Point to the My Computer window title bar (Figure 1-28).**

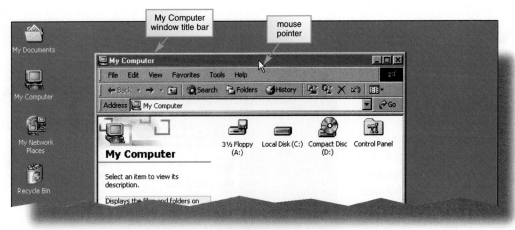

FIGURE 1-28

② **Hold down the left mouse button, move the mouse down so the window moves to the center of the desktop, and then release the left mouse button.**

As you drag the My Computer window, the window moves across the desktop. When you release the left mouse button, the window displays in its new location on the desktop (Figure 1-29).

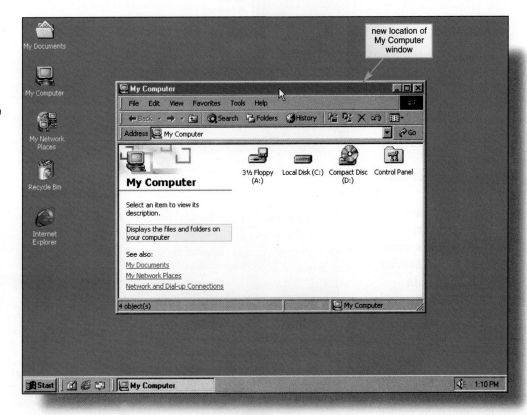

FIGURE 1-29

Sizing a Window by Dragging

As previously mentioned, sometimes when information displays in a window, the information is not completely visible. A second method to display information that is not visible is to change the size of the window by dragging the window. For example, you can drag the border of a window to change the size of the window. To change the size of the My Computer window, perform the following steps.

To Size a Window by Dragging

1 **Position the mouse pointer over the lower-right corner of the My Computer window until the mouse pointer changes to a two-headed arrow.**

When the mouse pointer is on top of the lower-right corner of the My Computer window, the pointer changes to a two-headed arrow (Figure 1-30).

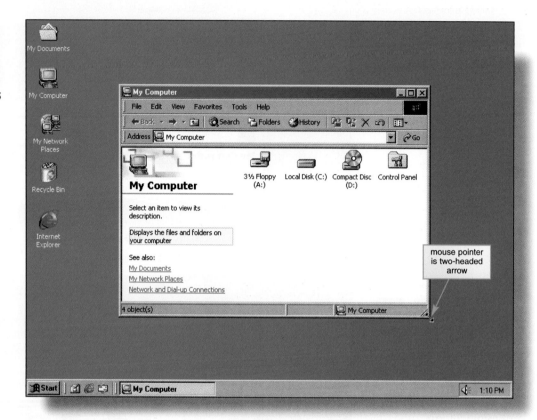

FIGURE 1-30

2 **Drag the lower-right corner upward and to the left until the window on the desktop resembles the window shown in Figure 1-31.**

As you drag the lower-right corner, the My Computer window changes size, the icons in the right panel display in two rows, a vertical scroll bar displays in the left panel, and a portion of the text in the left panel is not visible (Figure 1-31).

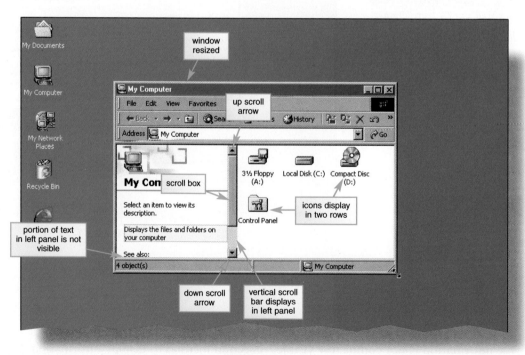

FIGURE 1-31

A **scroll bar** is a bar that displays when the contents of a window are not completely visible. A vertical scroll bar contains an **up scroll arrow**, a **down scroll arrow**, and a **scroll box** that enable you to view areas that currently are not visible. A vertical scroll bar displays along the right edge of the left panel of the My Computer window shown in Figure 1-31. In some cases, the vertical scroll bar also may display along the right edge of the right panel of a window.

In addition to dragging a corner of a window, you also can drag any of the borders of a window. If you drag a vertical border, such as the right border, you can move the border left or right. If you drag a horizontal border, such as the bottom border, you can move the border of the window up or down.

Scrolling in a Window

Previously, two methods were shown to display information that was not completely visible in the My Computer window. These methods were maximizing the My Computer window and changing the size of the My Computer window. The third method uses the scroll bar.

Scrolling can be accomplished in three ways: (1) click the scroll arrows; (2) click the scroll bar; and (3) drag the scroll box. On the following pages, you will use the scroll bar to scroll the contents of the left panel of the My Computer window. Perform the following steps to scroll the left panel of the My Computer window using the scroll arrows.

More *About*

Window Sizing

Windows 2000 remembers the size of the window when you close the window. When you reopen the window, it will display in the same size as when you closed it.

More *About*

Scrolling

Most people will either maximize a window or size it so all the objects in the window are visible to avoid scrolling because scrolling takes time. It is more efficient not to have to scroll in a window.

 To Scroll Using Scroll Arrows

1 **Point to the down scroll arrow on the vertical scroll bar (Figure 1-32).**

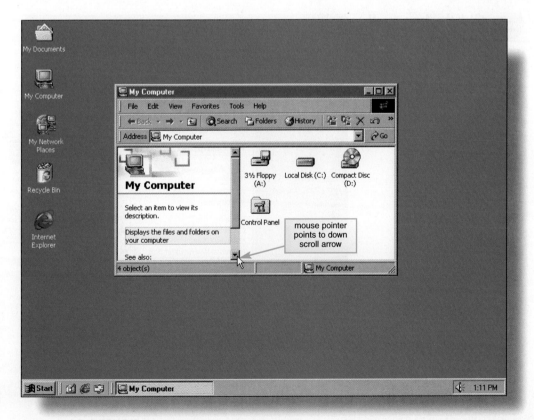

FIGURE 1-32

2 **Click the down scroll arrow one time.**

The left panel scrolls down (the contents in the left panel move up) and displays text at the bottom of the left panel that previously was not visible (Figure 1-33). Because the size of the left panel does not change when you scroll, the contents in the left panel will change, as seen in the difference between Figures 1-31 on the previous page and 1-33.

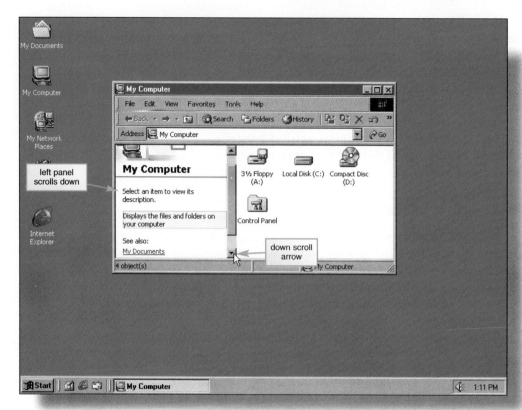

FIGURE 1-33

3 **Click the down scroll arrow two more times.**

The scroll box moves to the bottom of the scroll bar and the remaining text in the left panel displays (Figure 1-34).

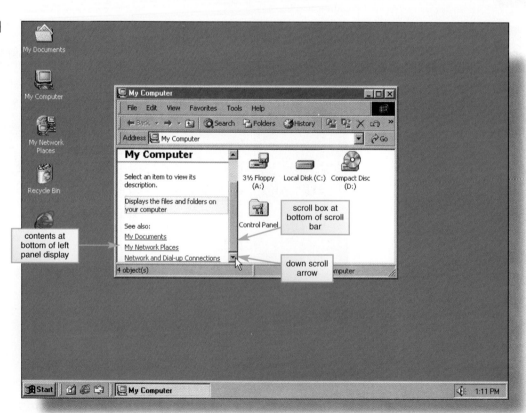

FIGURE 1-34

You can scroll continuously using scroll arrows by pointing to the up or down scroll arrow and holding down the left mouse button. The area being scrolled continues to scroll until you release the left mouse button or you reach the top or bottom of the area.

Scrolling by Clicking the Scroll Bar

You also can scroll by clicking the scroll bar itself. To scroll to the top of the left panel by clicking the scroll bar, complete the following steps.

 To Scroll Using the Scroll Bar

1 **Point to the scroll bar above the scroll box (Figure 1-35).**

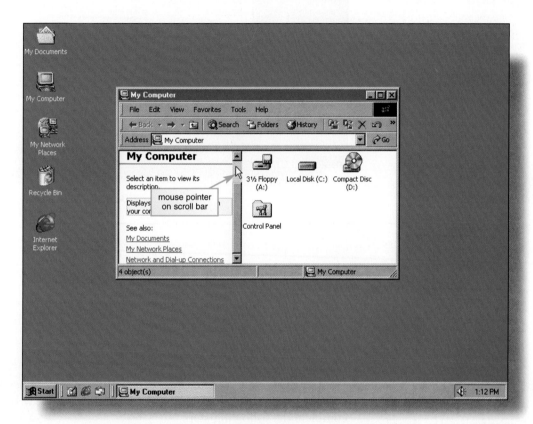

FIGURE 1-35

Click the scroll bar one time.

The scroll box moves to the top of the scroll bar and the top of the left panel displays (Figure 1-36).

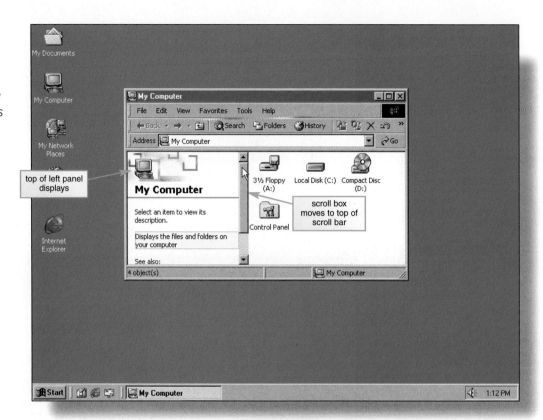

FIGURE 1-36

In the previous steps, you needed to click the scroll bar one time to move the scroll box to the top of the scroll bar and display the contents at the top of the left panel. In those cases where the scroll box is small and more contents are not visible, you may have to click three or more times to scroll to the top.

Scrolling by Dragging the Scroll Box

The third way in which you can scroll is by dragging the scroll box. To view the contents of the left panel of the My Computer window by dragging the scroll box, complete the following step.

The Scroll Box

Dragging the scroll box is the most efficient technique to scroll long distances. In many application programs, such as Microsoft Word, as you scroll using the scroll box, the page number of the document displays next to the scroll box.

To Scroll by Dragging the Scroll Box

1 **With the mouse pointer pointing to the scroll box on the scroll bar, drag the scroll box down the scroll bar until the scroll box is about halfway down the scroll bar.**

As you drag the scroll box down the vertical scroll bar, additional parts of the left panel become visible (Figure 1-37). Notice that the information in the window moves as you drag the scroll box.

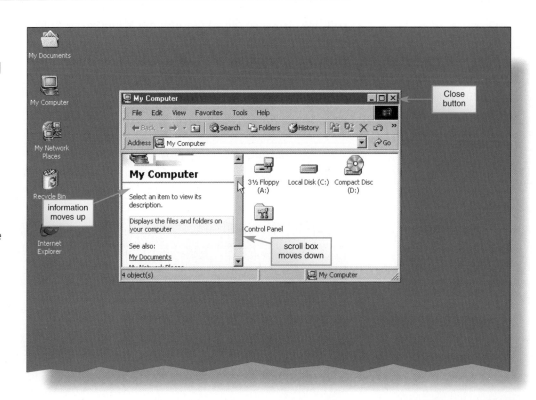

In previous examples, a vertical scroll bar displays in the left panel of the My Computer window. In addition, a sole vertical scroll bar may display in the right panel of a window or together with a scroll bar in the left panel of the window. In either case, the scroll arrows and scroll box allow you to view the contents of a window that currently are not visible. Being able to view the contents of a window by scrolling is an important Windows 2000 skill because in many cases the entire contents of a window are not visible.

Resizing a Window

After moving and resizing a window, you may wish to return the window to approximately its original size. To return the My Computer window to about its original size, complete the following steps.

TO RESIZE A WINDOW

1 Position the mouse pointer over the lower-right corner of the My Computer window border until the mouse pointer changes to a two-headed arrow.

2 Drag the lower-right corner of the My Computer window down and to the right until the window is the same size as shown in Figure 1-29 on page WIN 1.26 and then release the mouse button.

The My Computer window is approximately the same size as it was before you made it smaller.

 *About*

Scrolling Guidelines

General scrolling guidelines: (1) To scroll short distances (line by line), click the scroll arrows; (2) To scroll one screen at a time, click the scroll bar; and (3) To scroll long distances, drag the scroll box.

Closing a Window

After you have completed your work in a window, normally you will close the window. To close the My Computer window, complete the following steps.

TO CLOSE A WINDOW

1 Point to the Close button on the right of the title bar in the My Computer window (see Figure 1-37 on the previous page).

2 Click the Close button.

The My Computer window closes and the desktop contains no open windows (Figure 1-38). Because the My Computer window is closed, the My Computer button no longer displays in the taskbar button area.

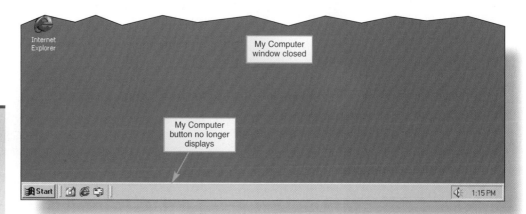

FIGURE 1-38

More About

Right-Dragging

Right-dragging was not available on some earlier versions of Windows, so you might find people familiar with Windows not even considering right-dragging. Because it always produces a shortcut menu, however, right-dragging is the safest way to drag.

Right-Drag

Right-drag means you point to an item, hold down the right mouse button, move the item to the desired location, and then release the right mouse button. When you right-drag an object, a shortcut menu displays. The shortcut menu contains commands specifically for use with the object being dragged. To right-drag the Launch Outlook Express icon on the Quick Launch toolbar below the icons to the desktop, perform the following steps. If the Launch Outlook Express icon does not display on the Quick Launch toolbar, you will be unable to perform Steps 1 through 4 that follow.

Steps **To Right-Drag**

1 **Point to the Launch Outlook Express icon on the Quick Launch toolbar (Figure 1-39).**

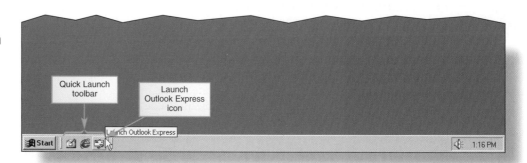

FIGURE 1-39

2 **Hold down the right mouse button, drag the icon below the other icons on the desktop, and then release the right mouse button.**

The dimmed Launch Outlook Express icon and a shortcut menu display on the desktop (Figure 1-40).

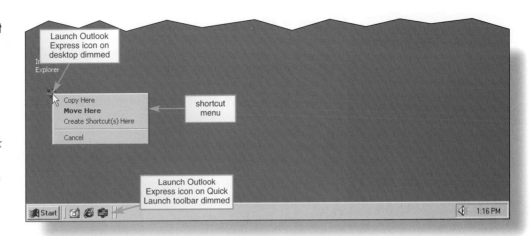

FIGURE 1-40

3 **Point to Cancel on the shortcut menu.**

The Cancel command is highlighted (Figure 1-41).

4 **Click Cancel.**

The shortcut menu and the dragged Launch Outlook Express icon no longer display on the desktop.

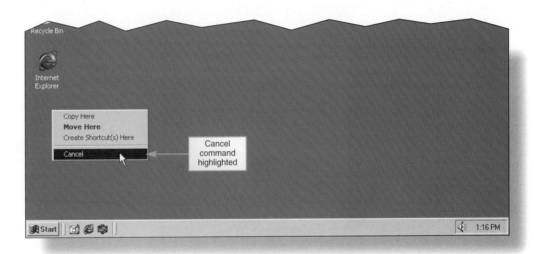

FIGURE 1-41

In Figure 1-40, the original Launch Outlook Express icon remains at its original location on the Quick Launch toolbar and the shortcut menu contains four commands: Copy Here, Move Here, Create Shortcut(s) Here, and Cancel. The Move Here command in bold (dark) font identifies what would happen if you were to drag the Launch Outlook Express icon with the left mouse button.

If you click **Move Here** on the shortcut menu shown, Windows 2000 will move the icon from its current location to the new location. If you click **Copy Here**, Windows 2000 will copy the icon to the new location and two icons will display. Windows 2000 automatically will give the second icon a different name. If you click **Create Shortcut(s) Here**, Windows 2000 will create a special object called a shortcut. You will learn more about shortcuts in Project 2 of this book.

Whenever you begin an operation but do not want to complete the operation, you can click Cancel on a shortcut menu or click the Cancel button in a dialog box. The **Cancel** command will reset anything you have done in the operation.

Although you can move icons by dragging with the primary (left) mouse button and by right-dragging with the secondary (right) mouse button, it is strongly suggested you right-drag because a menu displays and you can specify the exact operation you want to occur. When you drag using the left mouse button, a default operation takes place and the operation may not do what you want.

The Microsoft Keyboard

The Microsoft keyboard in Figure 1-39(b) has special keys for Windows 2000 and is designed ergonomically so you type with your hands apart. It takes a little time to adapt, but several Shelly Cashman Series authors report they type faster, more accurately, and with less fatigue when using the keyboard.

Summary of Mouse and Windows Operations

You have seen how to use the mouse to point, click, right-click, double-click, drag, and right-drag in order to accomplish certain tasks on the desktop. The use of a mouse is an important skill when using Windows 2000. In addition, you have learned how to move around and use windows on the Windows 2000 desktop.

The Keyboard and Keyboard Shortcuts

The **keyboard** is an input device on which you manually key in, or type, data. Figure 1-42a shows the enhanced IBM 101-key keyboard, and Figure 1-42b shows a Microsoft Natural keyboard designed specifically for use with Windows. Many tasks you accomplish with a mouse also can be accomplished using a keyboard.

FIGURE 1-42a

FIGURE 1-42b

Microsoft Keyboards

For additional information about Microsoft keyboards, visit the Microsoft Keyboard Web Site. To visit the site, launch the Internet Explorer browser (see pages WIN 1.37 and 1.38), type www.scsite.com/win2000/more.htm in the Address box and press the ENTER key. To purchase a keyboard, click the buy now button!!!

To perform tasks using the keyboard, you must understand the notation used to identify which keys to press. This notation is used throughout Windows 2000 to identify a **keyboard shortcut**.

Keyboard shortcuts consist of: (1) pressing a single key (such as press the ENTER key); or (2) pressing and holding down one key and pressing a second key, as shown by two key names separated by a plus sign (such as press CTRL+ESC). For example, to obtain Help about Windows 2000, you can press the F1 key; to display the Start menu, hold down the CTRL key and then press the ESC key (press CTRL+ESC).

Often, computer users will use keyboard shortcuts for operations they perform frequently. For example, many users find pressing the F1 key to launch Windows 2000 Help easier than using the Start menu as shown later in this project. As a user, you probably will find the combination of keyboard and mouse operations that particularly suit you, but it is strongly recommended that generally you use the mouse.

Launching an Application Program

One of the basic tasks you can perform using Windows 2000 is to launch an application program. A **program** is a set of computer instructions that carries out a task on the computer. An **application program** is a program that allows you to accomplish a specific task for which that program is designed. For example, a **word processing program** is an application program that allows you to create written documents; a **presentation graphics program** is an application program that allows you to create graphic presentations for display on a computer; and a **Web browser program** is an application program that allows you to search for and display Web pages.

The most common activity on a computer is to run an application program to accomplish tasks using the computer. You can launch an application program in a variety of ways. When several methods are available to accomplish a task, a computer user has the opportunity to try various methods and select the method that best fits his or her needs.

To illustrate the variety of methods available to launch an application program, three methods will be shown to launch the Internet Explorer Web browser program. These methods include using the Start button; using the Quick Launch toolbar; and using an icon on the desktop.

Launching an Application Using the Start Button

The first method of launching an application program is to use the Start menu. Perform the following steps to launch Internet Explorer using the Start menu and Internet Explorer command.

 To Launch a Program Using the Start Menu

1 **Click the Start button on the taskbar, point to Programs on the Start menu, and then point to Internet Explorer on the Programs submenu.**

The Start menu and Programs submenu display (Figure 1-43). The Programs submenu contains the Internet Explorer command to launch the Internet Explorer program. You might find more, fewer, or different commands on the Start menu and Programs submenu on your computer.

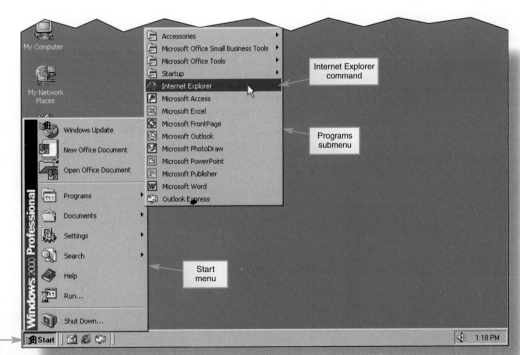

FIGURE 1-43

2 **Click Internet Explorer. If necessary, maximize the Microsoft Internet Explorer window.**

Windows 2000 launches the Internet Explorer program by displaying the Welcome to MSN.COM – Microsoft Internet Explorer window on the desktop, displaying the MSN.COM Web page in the window, and adding a recessed button in the taskbar button area (Figure 1-44). The URL for the Web page displays in the Address bar. Because Web pages change frequently, the Web page that displays on your desktop may be different.

3 **Click the Close button in the Microsoft Internet Explorer window.**

The Microsoft Internet Explorer window closes.

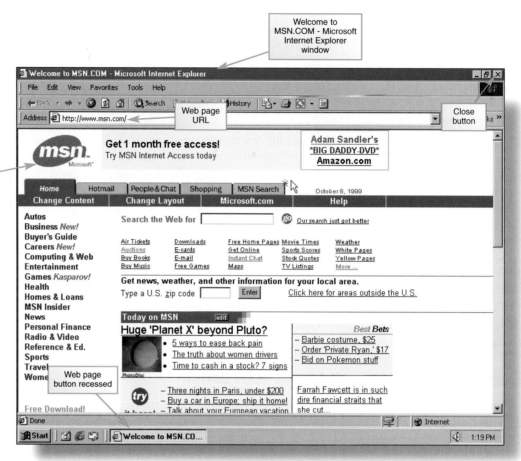

FIGURE 1-44

Other Ways

1. Click Start button, click Run, type iexplore, click OK button
2. Press WINDOWS+R (WINDOWS key on Microsoft Natural keyboard), type iexplore, press ENTER
3. Press CTRL+ESC, press P, press I

Any computer connected to the Internet that contains Web pages you can reference is called a **Web site**. The **MSN.COM Web site**, one of millions of Web sites around the world, is stored on a computer operated by Microsoft Corporation and can be accessed using Internet Explorer. The Welcome to MSN.COM **Web page** in Figure 1-44 is the first Web page you see when you access the MSN.COM Web site and is, therefore, referred to as a **home page**, or **start page**.

After you have launched Internet Explorer, you can use the program to search for and display additional Web pages located on different Web sites around the world.

Launching an Application Using the Quick Launch Toolbar

The second method of launching an application is to use an icon on the Quick Launch toolbar. Currently, the Quick Launch toolbar contains three icons that allow you to view an uncluttered desktop at any time, launch Internet Explorer, and launch Outlook Express (see Figure 1-45). Perform the following steps to launch the Internet Explorer program using the Launch Internet Explorer Browser icon on the Quick Launch toolbar.

To Launch a Program Using the Quick Launch Toolbar

1 **Point to the Launch Internet Explorer Browser icon on the Quick Launch toolbar (Figure 1-45).**

2 **Click the Launch Internet Explorer Browser icon.**

Windows 2000 launches the Internet Explorer program as shown in Figure 1-44.

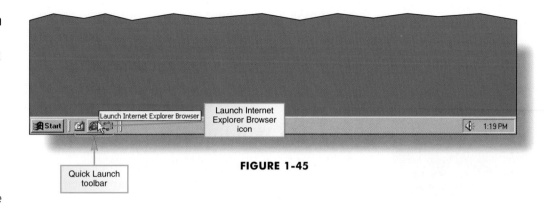

FIGURE 1-45

3 **Click the Close button in the Microsoft Internet Explorer window.**

Windows 2000 closes the Microsoft Internet Explorer window.

Launching an Application Using an Icon on the Desktop

The third method of launching an application is to use an icon on the desktop. Perform the following steps to launch the Internet Explorer program using the Internet Explorer icon on the desktop.

 To Launch a Program Using an Icon on the Desktop

1 **Point to the Internet Explorer icon on the desktop (Figure 1-46).**

2 **Double-click the Internet Explorer icon.**

Windows 2000 launches the Internet Explorer program as shown in Figure 1-44.

3 **Click the Close button in the Microsoft Internet Explorer window.**

The Microsoft Internet Explorer window closes.

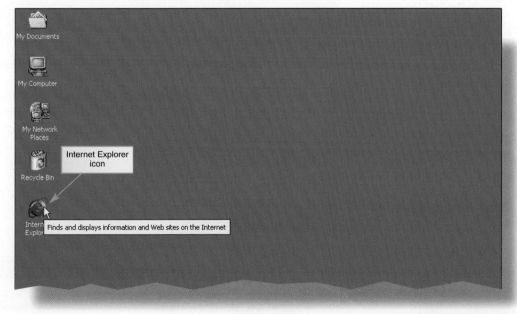

FIGURE 1-46

Windows 2000 provides a number of ways in which to accomplish a particular task. Previously, three methods to launch the Internet Explorer program were illustrated. In the remainder of this book, a single set of steps will illustrate how to accomplish a task. Those steps may not be the only way in which the task can be completed. If you can perform the same task using other methods, the Other Ways box specifies the other methods. In each case, the method shown in the steps is the preferred method, but it is important for you to be aware of all the techniques you can use.

Using Windows Help

One of the more powerful application programs for use in Windows 2000 is Windows Help. Windows Help is available when using Windows 2000, or when using any application program running under Windows 2000, to assist you in using Windows 2000 or the various application programs. It contains answers to many questions you may ask with respect to Windows 2000.

Contents Sheet

Windows Help provides a variety of ways in which to obtain information. One method of finding a Help topic involves using the **Contents sheet** to browse through Help topics by category. To illustrate this method, you will use Windows Help to determine how to find a Help topic. To launch Help, complete the following steps.

Windows 2000 Help

If you purchased an operating system or application program six years ago, you received at least one, and more often several, thick and heavy technical manuals that explained the software. With Windows 2000, you receive a skinny manual with less than 100 pages. The online Help feature of Windows 2000 replaces reams and reams of printed pages in hard-to-understand technical manuals.

 To Launch Windows Help

1 Click the Start button on the taskbar and then point to Help on the Start menu (Figure 1-47).

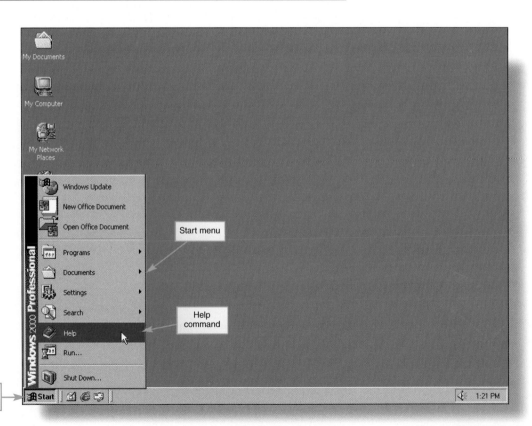

FIGURE 1-47

② **Click Help and then click the Maximize button on the Windows 2000 title bar. If necessary, click the Contents tab.**

*The Windows 2000 window opens and maximizes (Figure 1-48). The window contains the Help toolbar and two panes. The left pane, called the naviga- tion pane, contains four **tabs**. Clicking the Contents tab dis- plays the Contents sheet. The right pane, called the topic pane, contains the Start Here screen, containing the Microsoft 2000 Professional title and Start Here table of contents.*

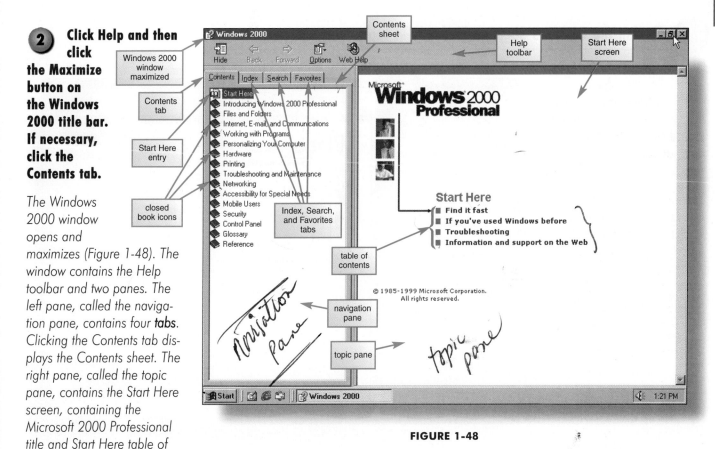

FIGURE 1-48

The Contents sheet in the navigation pane contains 16 entries. The first entry is identified by an open book and document icon, and the highlighted Start Here name. The **open book and document icon** indicates additional information or an overview is available for the entry. The Start Here entry is highlighted to indicate additional information about the entry displays in the topic pane. The topic pane contains the **Start Here screen**. The Start Here screen contains a table of contents consisting of four items (Find it fast, If you've used Windows before, Troubleshooting, and Information and support on the Web).

A closed book icon precedes each of the remaining 15 entries in the Contents sheet. The **closed book icon** indicates that Help topics or more books are contained in a book but do not display in the Contents sheet. Clicking the Index tab, Search tab, or Favorites tab in the navigation pane displays the Index, Search, or Favorites sheet, respectively.

In addition to launching Help by using the Start button, you also can launch Help by clicking an open area of the desktop and pressing the F1 key.

After launching Help, the next step is to find the topic in which you are inter- ested. Assume you want to find information about locating a Help topic. Perform the steps on the next page to find the topic that describes how to find a topic in Help.

Other Ways

1. Click open area of desktop, press F1
2. Press WINDOWS+F1 (WINDOWS key on Microsoft Natural keyboard)

To Use the Contents Sheet to Find a Help Topic

1 **Point to the Introducing Windows 2000 Professional closed book icon in the navigation pane.**

The mouse pointer changes to a hand when positioned on the icon and the Introducing Windows 2000 Professional book name displays in blue font and underlined (Figure 1-49).

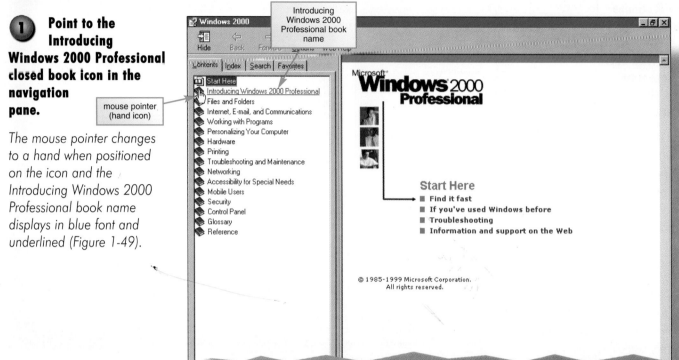

FIGURE 1-49

2 **Click the Introducing Windows 2000 Professional closed book icon and then point to the How to Use Help closed book icon.**

Windows 2000 opens the Introducing Windows 2000 Professional book, changes the closed book icon to an open book icon, highlights the Introducing Windows 2000 Professional book name, underlines the How to Use Help book name, and displays the name and underline in blue font (Figure 1-50). The open book icon indicates that Help topics or books contained in the book display indented below the book.

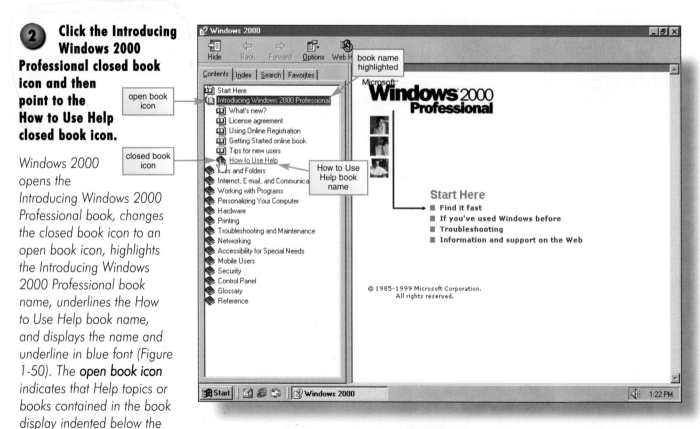

FIGURE 1-50

3 **Click the How to Use Help closed book icon and then point to Find a Help topic.**

Windows 2000 opens the How to Use Help book, changes the closed book icon to an open book icon, highlights the How to Use Help book name, under-lines the Find a Help topic name, and displays the topic name and underline in blue font (Figure 1-51). The **question mark icon** *indicates a Help topic without further subdivisions. Clicking the* **Help overview** *icon displays an overview of the Help system.*

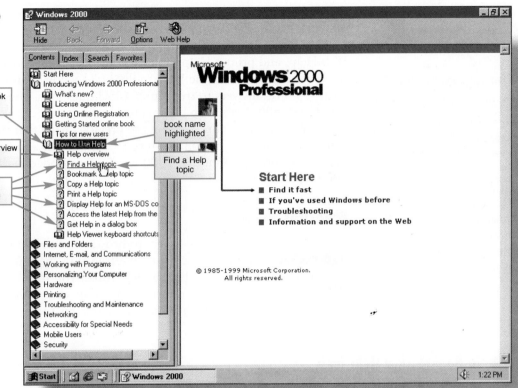

FIGURE 1-51

4 **Click Find a Help topic and then read the information about finding a Help topic in the topic pane.**

Windows 2000 highlights the Find a Help topic name and displays information about finding a Help topic in the topic pane (Figure 1-52). Clicking the **plus sign** *in the small box to the left of the Contents tab, Index tab, Search tab, or Favorites tab entries displays additional information about the entry.*

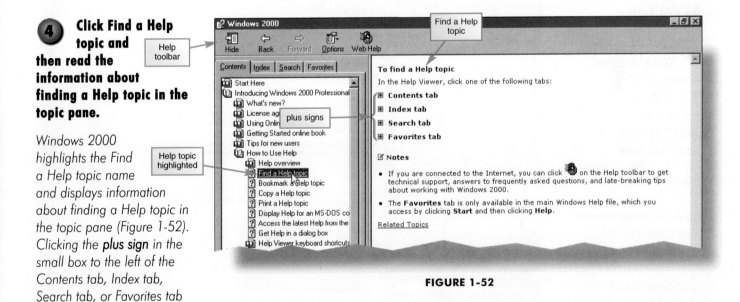

FIGURE 1-52

In Figure 1-52, the Help toolbar contains five icons. If you click the **Hide button** on the Help toolbar, Windows 2000 hides the tabs in the navigation pane and displays only the topic pane in the Windows 2000 window. Clicking the **Back button** or **Forward button** displays a previously displayed Help topic in the topic pane. Clicking

Other **Ways**

1. Press DOWN ARROW until book name is highlighted, press RIGHT ARROW (or ENTER), continue until Help topic displays, press ENTER, read Help topic

The Favorites Sheet

The idea for a Favorites sheet came from surfing the Web. When you find an interesting Web page, you add it to your favorites list, making it possible to return to the page in the future. In Help, you find a helpful topic and add it to your list using the Favorites sheet.

the **Options button** allows you to hide or display the tabs in the navigation pane, display previously displayed Help topics in the topic pane, stop the display of a Help topic, refresh the currently displayed Help topic, access the Internet options, access Web Help, and print a Help topic. The **Web Help command** on the Options menu and the **Web Help button** on the Help toolbar allow you to use the Internet to obtain technical support, answers to frequently asked questions, and tips about working with Windows 2000. Web Help is explained in Project 2.

Notice also in Figure 1-52 on the previous page that the Windows 2000 title bar contains a Minimize button, Restore Down button, and Close button. You can minimize or restore the Windows 2000 window as needed and also close the Windows 2000 window.

Favorites Sheet

After using the Contents sheet to browse for a Help topic, you may want to **bookmark**, or save, the topic for easy retrieval in the future. Assume you want to bookmark the Help topic (Find a Help topic) you found while using the Contents sheet (see Figure 1-52) and return to this topic in the future. Perform the following steps to use the Favorites sheet to bookmark this topic.

 To Bookmark a Help Topic

1 **Click the Favorites tab and then point to the Add button.**

The Favorites sheet, containing the Topics list box, Remove and Display buttons, Current topic text box, and Add button, displays in the navigation pane (Figure 1-53). The Topics list box is empty, indicating no topics have been bookmarked, and the Current topic text box contains the insertion point and the name of the last topic found (Find a Help topic).

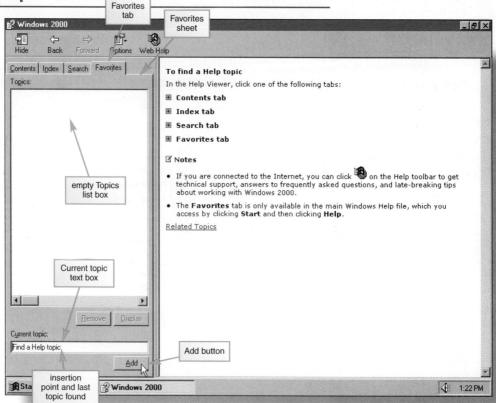

FIGURE 1-53

2 **Click the Add button.**

The Find a Help topic name displays in the Topics list box (Figure 1-54).

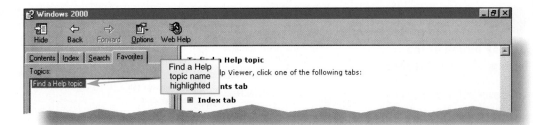

FIGURE 1-54

> **Other Ways**
>
> 1. Press ALT+I, press ALT+A
> 2. Press ALT+I, press TAB key four times, press ENTER

In the future, if you want to return to a topic, click the Favorites tab, click the topic name in the Topics list, and click the Display button in the Favorites sheet. The topic will display in the topic pane of the Windows 2000 window. The steps to display a topic are illustrated later in this project.

Index Sheet

A second method of finding answers to your questions about Windows 2000 or application programs running under Windows 2000 is to use the Index sheet. The **Index sheet** contains a list of index entries, each of which references one or more Help screens. Assume you want more information about the desktop and the objects on the desktop. Perform the following steps to learn more about the desktop and the objects on the desktop.

More About

The Index Sheet

The Index sheet probably is the best source of information in Windows Help because you can enter the subject in which you are interested. Sometimes, however, you will have to be creative to discover the index entry that answers your question because the most obvious entry will not always lead to your answer.

Steps **To Use the Index Sheet**

1 **Click the Index tab, type** desktop **in the Type in the keyword to find text box, and then point to overview in the list.**

The Index sheet, containing the Type in the keyword to find text box, a list box, and Display button, displays (Figure 1-55). When you type an entry in the text box, the list of index entries in the list box automatically scrolls and the entry you type (desktop) is highlighted in the list. Several entries display indented below the desktop entry.

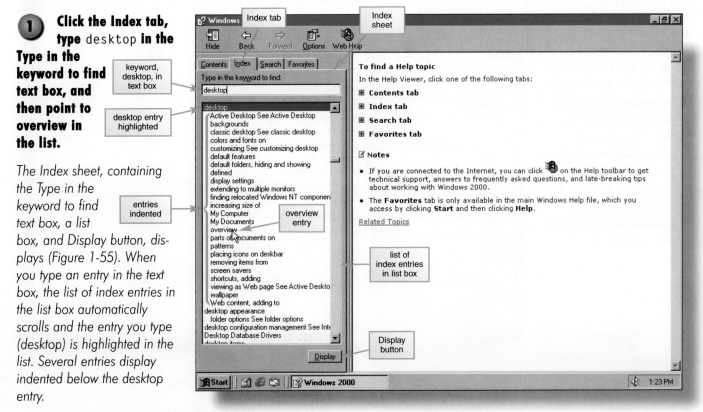

FIGURE 1-55

2 Click overview and then point to the Display button at the bottom of the Index sheet.

Windows 2000 displays the desktop, overview entry in the text box and highlights the overview entry in the list (Figure 1-56).

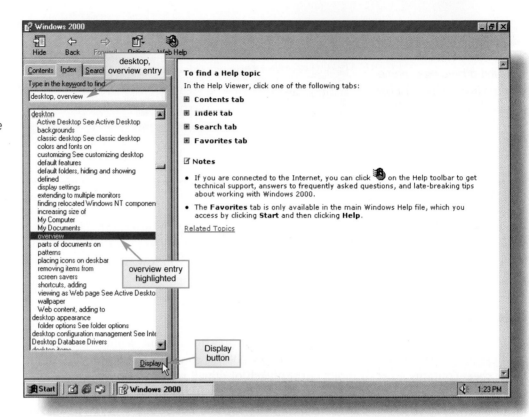

FIGURE 1-56

3 Click the Display button.

The Desktop overview topic displays in the topic pane (Figure 1-57). The topic contains an overview of the desktop, a list of desktop features, and several links (shortcuts, programs, active content, channel, Windows 2000 Professional Getting Started, and Related Topics). Clicking the plus sign in the small box to the left of a desktop feature displays additional information about that feature.

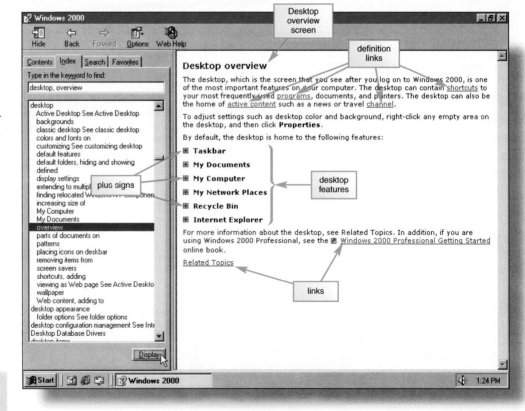

FIGURE 1-57

Other Ways

1. Press ALT+N, type keyword, press DOWN ARROW until topic is highlighted, press ALT+D (or ENTER)

In Figure 1-57, the shortcuts, programs, active content, and channel links are underlined and display in green font to indicate that clicking a link will display its definition. Clicking anywhere off the definition removes the definition.

The Windows 2000 Professional Getting Started and Related Topics links are underlined and display in blue font. Clicking the Windows 2000 Professional Getting Started link displays the Getting Started online book that helps you install Windows 2000, use the desktop, learn about new features, connect to a network, and find answers to commonly asked questions. Clicking the Related Topics link displays a pop-up window that contains topics related to the desktop overview topic.

Bookmarking a Help Topic

After using the Index sheet to search for and display a Help topic, assume you want to bookmark the desktop overview topic and return to this topic in the future (see Figure 1-57). Perform the following steps to bookmark this topic.

TO BOOKMARK A HELP TOPIC

1 Click the Favorites tab in the Windows 2000 window.

2 Click the Add button in the Favorites sheet.

The Favorites sheet displays and the Desktop overview topic name is added to the list of favorite topics in the Topics list (Figure 1-58).

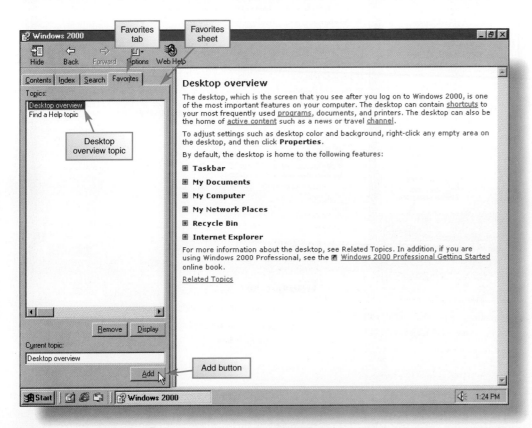

FIGURE 1-58

More About

The Search Sheet

The Search sheet allows you to use logical operators and other search techniques to improve the search results. For additional information, launch Help, click the Search tab, type find it fast in the Type in the keyword to find text box, click the Display button, and read about additional search techniques.

In the future, if you want to return to a topic, click the Favorites tab, click the topic name in the Topics list, and then click the Display button. The topic will display in the topic pane of the Windows 2000 window. The steps to display a topic are illustrated later in this project.

Search Sheet

A third method of obtaining help about Windows 2000 is to use the Search sheet. The **Search sheet** allows you to enter a keyword and display all Help topics containing the keyword. Assume you want more information about computer viruses. Perform the following steps to learn more about viruses.

Steps To Use the Search Sheet

1 Click the Search tab, type virus in the Type in the keyword to find text box and then point to the List Topics button.

The Search sheet, containing the Type in the keyword to find text box, List Topics button, Select Topic to display list box, and dimmed Display button, displays in the navigation pane (Figure 1-59). The text box contains the word, virus, and the insertion point.

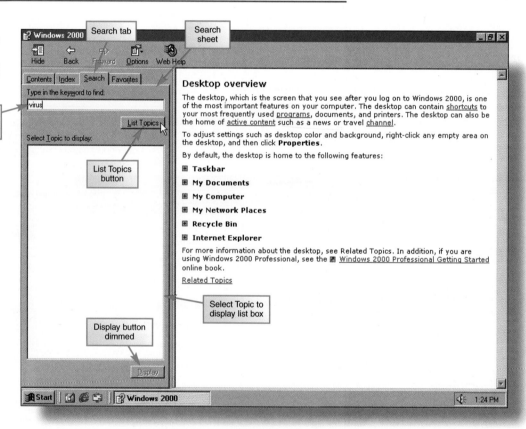

FIGURE 1-59

2 **Click the List Topics button, click the Protecting against viruses and Trojan horses topic in the Select Topic to display list box, and then point to the Display button.**

A Searching dialog box displays momentarily while the search is performed, two topics display in the Select Topic to display list box, and the second topic, Protecting against viruses and Trojan horses, is highlighted (Figure 1-60).

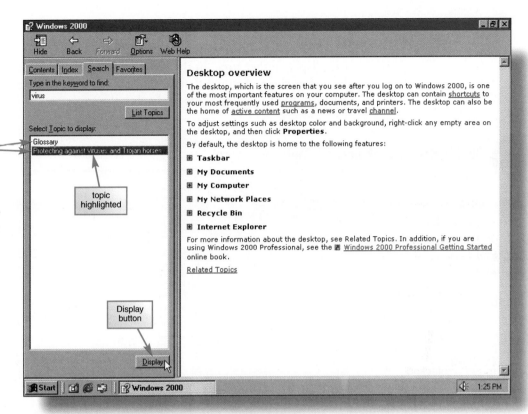

FIGURE 1-60

3 **Click the Display button.**

The Protecting against viruses and Trojan horses topic, which contains information about viruses, displays in the topic pane (Figure 1-61). Each occurrence of the keyword, virus, is highlighted and the Trojan horses link displays in green font. Clicking the Trojan horses link displays its definition.

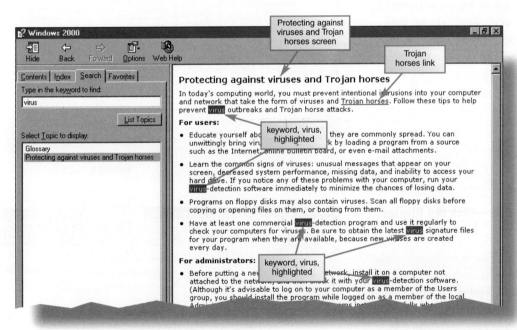

FIGURE 1-61

Other Ways

1. Press ALT+S, type keyword, press ALT+L, press TAB twice, press DOWN ARROW to highlight topic, press ALT+D (or ENTER)

Displaying a Bookmarked Help Topic

After bookmarking the Find a Help topic and Desktop overview topics, you can display either topic in the topic pane by clicking the appropriate name in the Favorites sheet. Assume that you want to display the Find a Help topic Help topic. Perform the following steps to display the topic.

 To Display a Bookmarked Topic

1 **Click the Favorites tab, click Find a Help topic in the Topics list box, and then point to the Display button.**

The Topics list in the Favorites sheet contains two topics, the Current topic text box contains the name of the last topic found (Protecting against viruses and Trojan horses), and the topic pane contains the Protecting against viruses and Trojan horses topic (Figure 1-62). The Find a Help topic name is highlighted in the Topics list box.

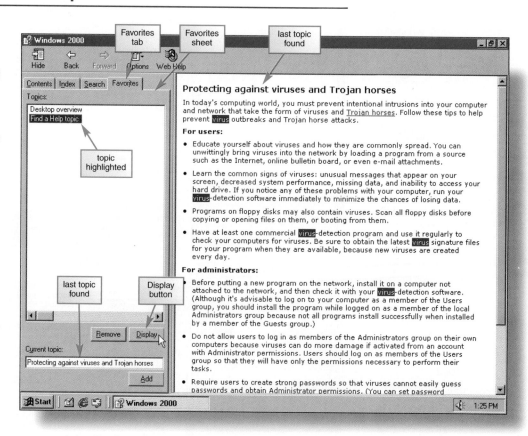

FIGURE 1-62

2 **Click the Display button.**

The Find a Help topic Help topic is no longer highlighted in the list in the navigation pane and the To find a Help topic Help topic displays in the topic pane (Figure 1-63).

 Ways

1. Press ALT+I, press DOWN ARROW to highlight topic, press ALT+D

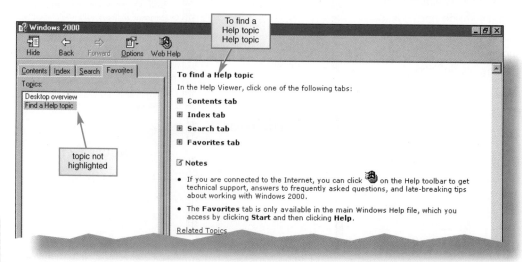

FIGURE 1-63

Removing a Bookmark

In addition to viewing a Help topic using the Favorites sheet, you also may want to remove a Help topic. Assume that you want to remove the Desktop overview and Find a Help topic Help topics from the list of favorite topics in the Topics list box. Perform the following steps to remove the two topics.

 To Remove a Bookmark

1 **Click Desktop overview in the Topics list box and then point to the Remove button.**

The Topics list box in the Favorites sheet contains two Help topics (Desktop overview and Find a Help topic) (Figure 1-64). Desktop overview is highlighted.

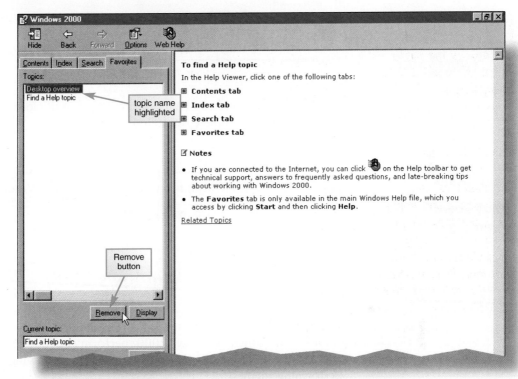

FIGURE 1-64

2 **Click the Remove button.**

The Desktop overview topic name is removed from the Topics list box and the Find a Help topic name displays in the list box (Figure 1-65).

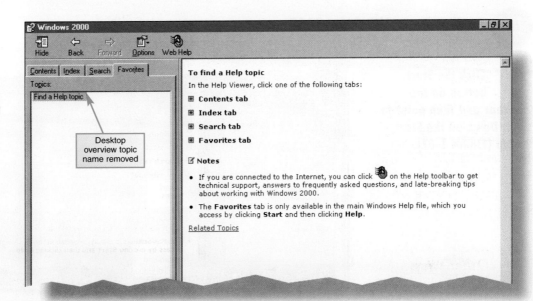

FIGURE 1-65

3 **Click Find a Help topic in the Topics list box and then click the Remove button.**

The Find a Help topic name is removed from the Topics list box (Figure 1-66).

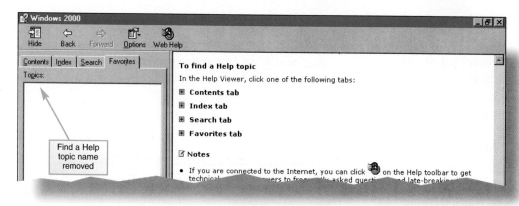

FIGURE 1-66

More *About*

Shut Down Procedures

Some users of Windows 2000 have turned off their computers without following the shut down procedure only to find data they thought they had stored on disk was lost. Because of the way Windows 2000 writes data on the disk, it is important you shut down Windows properly so you do not lose your work.

After using Windows Help, normally you will close Windows Help. To close Windows Help, complete the following step.

TO CLOSE WINDOWS HELP

1 Click the Close button on the title bar of the Windows 2000 window.

Windows 2000 closes the Windows 2000 window.

Shutting Down Windows 2000

After completing your work with Windows 2000, you may want to shut down Windows 2000 using the **Shut Down command** on the Start menu. If you are sure you want to shut down Windows 2000, perform the following steps. If you are not sure about shutting down Windows 2000, read the following steps without actually performing them.

Steps **To Shut Down Windows 2000**

1 **Click the Start button on the taskbar and then point to Shut Down on the Start menu (Figure 1-67).**

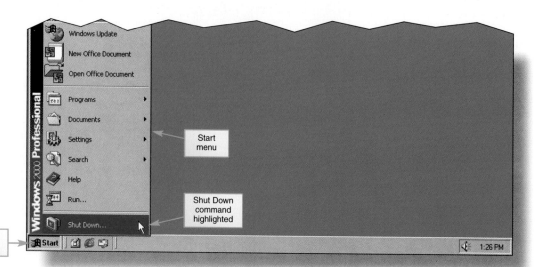

FIGURE 1-67

2 **Click Shut Down. If necessary, use the UP ARROW key or DOWN ARROW key to display the words, Shut down, in the What do you want the computer to do? box. Point to the OK button.**

The desktop darkens and the Shut Down Windows dialog box displays (Figure 1-68). The dialog box contains the What do you want the computer to do? box and three command buttons. The highlighted command, Shut down, displays in the box.

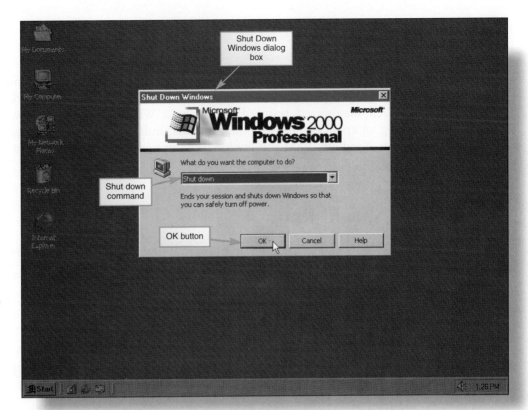

FIGURE 1-68

3 **Click the OK button.**

Windows 2000 is shut down.

While Windows 2000 is shutting down, two dialog boxes display momentarily on a blue background. First, the Please Wait dialog box containing the Windows 2000 logo, Windows 2000 name, and the text, saving your settings, displays momentarily. Then, the Shutdown in Progress dialog box, containing the text, Please wait while the system writes unsaved data to disk, displays. At this point you can turn off the computer. When shutting down Windows 2000, you should never turn off the computer before these two dialog boxes display.

If you accidentally click Shut Down on the Start menu and you do not want to shut down Windows 2000, click the Cancel button in the Shut Down Windows dialog box to return to normal Windows 2000 operation.

Other Ways

1. Press CTRL+ESC, press U, use ARROW keys to select Shut down, press ENTER
2. Press ALT+F4, use ARROW keys to select Shut down, press ENTER

CASE PERSPECTIVE SUMMARY

While continuing to answer questions about Windows 2000 Professional in the workplace, you spent nearly every free moment in the next two weeks learning about the newly installed operating system. Then, the daily training sessions kept you busy for the following three months. You taught 35 workshops and trained all of the 462 employees in the company. Your supervisor, who attended the Windows 2000 Professional seminar, complimented your success by giving you a sizable pay raise and time off to attend the annual Comdex computer convention in Las Vegas, Nevada.

Project Summary

Project 1 illustrated the Microsoft Windows 2000 graphical user interface. You launched Windows 2000, learned the parts of the desktop, and learned to point, click, right-click, double click, drag, and right-drag. You opened, minimized, maximized, restored, and closed a Windows 2000 window, as well as learning several methods of launching an application. Using the Contents, Index, Search, and Favorites sheets, you obtained Help about Microsoft Windows 2000 and bookmarked important Help topics. You shut down Windows 2000 using the Shut Down command on the Start menu.

What You Should Know

Having completed this project, you now should be able to perform the following tasks:

▶ Bookmark a Help Topic *(WIN 1.44, WIN 1.47)*
▶ Close a Window *(WIN 1.34)*
▶ Close and Reopen a Window *(WIN 1.25)*
▶ Close the Getting Started with Windows 2000 Window *(WIN 1.13)*
▶ Close Windows Help *(WIN 1.52)*
▶ Display a Bookmarked Topic *(WIN 1.50)*
▶ Launch a Program Using an Icon on the Desktop *(WIN 1.39)*
▶ Launch a Program Using the Quick Launch Toolbar *(WIN 1.39)*
▶ Launch a Program Using the Start Menu *(WIN 1.37)*
▶ Launch Windows Help *(WIN 1.40)*
▶ Maximize and Restore a Window *(WIN 1.22)*
▶ Minimize and Redisplay a Window *(WIN 1.20)*

▶ Move an Object by Dragging *(WIN 1.27)*
▶ Open a Window by Double-Clicking *(WIN 1.18)*
▶ Point and Click *(WIN 1.14)*
▶ Remove a Bookmark *(WIN 1.51)*
▶ Resize a Window *(WIN 1.33)*
▶ Right-Click *(WIN 1.17)*
▶ Right-Drag *(WIN 1.34)*
▶ Scroll by Dragging the Scroll Box *(WIN 1.33)*
▶ Scroll Using Scroll Arrows *(WIN 1.29)*
▶ Scroll Using the Scroll Bar *(WIN 1.31)*
▶ Shut Down Windows 2000 *(WIN 1.50)*
▶ Size a Window by Dragging *(WIN 1.28)*
▶ Use the Contents Sheet to Find a Help Topic *(WIN 1.42)*
▶ Use the Index Sheet *(WIN 1.45)*
▶ Use the Search Sheet *(WIN 1.48)*

Test Your Knowledge

Page 146

1 True/False

Instructions: Circle T if the statement is true or F if the statement is false.

T   F   1. A user interface is a combination of computer hardware and computer software.

T   F   2. The Quick Launch toolbar displays on the taskbar at the bottom of the desktop.

T   F   3. Click means press the right mouse button.

T   F   4. When you drag an object onto the desktop, Windows 2000 displays a shortcut menu.

T   F   5. Double-clicking the My Computer icon on the desktop opens a window.

T   F   6. You can maximize a window by dragging the title bar of the window.

T   F   7. One of the basic tasks you can perform using Windows 2000 is to launch an application program.

T   F   8. You can launch Windows Help by clicking the Start button and then clicking Help on the Start menu.

T   F   9. To find an entry in the Index sheet, type the first few characters of the entry in the text box in the Contents sheet.

T   F   10. You use the Bookmark tab to bookmark a Help topic.

2 Multiple Choice

Instructions: Circle the correct response.

1. Through a user interface, the user is able to _____ .
   a. control the computer
   b. request information from the computer
   c. respond to messages displayed by the computer
   d. all of the above

2. A shortcut menu displays when you _____ a(n) _____ .
   a. right-click, object
   b. click, menu name on the menu bar
   c. click, submenu
   d. click, recessed button in the taskbar button area

3. In this book, a dark blue title bar and a recessed button in the taskbar button area indicate a window is _____ .
   a. inactive
   b. minimized
   c. closed
   d. active

4. Text that is underlined and displays in blue font is a(n) _____ .
   a. uniform resource locator
   b. hyperlink
   c. hypertext document
   d. definition

(continued)

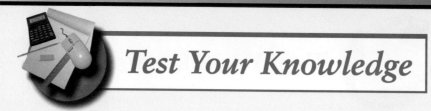

Test Your Knowledge

Multiple Choice (*continued*)

5. To view the contents of a window that are not currently visible in the window, use the _____ .
    a. title bar
    b. scroll bar
    c. menu bar
    d. Restore Down button

6. _____ is holding down the right mouse button, moving an item to the desired location, and then releasing the right mouse button.
    a. Double-clicking
    b. Right-clicking
    c. Right-dragging
    d. Pointing

7. Which method cannot be used to launch the Internet Explorer application?
    a. Click the Start button, point to Programs, and then click Internet Explorer.
    b. Click the Launch Internet Explorer Browser icon on the Quick Launch toolbar.
    c. Click the Internet Explorer button on the Standard Buttons toolbar.
    d. Click the Internet Explorer icon on the desktop.

8. To bookmark a Help topic, click the _____ , and then click the _____ .
    a. Favorites sheet, Bookmark button
    b. Favorites tab, Add button
    c. Help topic, Bookmark button
    d. Bookmark tab, Display button

9. For information about an index entry in the Index sheet, click the index entry and _____ .
    a. press the F1 key
    b. click the Forward button on the toolbar
    c. click the Search tab
    d. click the Display button

10. To shut down Windows 2000, _____ .
    a. click the Start button, select Shut Down, and then click the OK button
    b. click File on the menu bar and then click Shut Down
    c. right-click the taskbar, click Shut Down on the shortcut menu, and then click the OK button
    d. press the F10 key and then click the OK button

3 Identifying the Objects on the Desktop

Instructions: On the desktop shown in Figure 1-69, arrows point to several items or objects on the desktop. Identify the items or objects in the spaces provided.

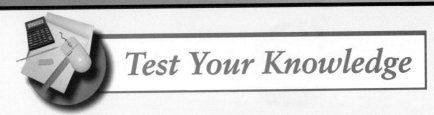

Test Your Knowledge

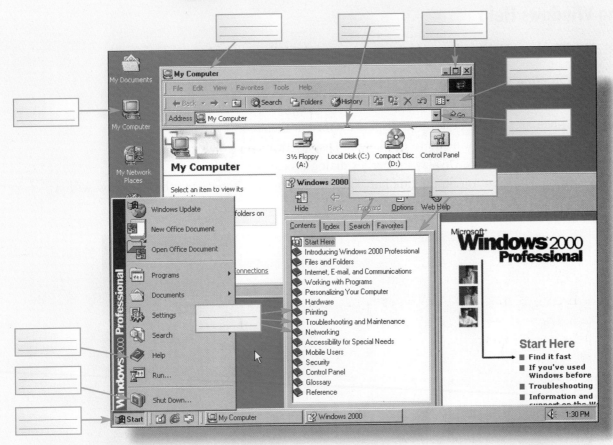

FIGURE 1-69

4 Launching the Internet Explorer Browser

Instructions: In the spaces provided, list the steps for the three methods used in this project of launching the Internet Explorer browser.

Method 1:

Step 1: _____

Step 2: _____

Step 3: _____

Step 4: _____

Method 2:

Step 1: _____

Method 3:

Step 1: _____

Use Help

1 Using Windows Help

Instructions: Use Windows Help and a computer to perform the following tasks.

Part 1: *Using the Question Mark Button*

1. If necessary, start Microsoft Windows 2000.
2. Right-click an open area of the desktop to display a shortcut menu.
3. Click Properties on the shortcut menu to display the Display Properties dialog box.
4. Click the Background tab in the Display Properties dialog box.
5. Click the Question Mark button on the title bar. The mouse pointer changes to a block arrow with a question mark (Figure 1-70).

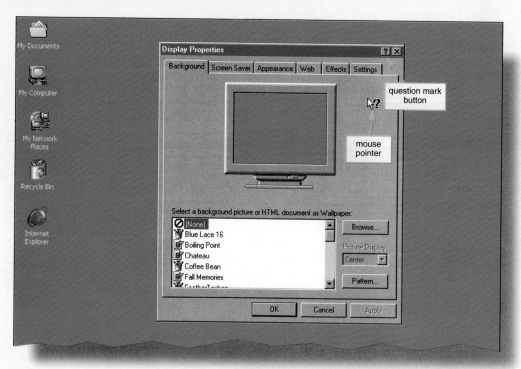

FIGURE 1-70

6. Click the list box in the Background sheet. A pop-up window displays explaining the list box. Read the information in the pop-up window and summarize the function of the list box. *lists the designs that you can use for a background, displays it.*
7. Click an open area of the Background sheet to remove the pop-up window.
8. Click the question mark button on the title bar and then click the Pattern button. A pop-up window displays explaining what happens when you click this button. Read the information in the pop-up window and summarize the function of the button. *click to select a pattern to use on your desktop or create a new one.*
9. Click an open area in the Background sheet to remove the pop-up window.

Use Help

10. Click the question mark button on the title bar and then click the monitor icon in the Background sheet. A pop-up window displays explaining the function of the monitor. Read the information in the pop-up window and summarize the function of the monitor. *Displays how a pattern will look on your screen*

11. Click an open area in the Background sheet to remove the pop-up window.

12. Click the question mark button on the title bar and then click the Cancel button. A pop-up window displays explaining what happens when you click the button. Read the information in the pop-up window and summarize the function of the Cancel button. *Closes the box with out saving any changes I made*

13. Click an open area in the Background sheet to remove the pop-up window.

14. Click the Cancel button in the Display Properties dialog box.

Part 2: *Finding What's New in Windows 2000*

1. Click the Start button and then click Help on the Start menu.

2. Click the Maximize button on Windows 2000 title bar.

3. If the Contents sheet does not display, click the Contents tab in the navigation pane. Click the Introducing Windows 2000 Professional closed book icon.

4. Click the What's new? icon in the Contents sheet and then click the plus sign in a small box preceding the More powerful entry in the topic pane. The three ways that Windows 2000 Professional makes using a computer more powerful display in the topic pane (Figure 1-71).

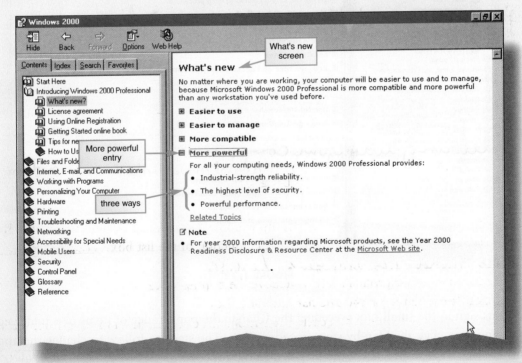

FIGURE 1-71

(continued)

Use Help

Using Windows Help *(continued)*

5. Click the Options button on the Help toolbar to display the Options menu and then click Print.
6. Click the OK button in the Print Topics dialog box. Click the Print button in the Print dialog box to print the What's new topic.
7. Click the Related Topics link in the topic pane to display a pop-up window containing three related topics. List the three topics. <u>*performance, reliability, Security*</u>
8. Click the Reliability topic in the pop-up window.
9. Click the Options button on the Help toolbar to display the Options menu and then click Print.
10. Click the OK button in the Print Topics dialog box. Click the Print button in the Print dialog box to print the What's new topic screen.

Part 3: *Viewing Tips for New Windows 2000 Users*

1. Click the Tips for new users icon in the Contents sheet. The Tips for new users screen displays in the topic pane (Figure 1-72).

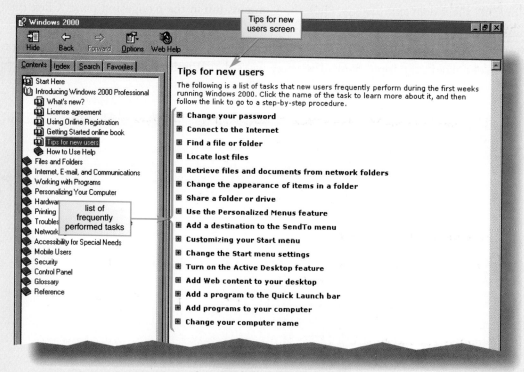

FIGURE 1-72

2. Click the plus sign in the small box preceding the Change the appearance of items in a folder entry in the topic pane and then click the Step-by-step procedure link. The steps to follow to change the appearance of the items in a folder display. What is the first step in the procedure? <u>*Open Windows explorer*</u>
3. Click the Back button on the Help toolbar to display the Tips for new users screen.

Use Help

4. Click the plus sign in the small box preceding the Add Web content to your desktop entry in the topic pane. What types of content can you add to the desktop? _picture from the net, news, entertainment, weather_

5. Click the Step-by-step procedure link. What are the three instructions to follow to add content to the desktop? _1) right click a blank area on the desktop to activate desktop._ _2) click new desktop Item   3) follow instructions on screen_

Part 4: *Reading About the Getting Started Online Book*

1. Click the Getting Started online book icon in the navigation pane. Read the information Windows 2000 displays about the *Getting Started online book* in the topic pane. The *Getting Started online book* is the printed manual for Windows 2000.

2. Click the Windows 2000 Professional Getting Started link in the topic pane to display the Windows 2000 Professional Getting Started window.

3. If the Contents sheet does not display, click the Contents tab. Click the Preface closed book icon. Click and read the three Help topics.

4. Click the open book icon (followed by a right arrow) in the upper-right corner of the topic pane until you have displayed and read each topic in the Ch.1 - Welcome book.

5. Click the open book icon (preceded by a left arrow) in the upper-left corner of the topic pane to display previously displayed topics.

6. Read the remaining chapters and appendices in the *Getting Started online book*.

7. Click the Close button in the Windows 2000 Professional Getting Started window.

8. Click the Close button in the Windows 2000 window.

2 Using Windows Help to Obtain Help

Instructions: Use Windows Help and a computer to perform the following tasks.

1. Find Help about keyboard shortcuts by looking in the Reference book in the Contents sheet. Answer the following questions in the spaces provided.

   a. What Windows 2000 keyboard shortcut is used to view properties for a selected item?
   Alt + enter.

   b. What Windows 2000 keyboard shortcut is used to display the shortcut menu for a selected item?
   Shift + F10

   c. What Help Viewer keyboard shortcut is used to display the Options menu?
   ALT + O

   d. What Help Viewer keyboard shortcut is used to display the Index tab? _ALT + N_

   e. What Natural Keyboard shortcut is used to display or hide the Start menu? _Windows Key_

   f. What Natural Keyboard shortcut is used to open My Computer? _Windows Key + E_

(continued)

Use Help

Using Windows Help to Obtain Help *(continued)*

2. Use the Index sheet to answer the following questions in the spaces provided.
   a. How do you get Help in a dialog box? *type help + click on the topic you want then click on display.*
   b. What dialog box do you use to change the appearance of the mouse pointer? *mouse pointers, changing*
   c. How do you minimize all windows? *click ▢ on the taskbar (Show Desk Top icon)*
   d. What is a server? *a computer that controls access to the hardware + software on a network + provides a centralized storage area for programs, data + info.*

3. Find Help about viewing the Start Here screen (also called the **Welcome** screen) that displays when you launch Windows 2000. Use the search word, welcome, and the Search sheet. The Viewing the Welcome screen should display. Answer the following questions in the spaces provided.
   a. How can you open the Welcome screen from the Viewing the Welcome screen? *should come on when you start Windows 2000 unless you clear the screen (show this screen at startup)*
   b. How can you open the Welcome screen using the Start menu? *start, run, type welcome*
   c. Open the Welcome screen. How many entries display in the Table of Contents in the Getting Started screen? *3*
   d. Point to Discover Windows 2000 in the table of contents. What does the Discover Windows 2000 Professional tour highlight? *all the newest + coolest features*
   e. Close the Getting Started with Windows 2000 window.

4. Find Help about what to do if you have a problem in Windows 2000. The tools to solve a problem while using Windows 2000 are called troubleshooters. Using Help, locate the Troubleshooters overview. Answer the following questions in the spaces provided.
   a. What does a troubleshooter allow you to diagnose and solve? *technical problems that are occurring with your computer.*
   b. List five of the Windows 2000 troubleshooters. *display, hardware, modem, multi media games, print, sound.*

5. Obtain information on software licensing by answering the following questions. Find and then print information from Windows Help that supports your answers.
   a. How does the law protect computer software? *by copyright law + int. copyright treaties, owner has exclusive rights*
   b. What is software piracy? *is the unauthorized copying, reproduction, or use or manufacture of software products.*
   c. Why should I be concerned about it? *higher prices for licensed users, reduced support, delays in funding + development of new products, harms local + national economies*
   d. What is an EULA (end user licensing agreement)? *Commercial computer software is licensed directly or indirectly from the author (software publisher) for use by the customer through a contract called a EULA.*

Use Help

e. Can you make a second copy of an operating system (Windows 2000) for use at home, work, or on a *operating systems* portable computer? *No, the right to copy only applies to some application product not operating systems*

f. How can you identify illegal Microsoft software? *prices too good to be true, NO EULA, no product ID #, no registration card, manuals photocopyed,*

6. Find the definition for the following terms using the Glossary book in the Contents sheet. Write the definitions in the spaces provided.
   a. desktop pattern *a design that appears across your desktop. you can create your own or select a pattern provided by Windows.*
   b. My Documents *Convenient place to store documents, graphics, files, you want to access quickly.*
   c. screen saver *a moving picture or pattern that appears on your screen when you have not used the keyboard or mouse for a specific time.*
   d. server *a computer that provides shared resources to network users.*
   e. virus *Program that attempts to spread from computer to computer + either cause damage (erasing computer data) or annoy users (by printing messages or altering what on the screen).*

7. Use the Reference book in the Contents sheet to view the Programs list. Answer the following questions in the spaces provided.
   a. What is the purpose of the Address Book? *provide a convenient place to store contact info. for easy retrieval from programs such as outlook, outlook express, Int. explorer,*
   b. For what purpose would you use a certificate? *used to assure the end user that the software program is not counterfeit.*
   c. What information does Device Manager provide? *Tells you how your hardware on your computer is installed + configured. + how it interacts with your computer programs.*
   d. What does Outlook Express allow you to do? *E mail program exchange mail with friends etc. to trade ideas + info.*
   e. What is Paint? *drawing tool you can use to create black & white or color drawings that you can save*

8. Close all open windows. *as bit files.*

In the Lab

1 Improving Your Mouse Skills

Instructions: Use a computer to perform the following tasks.

1. If necessary, start Microsoft Windows 2000.
2. Click the Start button on the taskbar, point to Programs on the Start menu, point to Accessories on the Programs submenu, point to Games on the Accessories submenu, and click Solitaire on the Games submenu.
3. Click the Maximize button in the Solitaire window (Figure 1-73).

FIGURE 1-73

4. Click Help on the Solitaire menu bar and then click Contents. If the Contents sheet does not display, click the Contents tab.
5. Read the Solitaire overview and the three Help topics (Play Solitaire, Change game options, and Choose a scoring system) in the Solitaire book.
6. After reviewing the Help topics, close the Solitaire window.
7. Play the game of Solitaire.
8. Click the Close button on the Solitaire title bar to close the game.

2 Using the Discover Windows 2000 Professional Tour

Instructions: To use the Discover Windows 2000 Professional tour you will need a copy of the Windows 2000 Professional CD-ROM. If this CD-ROM is not available, skip this lab assignment. Otherwise, use a computer and the CD-ROM to perform the following tasks.

Part 1: *Launching the Discover Windows 2000 Professional Tour*

1. If necessary, start Microsoft Windows 2000.
2. Insert the Windows 2000 Professional CD-ROM in the CD-ROM drive. If the Microsoft Windows 2000 CD window displays, click the Close button in the window to close the window.

In the Lab

3. Click the Start button on the taskbar, click Run on the Start menu, type `welcome` in the Open box in the Run dialog box, and click the OK button. The Getting Started with Windows 2000 window, containing a table of contents, displays.

4. Click Discover Windows in the table of contents. The Discover screen displays (Figure 1-74). The right panel contains four categories (Easier to Use, Easier to Manage, More Compatible, and More Powerful), and the left panel contains instructions for selecting a category in the right panel.

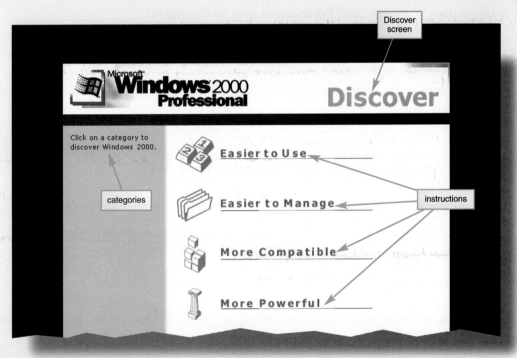

FIGURE 1-74

Part 2: *Starting the Tour*

1. Click Easier to Use in the right panel. A toolbar containing the four categories displays, the five topics in the Easier to Use category display in the left panel, and the right panel contains information about the Easier to Use category. Read the information.

Part 3: *Touring the Easier to Use Category*

1. Click Work with Files in the left panel. Four subtopics display indented below the Work with Files topic in the left panel and the right panel contains information about the Work with Files topic. Read the information.

2. Click Track Your Documents. Four subtopics display indented below the Track Your Documents subtopic in the left panel, and the right panel contains information about the Track Your Documents subtopic. Read the information.

(continued)

In the Lab

Using the Discover Windows 2000 Professional Tour *(continued)*

3. Click My Network Places. Information about the My Network Places subtopic displays in right panel. Read the information.

4. Click each of the remaining subtopics (My Documents, File Open/Save As, and History Folder) in the Track Your Documents subtopic. When a Play Animation button displays, click the button to view an animated explanation of the subtopic. Answer the following question.

    a. In what folder does Windows 2000 Professional save all documents? _____

    _____

5. Click the remaining subtopics in the Track Your Documents topic (Associate File Types, Work with Images, and Manage Your Printing) in the Work with Files topic.

6. Tour the remaining topics (Find Information, Personalize, Work on the Web, and Work Remotely) in the Easier to Use category. Answer the following questions.

    a. Which dialog box do you use to search the disk drive, network, or Internet?_____

    _____

    b. Which wizard do you use to establish a new Internet user account?_____

    _____

    c. If you lose your portable computer, what prevents others from viewing the files on the computer?

    _____

Part 4: *Touring the Other Categories*

1. Tour the other three categories (Easier to Manage, More Compatible, and More Powerful) and answer the following questions.

    a. The ability to upgrade from Windows 95 and Windows 98 to Windows 2000 is based on what requirement?_____

    b. What is the comprehensive list of devices supported by Windows 2000 called? _____

    _____

    c. What is IEEE 1394? _____

    _____

    d. What is a self-healing program? _____

    e. Disk space storage is more efficient because of what storage system?_____

    _____

2. Click Exit in the left panel to quit the tour.

3. Click the Close button in the Getting Started with Windows 2000 window.

4. Remove the Windows 2000 CD-ROM from the CD-ROM drive.

3 Launching and Using the Internet Explorer Application

Instructions: Perform the following steps to launch the Internet Explorer application.

Part 1: *Launching the Internet Explorer Application*

1. Start Microsoft Windows 2000 and, if necessary, connect to the Internet.
2. Click the Launch Internet Explorer Browser icon on the Quick Launch toolbar. Maximize the Microsoft Internet Explorer window.
3. If the Address bar does not display below the Standard Buttons toolbar in the Microsoft Internet Explorer window, click View on the menu bar, point to Toolbars, and click Address bar on the Toolbars submenu.

Part 2: *Entering a URL in the Address Bar*

1. Click the URL in the Address bar to highlight the URL.
2. Type www.microsoft.com in the Address bar and then press the ENTER key.
3. Answer the following questions.
   a. What URL displays in the Address bar? _http! /www. micRosoft .com /_
   b. What window title displays on the title bar? _MicRosoft CoRporation - microsoft Internet ExpLoreR_
4. If necessary, scroll the Web page to view the contents of the Web page. List five hyperlinks (underlined text) that are shown on this Web page. _at home, WindowsxP, Clip art, micRosoft hardware, at work,_
5. Click any hyperlink on the Web page. What hyperlink did you click? _clipart,_
6. Describe the Web page that displayed when you clicked the hyperlink? _display all the different types of clipart,_
7. Click the Print button on the Standard Buttons toolbar to print the Web page.

Part 3: *Entering a URL in the Address Bar*

1. Click the URL in the Address bar to highlight the URL.
2. Type www.disney.com in the Address bar and then press the ENTER key.
3. What window title displays on the title bar? _Disney online -The official Site Home page the WDC! micuosof.Exp_
4. Scroll the Web page to view the contents of the Web page. Do any graphic images display on the Web page? _yes,_
   If so, describe two images. _advertises Cinderella, frosted flakes_
5. Pointing to an image on a Web page and having the mouse pointer change to a hand indicates the image is a hyperlink. Does the Web page include an image that is a hyperlink? _Yes. what is Toontown_
   If so, describe the image. _multiplayer internet game_
6. Click the hyperlink to display another Web page. What window title displays on the title bar? _Disney's Toontown Online - Microsoft Internet Explorer_
7. Click the Print button on the Standard Buttons toolbar to print the Web page.

(continued)

In the Lab

Launching and Using the Internet Explorer Application *(continued)*

Part 4: *Displaying Previously Displayed Web Pages*

1. Click the Back button on the Standard Buttons toolbar. What Web page displays? *last page*
2. Click the Back button on the Standard Buttons toolbar twice. What Web page displays? *microsoft*
3. Click the Forward button on the Standard Buttons toolbar bar. What Web page displays? *toontown*

Part 5: *Entering a URL in the Address Bar*

1. Click the URL in the Address bar to highlight the URL.
2. Type www.scsite.com in the Address bar and then press the ENTER key.
3. Scroll the Web page to display the Operating Systems link.
4. Click the Operating Systems link.
5. Click the textbook title of your Windows 2000 textbook.
6. Click the Steve's Cool Sites hyperlink on the Web page.
7. Click any hyperlinks that are of interest to you. Which hyperlink did you like the best? _____
8. Use the Back button or Forward button to display the Web site you like the best.
9. Click the Print button on the Standard Buttons toolbar to print the Web page.
10. Click the Close button on the Microsoft Internet Explorer title bar.

4 Launching an Application

Instructions: Perform the following steps to launch the Notepad application using the Start menu and create the homework list shown in Figure 1-75. **Notepad** is a popular application program available with Windows 2000 that allows you to create, save, and print simple text documents.

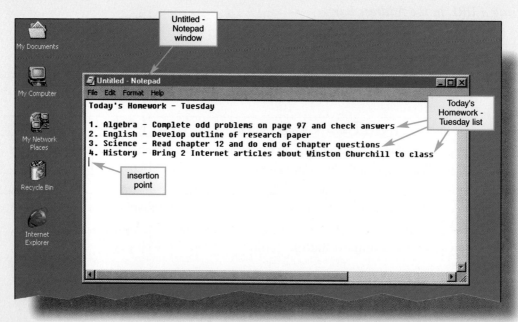

FIGURE 1-75

In the Lab

Part 1: *Launching the Notepad Application*

1. If necessary, start Microsoft Windows 2000.
2. Click the Start button.
3. Point to Programs on the Start menu, point to Accessories on the Programs submenu, and click Notepad on the Accessories submenu. The Untitled - Notepad window displays and an insertion point (flashing vertical line) displays in the blank area below the menu bar.

Part 2: *Creating a Document Using Notepad*

1. Type Today's Homework - Tuesday and then press the ENTER key twice.
2. Type 1. Algebra - Complete odd problems on page 97 and check answers and then press the ENTER key.
3. Type 2. English - Develop outline of research paper and then press the ENTER key.
4. Type 3. Science - Read chapter 12 and do end of chapter questions and then press the ENTER key.
5. Type 4. History - Bring 2 Internet articles about Winston Churchill to class and then press the ENTER key.

Part 3: *Printing the Today's Homework Document*

1. Click File on the menu bar and then click Print. Click the Print button in the Print dialog box to print the document.
2. Retrieve the printed Today's Homework list from the printer.

Part 4: *Closing the Notepad Window*

1. Click the Close button on the Notepad title bar.
2. Click the No button in the Notepad dialog box to not save the Today's Homework document.

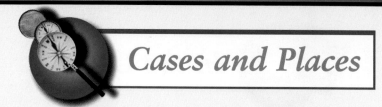

Cases and Places

The difficulty of these case studies varies:
▶ are the least difficult; ▶▶ are more difficult; and ▶▶▶ are the most difficult.

1 ▶ Using Windows Help, locate the *Getting Started* online book. Using the online book, read about the following ten topics: Connecting to a Local Area Network, Customizing Your Desktop, Emergency Repair Disk, NTFS File System, Hardware Compatibility List, Microsoft NetMeeting, Active Desktop, Search Tips, Universal Serial Bus (USB), and Watching TV. Select five of the ten topics. In a brief report, summarize the five topics you have selected.

2 ▶ Technical support is an important consideration when installing and using an operating system or an application software program. The ability to obtain a valid answer to a question at the moment you have the question can be the difference between a frustrating experience and a positive experience. Using Windows 2000 Help, the Internet, or another research facility, write a brief report on the options that are available for obtaining help and technical support while using Windows 2000.

3 ▶ The Windows 2000 operating system can be installed only on computers found in the Windows 2000 hardware compatibility list. Locate three older personal computers. Look for them in your school's computer lab, at a local business, or in your house. Use Windows Help and the Internet to find the Microsoft Web page that contains the Windows 2000 hardware compatibility list. Check each computer against the list and write a brief report summarizing your results.

4 ▶▶ Early personal computer operating systems were adequate, but they were not user-friendly and had few advanced features. Over the past several years, however, personal computer operating systems have become increasingly easy to use, and some now offer features once available only on mainframe computers. Using the Internet, a library, or other research facility, write a brief report on three personal computer operating systems. Describe the systems, pointing out their similarities and differences. Discuss the advantages and disadvantages of each. Finally, tell which operating system you would purchase and explain why.

5 ▶▶ Microsoft's decision to make the Internet Explorer 5 Web browser part of the Windows 2000 operating system caused many legal problems for Microsoft. Using the Internet, computer magazines and newspapers, or other resources, prepare a brief report on these legal problems. Explain the arguments for and against combining the browser and operating system. Identify the key players on both sides of the legal battle and summarize the final decision. Did the legal process or final decision affect the release date and contents of Windows 2000? Do you think computer users benefited from this decision? Explain your answers.

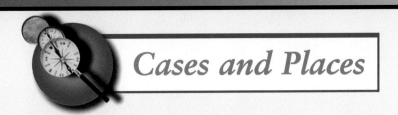

Cases and Places

6 ▶▶▶ In addition to Windows 2000, Microsoft also sells the Windows 98 operating system. Some say Windows 2000 will replace Windows 98 in the future. Using the Internet, computer magazines, or other resources, prepare a brief report comparing and contrasting the operating systems. How do their graphical user interfaces compare? What features and commands are shared by both operating systems? Does either operating system have features or commands that the other operating system does not have? Explain whether you think Windows 2000 could replace Windows 98.

7 ▶▶▶ Because of the many important tasks an operating system performs, most businesses put a great deal of thought into choosing an operating system. Interview a person at a local business about the operating system it uses with its computers. Based on the interview, write a brief report on why the business chose that operating system, how satisfied it is with it, and under what circumstances it may consider switching to a different operating system.

Microsoft Windows 2000

Working on the Windows 2000 Desktop

P R O J E C T

2

O B J E C T I V E S

You will have mastered the material in this project when you can:

- Launch an application, create a text document, and save the document on the desktop
- Create, name, and save a text document directly on the desktop
- Open and modify a document on the desktop
- Create and name a folder on the desktop
- Move documents to a folder on the desktop
- Display the contents of a folder
- Modify and print documents in a folder
- Open, modify, and delete multiple documents
- Copy a folder from the desktop onto a floppy disk
- Open a folder stored on a floppy disk
- Minimize all open windows
- Add and delete shortcuts on the Start menu
- Create and delete shortcuts on the desktop
- Open a document using a shortcut
- Share a folder on a network
- Delete shortcut icons, document icons, and folder icons from the desktop
- Describe active content and channels
- Turn the Active Desktop on and off
- Display the current home page on the Active Desktop
- Add and remove a desktop item on the Active Desktop
- Use Web Help

Performance and Flexibility

Next-Generation PC Computing Clicks with Users

In today's fast-paced world of instant access via the Internet and a booming e-commerce, business and individuals are taking advantage of the new laptops, smart cards, scanners, digital cameras, music players, and other devices being introduced every day. When choosing an operating system or upgrading, performance and flexibility are two of the major factors that determine how users want to manage their resources. Windows 2000, which supports more than 11,000 hardware devices, is available as a desktop and laptop product, making it an easy choice. One of its more important features is the ease with which users can access documents and files on the desktop.

In Project 2, two methods to create documents on the desktop are presented: launching an application program and using a shortcut menu.

You will create folders, use shortcuts, and access Web Help. Using the Active Desktop™, you will display constantly changing content from the Web directly on your desktop. Working on the Windows desktop in this project, you will find out for yourself how these features can save time and help you work efficiently.

Windows has come a long way since Bill Gates announced plans to add graphical capabilities to the IBM personal computer in 1983. The Microsoft chairman took this step to help current personal computer users work more effectively and, of course, to entice others to buy systems. More than three million computers were sold that year.

Gates's graphical intentions were fueled by work being done at Xerox's Palo Alto Research Center in California. He saw researchers there using an invention they called a mouse to move a pointer instead of using arrow keys on the keyboard to move a cursor.

Then, working with Apple, Microsoft developed software for the Macintosh computer. Combining its original innovations with those of Xerox, Microsoft created the graphical user interface and experimented with the use of various icons and fonts to make the screen user-friendly. In addition, Microsoft introduced Word and Excel for the Macintosh platform. When the Mac was released in 1984, it became a success among users, particularly students.

Microsoft's next step was to develop these applications for the IBM-PC and IBM-compatible computers. The company's innovations resulted in the release of Windows 3.1

in 1992, which sold three million copies within two months; Windows 95, a major upgrade to the Windows operating system; and Windows 98, boasting global sales of ten million copies within the first six months. Other Windows releases including Windows NT and Windows 2000 have been received with equal enthusiasm as the wave of computer users continues to swell. More than 100 million computers worldwide use the Windows operating system.

Programmers at Microsoft use a process the corporation calls continuous reinvention to constantly add new features to enhance Windows performance. Microsoft also allows anyone to write programs for the Windows platform without requiring prior permission. Today, many of the thousands of Windows-based programs compete with Microsoft's own programs.

Gates has indicated that Microsoft will continue to release new Windows versions every two or three years, evident in the recent release of Windows 2000. He is convinced that individuals will want to take advantage of user interface enhancements and innovations that make computing easier, more reliable, faster, and integrated with the Internet.

Adding performance and flexibility, Windows 2000 takes the next PC generation to advanced computing potential.

Microsoft Windows 2000

Working on the Windows 2000 Desktop

P R O J E C T

2

C A S E   P E R S P E C T I V E

As you work with Windows 2000, you will find one essential feature is the ease with which you can access documents and files you use constantly. You also will find that working with multiple documents at the same time is vital. The company where you work has placed you in charge of developing the text documents to keep track of the daily reminders. As you begin the assignment, you ascertain that reminders seem to change constantly. You realize that if you could work on the Windows 2000 desktop, you would save a great deal of time. In this project, you will learn the skills that are essential to your success and gain the knowledge required to work efficiently on the Windows 2000 desktop.

Introduction

In Project 1, you learned three methods of launching the Internet Explorer application. To launch Internet Explorer, you used the Start button and Start menu, an icon on the Quick Launch toolbar, or a shortcut icon on the desktop. The capability of accomplishing a task, such as launching an application, in a variety of ways is one of Windows 2000's more powerful features.

In Project 2, you will learn two methods of creating documents on the desktop. You also will discover the intuitive nature of the Windows 2000 desktop by creating a folder on the desktop in which to store multiple documents, storing documents in the folder, and then moving the folder from the desktop onto a disk. In addition, you will turn on the Active Desktop and add an Active Desktop item to the desktop. An **Active Desktop item** allows you to display the constantly changing content of a Web page directly on the Active Desktop and update the content automatically.

Assume each morning you create two daily reminders lists: one for Mr. Cortez and one for Ms. Nelson. Mr. Cortez and Ms. Nelson review the lists throughout the day. You must update the lists as reminders are added during the day. In addition, Mr. Cortez and Ms. Nelson must be able to view, add, and delete reminders on either list. You decide to use **Notepad**, a popular application program available with Windows 2000, to create the daily reminders lists. The finished documents are shown in Figure 2-1.

The name of each document displays at the top of the printed page, the text of the document (the daily reminders) displays below the document name, and a page number displays at the bottom of the page. The first printed document contains a list of Monday's reminders for Mr. Cortez. The second printed document contains a list of Monday's reminders for Ms. Nelson. The following sections illustrate two methods of creating these documents.

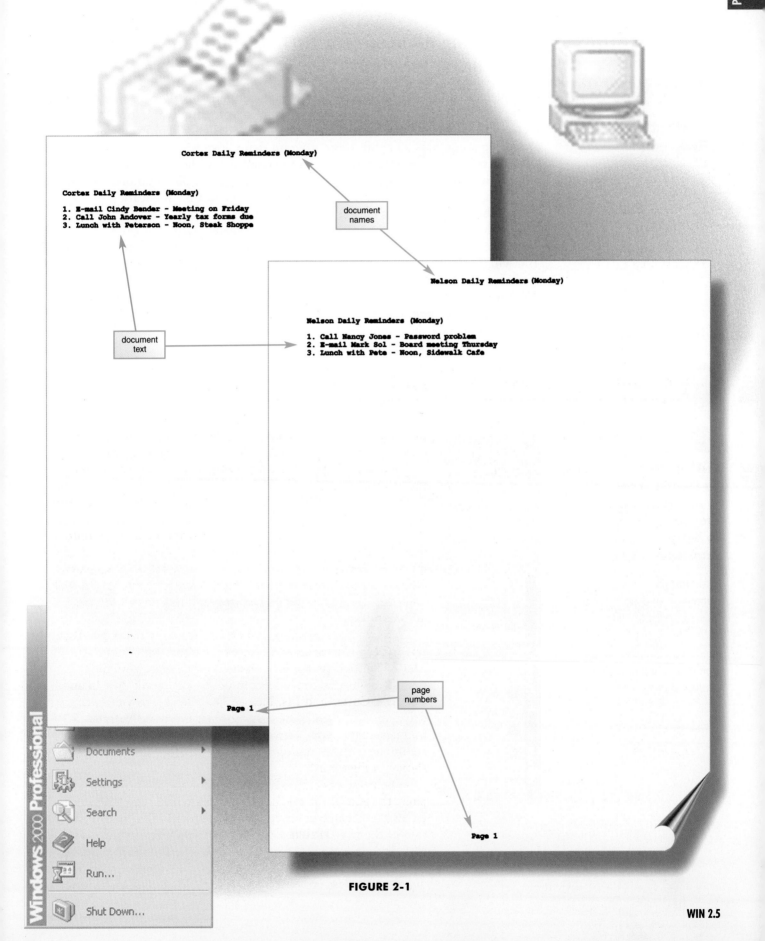

Cortez Daily Reminders (Monday)

Cortez Daily Reminders (Monday)

1. E-mail Cindy Bender - Meeting on Friday
2. Call John Andover - Yearly tax forms due
3. Lunch with Peterson - Noon, Steak Shoppe

document names

document text

Nelson Daily Reminders (Monday)

Nelson Daily Reminders (Monday)

1. Call Nancy Jones - Password problem
2. E-mail Mark Sol - Board meeting Thursday
3. Lunch with Pete - Noon, Sidewalk Cafe

page numbers

Page 1

Page 1

Documents

Settings

Search

Help

Run...

Shut Down...

Windows 2000 Professional

FIGURE 2-1

Creating a Document by Launching an Application Program

As explained in Project 1, a **program** is a set of computer instructions that carries out a task on the computer. An **application program** is a program that allows you to accomplish a specific task for which the program is designed. For example, a **word processing program** is an application program that allows you to create written documents, a **spreadsheet program** allows you to create spreadsheets and charts, and a **presentation graphics program** allows you to create graphic presentations for display on a computer. Project 1 illustrated three methods to start an application program. One method used the Start button on the taskbar.

To illustrate using an application program to create a written document, you will create the document to contain the daily reminders for Mr. Cortez using Notepad. You will create the document by launching the Notepad application, typing the reminders for Mr. Cortez, and then saving the document on the desktop. In Windows terminology, opening an application program and then creating a document is called the **application-centric approach**. Perform the following steps to launch Notepad and enter the reminders for Mr. Cortez.

Steps To Launch a Program and Create a Document

1 Click the Start button on the taskbar. Point to Programs on the Start menu. Point to Accessories on the Programs submenu. Point to Notepad on the Accessories submenu.

The Start menu, Programs submenu, and Accessories submenu display (Figure 2-2). The Accessories submenu contains the Notepad command to launch the Notepad program.

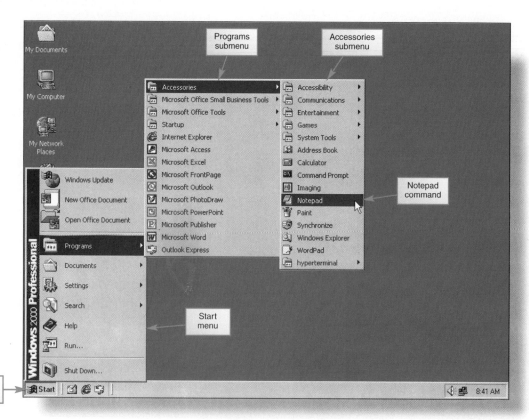

FIGURE 2-2

2 **Click Notepad. Type** `Cortez Daily Reminders (Monday)` **and then press the ENTER key twice. Type** `1. E-mail Cindy Bender - Meeting on Friday` **and then press the ENTER key. Type** `2. Call John Andover - Yearly tax forms due` **and then press the ENTER key. Type** `3. Lunch with Peterson - Noon, Steak Shoppe` **and then press the ENTER key.**

The Notepad program launches, the text of the document is entered, and a recessed Notepad button displays in the taskbar button area (Figure 2-3).

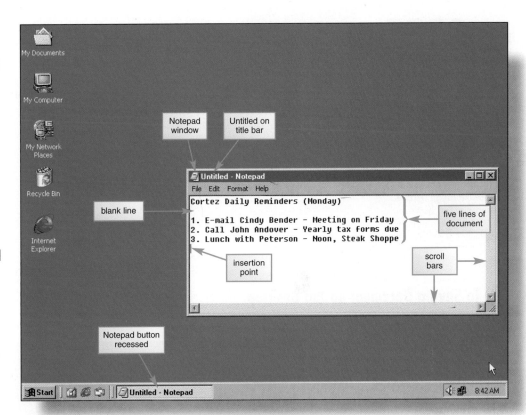

FIGURE 2-3

In Figure 2-3, the word, Untitled, in the window title bar (Untitled - Notepad) and on the Notepad button indicates the document has not been saved on disk. The area below the menu bar contains the five lines of the document, including the blank line, a line containing an insertion point, and two scroll bars. The **insertion point** is a flashing vertical line that indicates the point at which text typed on the keyboard will display. The scroll bars do not contain scroll boxes, indicating the document is not large enough to require scrolling.

Saving a Document on the Desktop

When you create a document using a program such as Notepad, the document is stored in the main memory (RAM) of the computer. If you close the program without saving the document or if the computer accidentally loses electrical power, the document will be lost. To protect against the accidental loss of a document and to allow you to modify the document easily in the future, you can save the document on disk (hard disk or floppy disk) or on the desktop. When you save a document on the desktop, a document icon displays on the desktop and the document is stored on the hard disk.

When you save a document, you must assign a file name to the document. All documents are identified by a **file name**. A file name should be descriptive of the saved file. Examples of possible file names are Cortez Reminders (Monday), Office Supplies List, and Automobile Maintenance. A file name can contain up to 255 characters, including spaces. Any uppercase or lowercase character is valid when creating a file name, except a backslash (\), slash (/), colon (:), asterisk (*), question mark (?), quotation mark ('), less than symbol (<), greater than symbol (>), or vertical bar (|). File names cannot be CON, AUX, COM1, COM2, COM3, COM4, LPT1, LPT2, LPT3, PRN, or NUL.

Other Ways

1. Right-click desktop, point to New, click Text Document, double-click New Text Document icon, enter text
2. Click Start button, click Run, type Notepad, click OK button, enter text
3. Press CTRL+ESC, press R, type Notepad, press ENTER key, enter text

More About 2000

Saving a Document

Many computer users can tell at least one horror story of working on their computer for a long period of time and then losing their work because of a power failure or software problem. Be Warned: Save and save often to protect the work you have completed on your computer.

File Names

The earliest versions of Windows allowed file names of only eight or fewer characters. F56QPSLA and similar indecipherable names were common. In 1995, Microsoft introduced long file names and touted them as a significant breakthrough. Apple Macintosh users, however, had used long file names for years.

To associate a document with an application, Windows 2000 assigns an extension of a period and up to three characters to each document. All documents created using the Notepad program are text documents and are saved with the .txt extension.

To save the document you created using Notepad on the desktop of the computer using the file name, Cortez Reminders (Monday), perform the following steps.

 ## To Save a Document on the Desktop

1 **Click File on the menu bar and then point to Save As.**

The File menu opens in the Notepad window (Figure 2-4). The ellipsis (...) following the Save As command indicates Windows 2000 requires more information to carry out the Save As command and will open a dialog box when you click Save As.

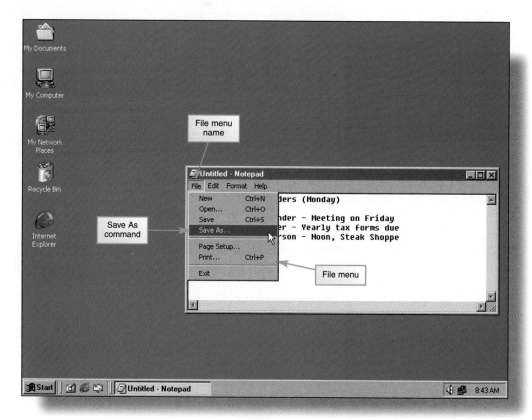

FIGURE 2-4

2 **Click Save As. Type** Cortez Reminders (Monday) **in the File name text box. Point to the Desktop button on the Shortcut bar.**

The Save As dialog box displays (Figure 2-5). The My Documents entry in the Save in box and the indented My Documents button on the Shortcut bar indicate the file will be saved to the My Documents folder. The File name text box contains the document name. When you save this document, Notepad will add the .txt extension to the file name automatically.

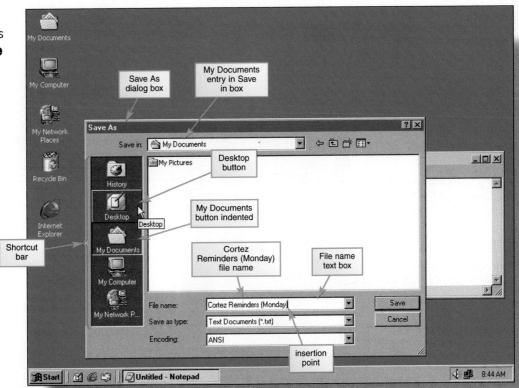

FIGURE 2-5

3 **Click the Desktop button and then point to the Save button in the Save As dialog box.**

The Desktop entry displays in the Save in box, the names of three folders on the desktop display in the list box, and the Shortcut bar contains the recessed Desktop button (Figure 2-6).

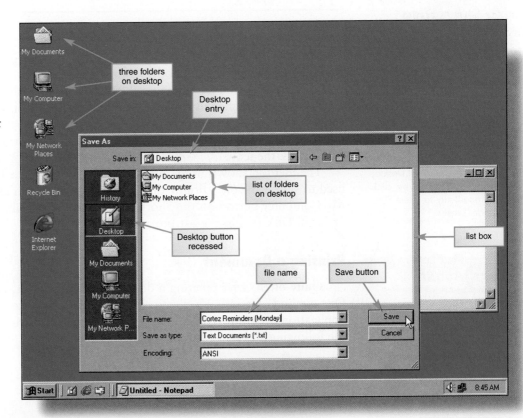

FIGURE 2-6

Click the Save button.

Windows 2000 displays an **hourglass icon** *while saving the Cortez Reminders (Monday) document on the desktop. The Save As dialog box closes. The Cortez Reminders (Monday) document icon displays on the desktop, and the file name becomes part of the Notepad window title and the button name in the taskbar button area (Figure 2-7).*

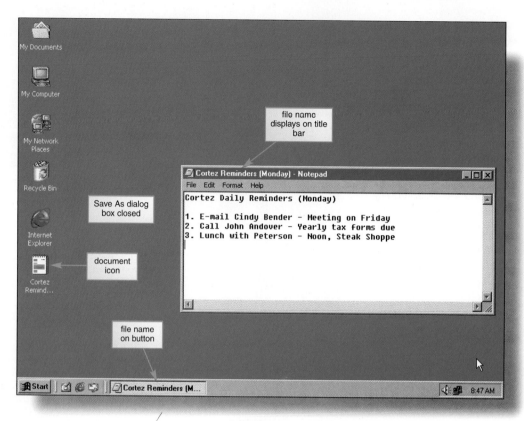

FIGURE 2-7

The Cortez Reminders (Monday) icon may display on the desktop next in line in the columns of icons or at another location, depending on the computer's settings.

In Figure 2-7, the file name on the button in the taskbar button area contains an ellipsis to indicate the entire button name does not fit on the button. To display the entire button name in the taskbar button area, point to the button. The file name on the document icon on the desktop also contains an ellipsis. To display the entire icon name, click the icon.

The method shown in the previous steps for saving a file on the desktop can be used to save a file on a floppy disk or on a hard disk on the computer by clicking the My Computer button on the Shortcut bar and then double-clicking 3½ Floppy (A:) or Local Disk (C:) in the list box.

 *About*

Printing

Printing is and will remain important for documents. Many sophisticated application programs, however, are extending the printing capability to include transmitting faxes, sending e-mail, and even posting documents on Web pages of the World Wide Web.

Printing a Document

Quite often, after creating a document and saving it, you will want to print it. One method of printing a document on the desktop is to print it directly from an application program. To print the Cortez Reminders (Monday) document, perform the following steps.

To Print a Document

1 **Click File on the menu bar and then point to Print.**

The File menu, containing the highlighted Print command, displays (Figure 2-8).

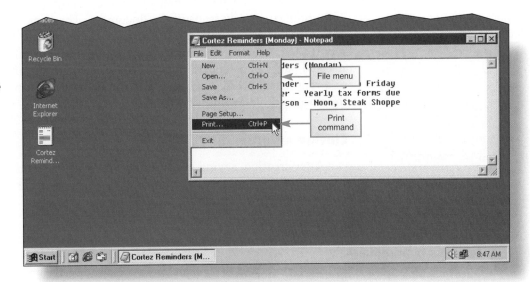

FIGURE 2-8

2 **Click Print and then point to the Print button in the Print dialog box.**

The Print dialog box, containing the General sheet, displays (Figure 2-9). The selected All option button and the value 1 in the Number of copies text box indicate one copy of all pages will print.

3  **Click the Print button.**

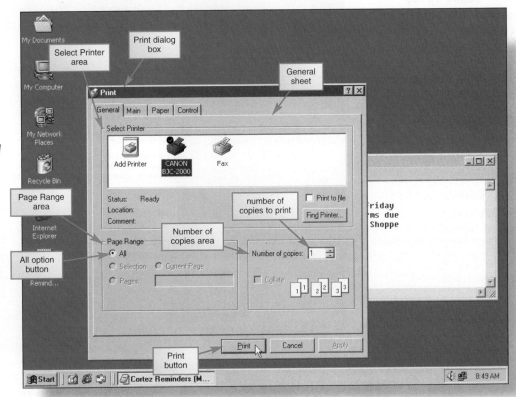

FIGURE 2-9

Other Ways

1. Right-click document icon on desktop, click Print
2. Press ALT+F, press P, press TAB key repeatedly to select Print button, press P

In Figure 2-9 on the previous page, the General sheet in the Printer dialog box contains the Select Printer, Page Range, and Number of copies areas. The highlighted printer icon in the Select Printer area indicates that, in this case, the Canon BJC-2000 printer is ready to print the document. The Page Range area contains three option buttons. The option buttons give you the choice of printing all pages of a report (All), selected parts of a report (Selection), current page (Current Page), or selected pages of a report (Pages). The selected All option button indicates all pages of a report will print. The value 1 in the Number of copies box indicates one copy of the document will print.

Closing a Document

After creating, saving, and printing the Cortez Reminders (Monday) document, your use of the document is complete. Perform the following steps to close the Notepad window containing the document.

To Close a Document

 1 **Point to the Close button on the Notepad title bar (Figure 2-10).**

 2 **Click the Close button.**

The Cortez Reminders (Monday) - Notepad window closes and the Cortez Reminders (Monday) - Notepad button no longer displays.

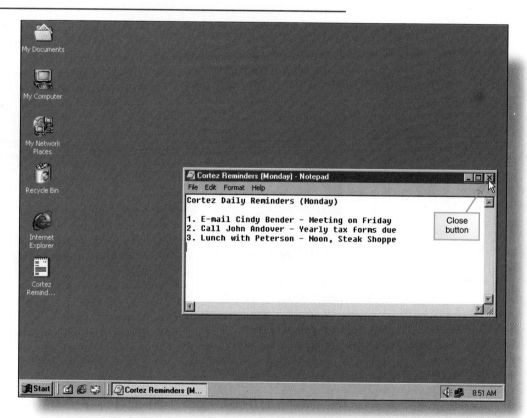

FIGURE 2-10

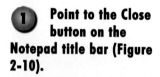

1. Double-click Notepad logo on title bar
2. Click Notepad logo on title bar, click Close
3. On File menu click Exit
4. Press ALT+F, press X; or press ALT+F4

After completing the reminders list for Mr. Cortez, the next step is to create a similar list for Ms. Nelson.

Creating and Naming a Document on the Desktop

Opening an application program and then creating a document (application-centric approach) was the method you used to create the first document. Although the same method could be used to create the second document for Ms. Nelson, another easier and more straightforward method, is to create the new document on the Windows 2000 desktop without first starting an application program. Instead of launching a program to create and modify a document, you create a blank document directly on the desktop and then use the Notepad program to enter data into the document. This method, called the **document-centric approach**, will be used to create the document to contain the reminders for Ms. Nelson.

To create a blank document directly on the desktop, perform the following steps.

More About

Document-Centric

The document-centric concept will progress to the point where you neither know nor care what application was used to create a document. For example, when you include a hyperlink to a Web page in a document, you will not care how the page was created. Only the content of the page is of interest.

 To Create a Blank Document on the Desktop

1 **Right-click an open area on the desktop, point to New on the shortcut menu, and then point to Text Document on the New submenu.**

The shortcut menu and New submenu display (Figure 2-11).

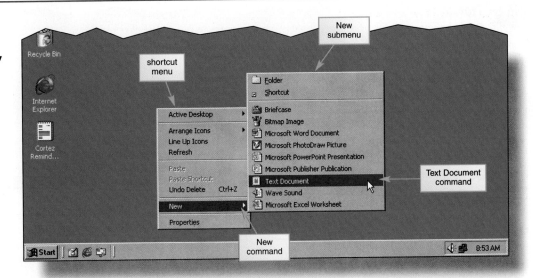

FIGURE 2-11

2 **Click Text Document.**

*The shortcut menu and New submenu close, a blank text document with the default name, New Text Document, is created and its icon displays on the desktop (Figure 2-12). The **icon title text box** below the icon contains the high-lighted default file name fol-lowed by an insertion point. Whenever highlighted text displays in a text box, any characters you type will replace the highlighted text.*

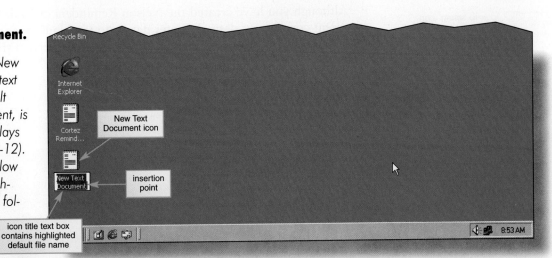

FIGURE 2-12

More About

Creating Blank Documents on the Desktop

The phrase, creating a document on the desktop, may be confusing. The document you actually create contains no data. It is blank. In effect, you are placing a blank piece of paper with a name on your desktop. The document has little value until you add text or other data to it.

A blank document has been created on the desktop to contain the daily reminders for Ms. Nelson. The icon may display on the desktop where you right-clicked the desktop or next in line in the columns of icons on the desktop, depending on the computer's settings.

Naming a Document

After you create a blank document on the desktop, normally you name the document so it is easily identifiable. In Figure 2-12 on the previous page, the default file name (New Text Document) is highlighted and the insertion point is blinking, so you can type the new name. To give the name, Nelson Reminders (Monday), to the document you just created, complete the following step.

 To Name a Document on the Desktop

 Type Nelson Reminders (Monday) **in the icon title text box and then press the ENTER key.**

The file name, Nelson Reminders (Monday), displays in the icon title text box, replacing the default name (Figure 2-13). The Nelson Reminders (Monday) icon is selected.

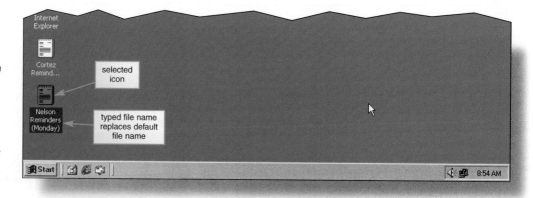

FIGURE 2-13

Other Ways

1. Right-click icon, click Rename, type name, press ENTER
2. Click icon to select icon, press F2, type name, press ENTER

Entering Data into a Blank Document on the Desktop

Although you have created the Nelson Reminders (Monday) document, the document contains no data. To enter data into the blank document, you must open the document. To open a document on the desktop, perform the following steps.

 To Open a Document on the Desktop

① Point to the Nelson Reminders (Monday) icon on the desktop.

The ToolTip indicates the file is a text file (Type: Text Document) and contains no text (Size: 0 bytes) (Figure 2-14).

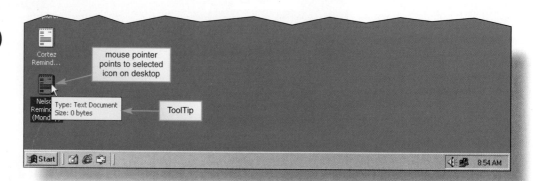

FIGURE 2-14

2 **Double-click the Nelson Reminders (Monday) icon.**

The Notepad window opens and the Nelson Reminders (Monday) document displays in the Notepad window (Figure 2-15). The document contains no text. The insertion point is located at the beginning of the first line of the document.

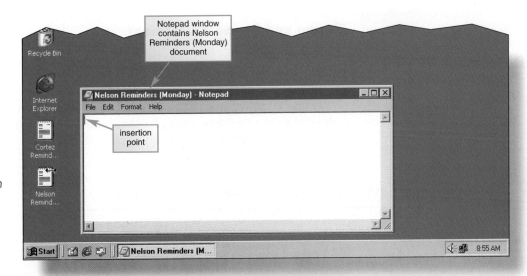

FIGURE 2-15

After the document is open, you can enter the required data by typing the text (the daily reminders) in the document. To enter the text for the Nelson Reminders (Monday) document, perform the following step.

To Enter Data into a Blank Document

1 **Type the text shown in Figure 2-16 for the Nelson Reminders (Monday) document.**

The text for Nelson Reminders (Monday) displays in the document (Figure 2-16).

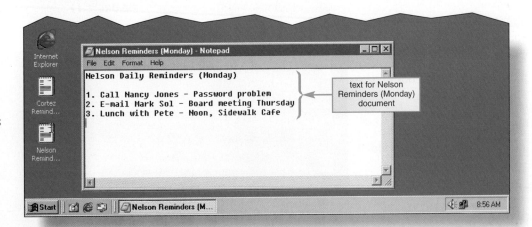

FIGURE 2-16

You can type as many words and lines as necessary for the document. The entry of the text into the Nelson Reminders (Monday) document modifies the document resulting in the need to save the document.

 Microsoft **Windows 2000**

Closing and Saving a Document

After entering the text into the Nelson Reminders (Monday) document, you will close and save the document so the text you entered will remain part of the document. You accomplish this by using the Save As command on the File menu as shown earlier in this project. In Windows 2000 applications, you can close and save a document in one set of steps. To close and save the Nelson Reminders (Monday) document, complete the following steps.

Steps **To Close and Save a Modified Document on the Desktop**

1 **Click the Close button on the Notepad title bar and then point to the Yes button in the Notepad dialog box.**

Because you changed the Nelson Reminders (Monday) document, Windows 2000 displays the Notepad dialog box asking if you want to save the changes you made in the document (Figure 2-17).

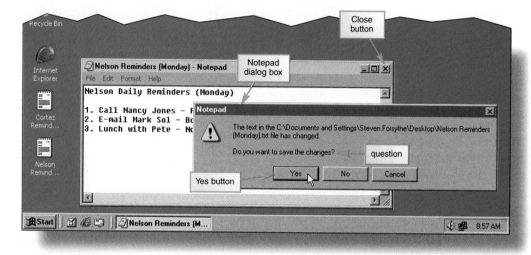

FIGURE 2-17

2 **Click the Yes button.**

The Notepad dialog box and Notepad window close and the modified Nelson Reminders (Monday) document is saved on the desktop (Figure 2-18).

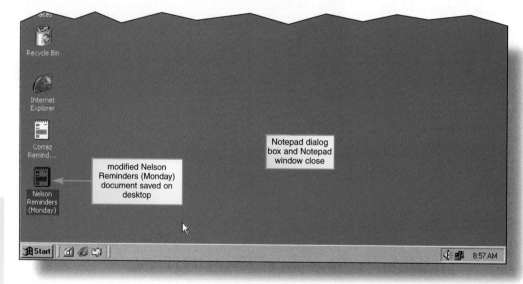

FIGURE 2-18

In most Windows 2000 application programs, if you attempt to close the program without saving the document, a dialog box displays asking if you want to save the document before closing the program. This is the way in which Windows 2000 ensures you accidentally do not lose changes made to a document.

After saving and closing the Nelson Reminders (Monday) document, the second document is complete.

More About

The Desktop

The desktop model for interfacing with a computer is quite popular. Critics insist, however, that more efficient and effective models exist. Can you think of any model that would be more efficient for you? What about the interfaces you use for interactive games?

Storing Documents in a Folder on the Desktop

When you have created one or more documents on the desktop, you will want to keep them together so you can find and reference them easily. In addition, sharing the folder with other users on the network allows them to view and modify the contents of the documents easily. Windows 2000 allows you to place one or more documents into a folder in much the same manner as you might take a document written on a piece of paper and place it in a file folder. To place a document in a folder, you first must create the folder. To create and name a folder on the desktop for the Cortez Reminders (Monday) and Nelson Reminders (Monday) documents, complete the following steps.

 To Create and Name a Folder on the Desktop

1 Right-click an open area on the desktop, point to New on the shortcut menu, and then point to Folder on the New submenu.

The shortcut menu and New submenu display (Figure 2-19). Clicking Folder on the New submenu will create a folder using the default folder name, New Folder.

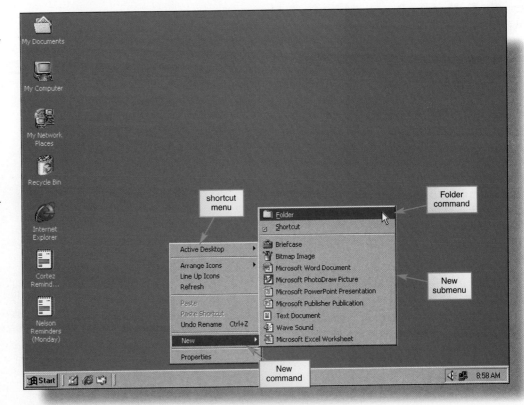

FIGURE 2-19

2 **Click Folder. Type**
Daily Reminders
in the icon title text box
and then press the ENTER
key.

The selected Daily Reminders folder icon displays on the desktop (Figure 2-20). The folder name, Daily Reminders, displays in the icon title text box.

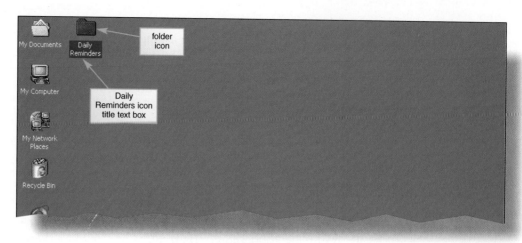

FIGURE 2-20

After you create a folder on the desktop, the next step is to move documents into the folder. For the Daily Reminders folder, you should move the Nelson Reminders (Monday) and the Cortez Reminders (Monday) documents into the folder. To accomplish this, complete the following steps.

Steps **To Move a Document into a Folder**

1 **Right-drag the**
Nelson Reminders
(Monday) icon on top of
the Daily Reminders folder
icon. Point to Move Here
on the shortcut menu.

The dimmed Nelson Reminders (Monday) icon displays on top of the dimmed Daily Reminders folder icon, and a shortcut menu displays (Figure 2-21). The Nelson Reminders (Monday) icon still displays on the desktop.

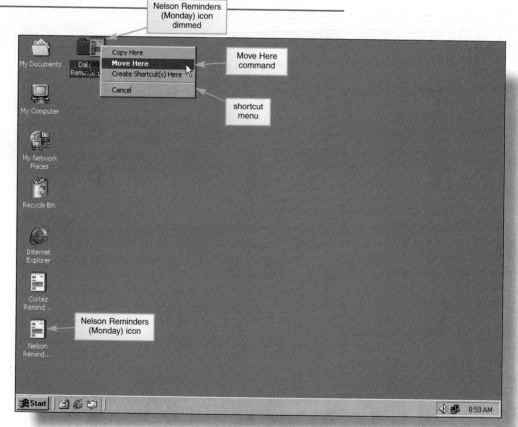

FIGURE 2-21

2 **Click Move Here.**

The Nelson Reminders (Monday) document is moved into the Daily Reminders folder, and the Nelson Reminders (Monday) icon no longer displays on the desktop (Figure 2-22). Windows 2000 rearranges the desktop, causing the Daily Reminders folder to display at the bottom of the icons on the desktop.

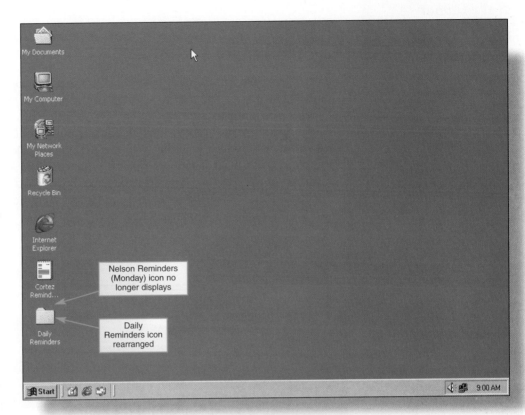

FIGURE 2-22

3 **Right-drag the Cortez Reminders (Monday) icon on top of the Daily Reminders icon. Click Move Here on the shortcut menu.**

The Cortez Reminders (Monday) document is moved into the Daily Reminders folder, and the Cortez Reminders (Monday) icon no longer displays on the desktop (Figure 2-23).

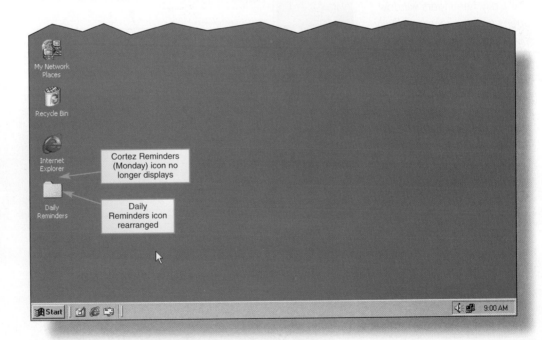

FIGURE 2-23

The ability to organize documents and files within a folder allows you to keep the desktop organized when using Windows 2000. Project 3 will discuss how to organize the files on the floppy and hard drives.

Other **Ways**

1. Right-click document icon, click Cut, right-click folder icon, click Paste
2. Drag document icon on top of folder icon

More About

Working with Documents

To modify a document, you are opening the document rather than starting an application program and then opening the document as you did previously in this project. Does this feel more natural? Research has indicated that people feel more at home dealing with documents instead of dealing with application programs and documents.

Opening and Modifying Documents Within a Folder

Documents stored in a folder on the desktop can be modified in a similar way as documents stored on the desktop. First, you must open the folder and then the document you want to modify.

Assume that you received further information about the daily reminders for Mr. Cortez. An Internet meeting with the Accounting Department in the Western United States has been scheduled for 2:00 p.m. and the Accounting Department must be notified of the meeting. To add this item to the schedule, first you must open the Daily Reminders folder that contains the Cortez Reminders (Monday) document. To do so, complete the following step.

Steps **To Open a Folder**

1 **Double-click the Daily Reminders folder icon on the desktop. Move and resize the Daily Reminders window to resemble the window shown in Figure 2-24.**

The Daily Reminders window opens and the recessed Daily Reminders button displays in the taskbar button area (Figure 2-24). The Daily Reminders folder icon remains on the desktop. Each of the document icons displays within the folder window, indicating the icons are contained within the folder.

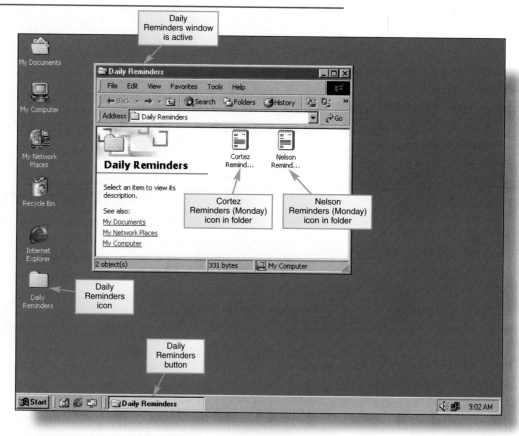

FIGURE 2-24

Other Ways

1. Right-click folder icon, click Open on shortcut menu
2. Click folder icon to select icon, press ENTER key

In Figure 2-24, the dark blue Daily Reminders title bar and the recessed button in the taskbar button area indicate the Daily Reminders window is the active window.

Opening and Modifying a Document Stored in a Folder

After opening the folder, you must open the document you want to modify. To open the Cortez Reminders (Monday) document in the Daily Reminders folder and enter the text about the Internet meeting, complete the following steps.

Steps To Open and Modify a Document in a Folder

1 **Double-click the Cortez Reminders (Monday) icon in the Daily Reminders window.**

Notepad launches, the Cortez Reminders (Monday) document displays in the Notepad window, and the Cortez Reminders (Monday) - Notepad button displays in the taskbar button area (Figure 2-25). The active Notepad window and inactive folder window now are open. The Daily Reminders folder button is no longer recessed.

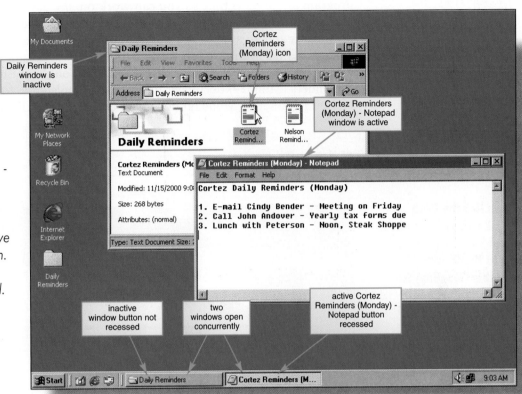

FIGURE 2-25

2 **Press the DOWN ARROW key five times to move the insertion point to the end of the document. Type** 4. Notify Accounting - NetMeeting at 2:00 p.m. **and then press the ENTER key.**

The insertion point moves to the end of the document and the entry is added to the document (Figure 2-26).

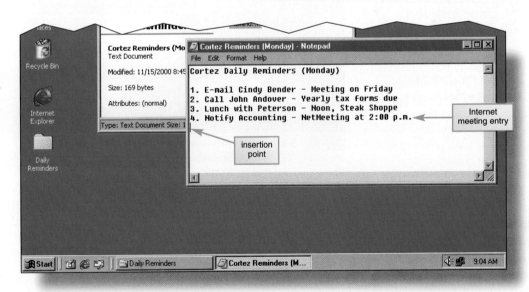

FIGURE 2-26

It is as easy to modify a document stored in a folder as it is to modify a document stored on the desktop. The method for opening and modifying a document, regardless of where the document is stored, is the same.

Other Ways

1. Right-click document icon, click Open on shortcut menu, enter text
2. Click document icon to select icon, press ENTER key, enter text

Opening Multiple Documents

Windows 2000 allows you to open more than one document and application program at the same time so you can work on any desired document. The concept of multiple programs running at the same time is called **multitasking**. To illustrate two documents and an application program open at the same time, assume you need to make a change to the Nelson Reminders (Monday) document to include a reminder to talk to Stan about Sarah's retirement party. You do not have to close the Cortez Reminders (Monday) document to do this. Complete the following steps to open the Nelson Reminders (Monday) document and make the changes.

 To Open and Modify Multiple Documents

1 **Click the Daily Reminders button in the taskbar button area. Point to the Nelson Reminders (Monday) icon in the Daily Reminders window.**

The Daily Reminders window moves on top of the Cortez Reminders (Monday) document and becomes the active window, denoted by the dark blue title bar (Figure 2-27). The Cortez Reminders (Monday) window becomes the inactive window, the Daily Reminders button is recessed, and the Cortez Reminders (Monday) - Notepad button is not recessed.

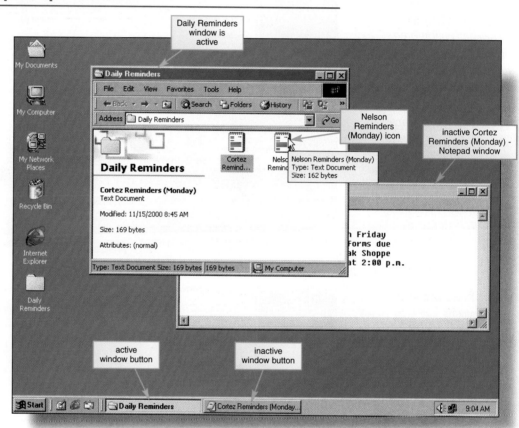

FIGURE 2-27

2 Double-click the Nelson Reminders (Monday) icon. Press the **DOWN ARROW** key five times to move the insertion point to the end of the document in the Notepad window. **Type** 4. Call Stan - Retirement party for Sarah **and then press the ENTER key.**

The Nelson Reminders (Monday) - Notepad window opens on top of the other two open windows, the recessed Nelson Reminders (Monday) - Notepad button displays in the taskbar button area, and the insertion point moves to the end of the document (Figure 2-28).

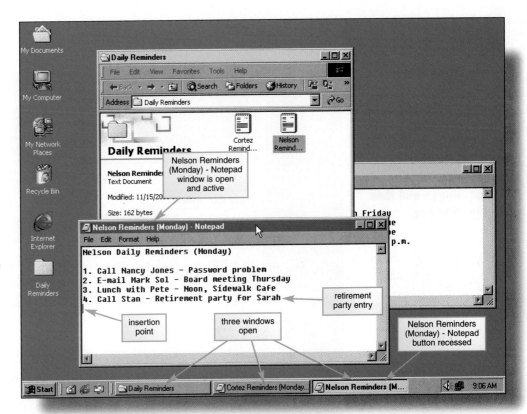

FIGURE 2-28

After you have modified the Nelson Reminders (Monday) document, you receive information that a dinner meeting with Larry Samuels has been scheduled for Mr. Cortez for 6:00 p.m. at the Seafood House. You are directed to add this entry to Mr. Cortez's reminders. To do this, you must open the Cortez Reminders (Monday) - Notepad inactive window. To open an inactive window and modify the document, complete the step on the next page.

Other Ways

1. Right-click document icon, click Open on shortcut menu, enter text

2. Click document icon, press ENTER, enter text

More About 2000

Opening Windows

In addition to clicking the taskbar button of an inactive window to make that window the active window, you also may click any open area of the window. Many people routinely click the title bar of a window to activate the window.

Steps **To Open an Inactive Window**

1 **Click the Cortez Reminders (Monday) - Notepad button in the taskbar button area. When the window opens, type** 5. Dinner with Samuels — 6:00 p.m., Seafood House **and then press the ENTER key.**

The Cortez Reminders (Monday) - Notepad window displays on top of the other windows on the desktop, and the dinner entry displays in the document (Figure 2-29).

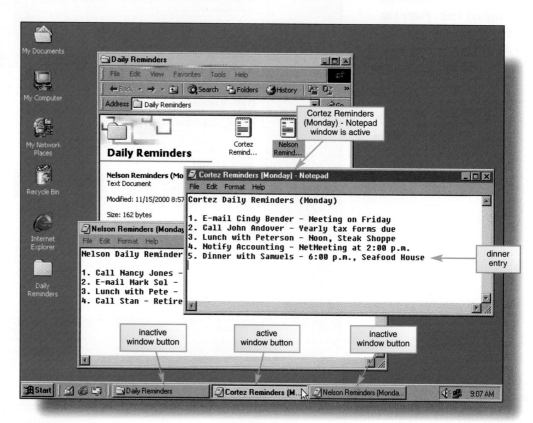

FIGURE 2-29

Other Ways

1. Press ALT+TAB until name of window displays, release keys
2. If visible, click title bar of window

Minimizing All Open Windows

Windows 2000 allows you to open multiple windows on the desktop and work within any of the open windows by clicking the appropriate button in the taskbar button area. As convenient as it may be to have multiple windows open on the desktop, too many windows or a single maximized window can limit the view of the objects on the desktop. To allow you to view the desktop easily without closing windows on the desktop, the Quick Launch toolbar contains the Show Desktop icon. The **Show Desktop icon** makes the desktop visible by minimizing all open windows on the desktop.

Currently, the Cortez Reminders (Monday) - Notepad, Daily Reminders, and Nelson Reminders (Monday) - Notepad windows are open on the desktop. A button for each window displays in the taskbar button area (see Figure 2-29). A recessed button displays for the active Cortez Reminders (Monday) - Notepad window and non-recessed buttons display for the remaining inactive windows. To minimize the open windows and view the objects on the desktop, perform the following steps.

To Minimize All Open Windows

1 **Point to the Show Desktop icon on the Quick Launch toolbar on the taskbar (Figure 2-30).**

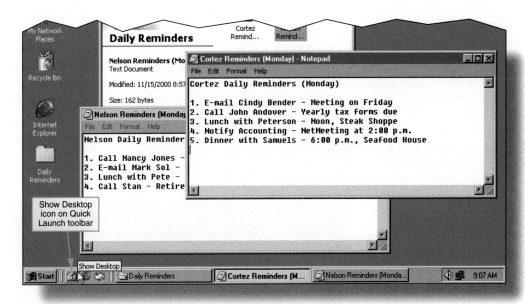

FIGURE 2-30

2 **Click the Show Desktop icon.**

Windows 2000 minimizes all three open windows (Figure 2-31). A button for each minimized window displays in the taskbar button area.

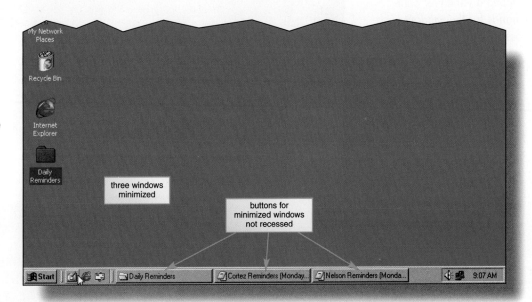

FIGURE 2-31

To open any of the minimized windows and be able to work in that window, click the corresponding button in the taskbar button area. To open all three windows and return the desktop to the way it looked before, click the Show Desktop icon (see Figure 2-30, and then click the Show Desktop button a second time.

1. Right-click open area of taskbar, click Minimize All Windows
2. Click the Minimize button on each window

 Microsoft **Windows 2000**

More About

Closing Windows

The choice of how to close windows is yours. In most cases, you will want to choose the method that causes the least amount of work.

Closing Multiple Windows

When you are finished working with multiple windows, close them. If the windows are open on the desktop, you can click the Close button on the title bar of each open window to close them. Regardless of whether the windows are open on the desktop or the windows are minimized using the Show Desktop icon, you also can close the windows using the buttons in the taskbar button area. To close the Cortez Reminders (Monday) - Notepad and Nelson Reminders (Monday) - Notepad windows from the taskbar, complete the following steps.

Steps To Close and Save Open Windows from the Taskbar

1 Right-click the Cortez Reminders (Monday) - Notepad button in the taskbar button area. Point to Close on the shortcut menu.

A shortcut menu displays containing a variety of commands for the window associated with the button that was clicked (Figure 2-32).

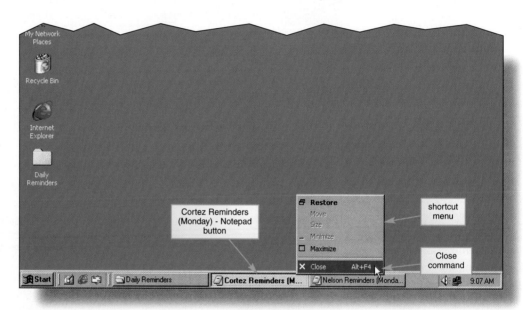

FIGURE 2-32

2 Click Close. Point to the Yes button in the Notepad dialog box.

The Notepad dialog box displays asking if you want to save the changes (Figure 2-33).

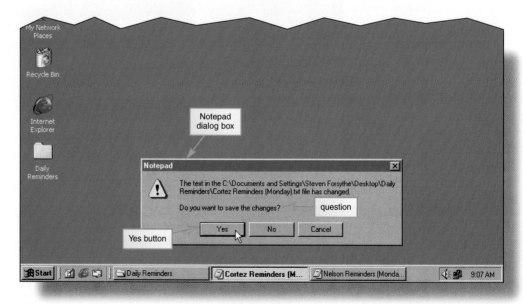

FIGURE 2-33

3 Click the Yes button. Right-click the Nelson Reminders (Monday) - Notepad button in the taskbar button area. Point to Close on the shortcut menu.

A shortcut menu displays (Figure 2-34). The modified Cortez Reminders (Monday) document is saved in the Daily Reminders folder and its button no longer displays in the taskbar button area.

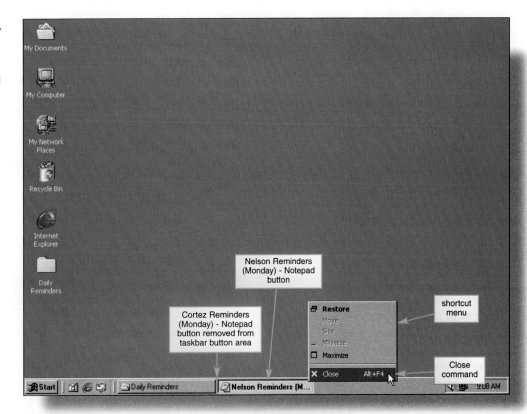

FIGURE 2-34

4 Click Close. When the Notepad dialog box displays asking if you want to save the changes, click the Yes button.

Only the Daily Reminders button remains in the taskbar button area (Figure 2-35).

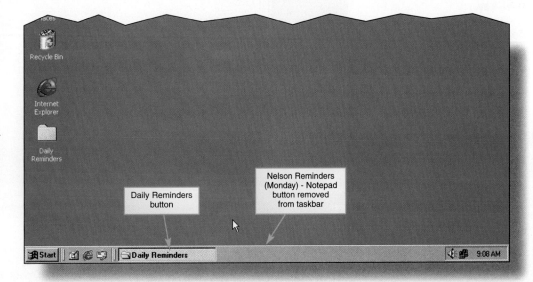

FIGURE 2-35

The capability of Windows 2000 to process multiple documents at the same time and perform multitasking with multiple programs running at the same time is a primary feature of the operating system.

Other Ways

1. Click taskbar button, on File menu click Save, click Close button
2. Click taskbar button, click Close button on title bar, click Yes button
3. Click taskbar button, on File menu click Exit, click Yes button

More About

Printing

Normally it is more efficient to print directly from the document within a folder or on the desktop than to open the document first. If the document were already open, of course, usually you would print from the open document.

Printing a Document from Within a Folder

After you modify and save documents on the desktop, print them so you have an updated hard copy of the Cortez Reminders (Monday) and the Nelson Reminders (Monday) documents. Earlier in this project, you used the Print command on the File menu to print an open document. You also can print multiple documents from a folder without opening the documents. To print both the Cortez Reminders (Monday) and the Nelson Reminders (Monday) documents from the Daily Reminders folder, perform the following steps.

Steps To Print Multiple Documents from Within a Folder

1 **Click the Daily Reminders button in the taskbar button area. Click the Cortez Reminders (Monday) icon in the Daily Reminders folder to select the icon, hold down the SHIFT key, and then click the Nelson Reminders (Monday) icon. Release the SHIFT key.**

Both icons are selected (Figure 2-36).

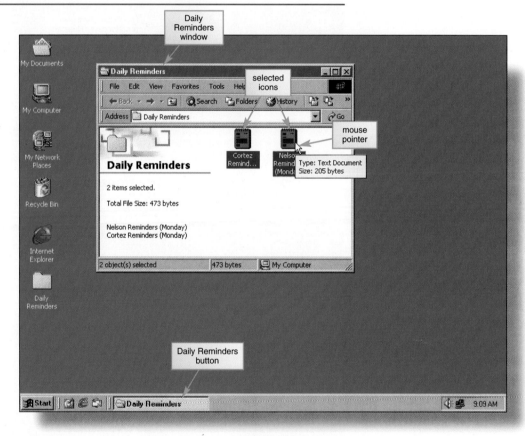

FIGURE 2-36

2 Right-click the Nelson Reminders (Monday) icon. Point to Print on the shortcut menu.

A shortcut menu, containing the Print command, displays (Figure 2-37).

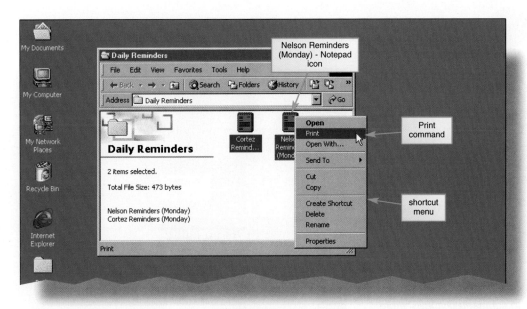

FIGURE 2-37

3 Click Print.

The modified documents print as shown in Figure 2-38.

4 Click the Close button on the Daily Reminders title bar.

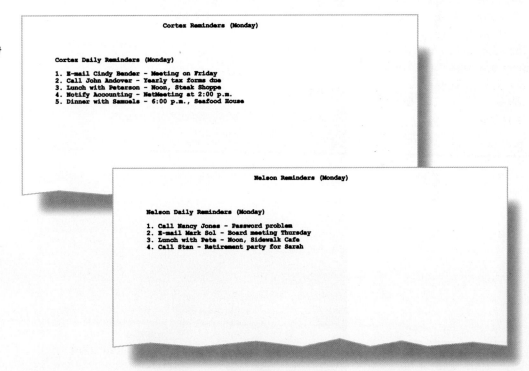

FIGURE 2-38

Other Ways

1. Select document icons, on File menu click Print

Copying a Folder onto a Disk

A folder on the desktop is useful when you are using one or more documents within the folder frequently. It is a good policy to make a copy of a folder and the documents within that folder so if the folder or its contents are accidentally lost or damaged, you do not lose your work. This is referred to as making a **backup** of the folders and files. To make a backup of the Daily Reminders folder on a floppy disk in drive A of the computer, complete the steps on the next page.

To Copy a Folder on the Desktop onto a Floppy Disk

1 **Insert a formatted floppy disk into drive A.**

2 **Right-click the Daily Reminders folder icon on the desktop. Point to Send To on the shortcut menu and then point to 3½ Floppy (A) on the Send To submenu.**

The shortcut menu and Send To submenu display (Figure 2-39).

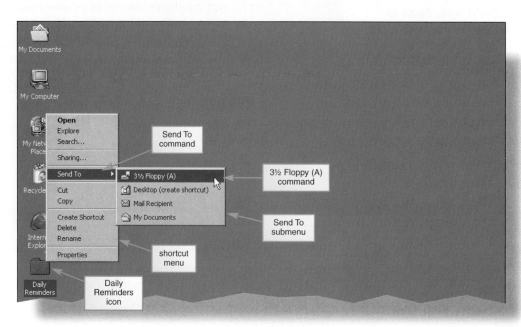

FIGURE 2-39

3 **Click 3½ Floppy (A).**

While the Daily Reminders folder and the documents within the folder are being copied, the Copying dialog box displays (Figure 2-40).

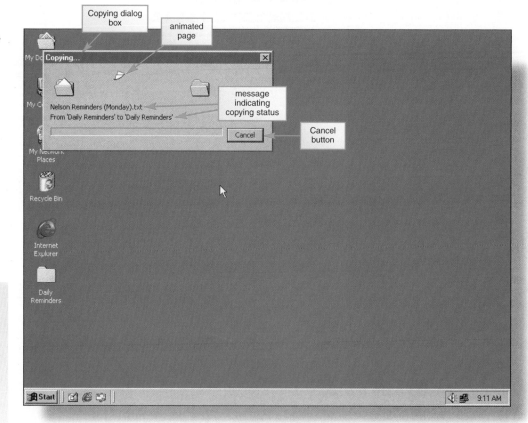

FIGURE 2-40

Other Ways

1. Double-click My Computer icon, right-drag folder icon to 3½ Floppy (A:) icon in My Computer window, click Copy Here

2. Double-click My Computer icon, drag folder icon to 3½ Floppy (A:) icon

3. Right-click the folder icon, click Copy, double-click My Computer icon, right-click 3½ Floppy (A:) icon, click Paste

In Figure 2-40, a message explains which folders and files are being copied, and animated pages fly from one folder to the other folder in the dialog box. After the folder and all documents have been copied, the Copying dialog box closes. When the copying process is complete, the Daily Reminders folder and the documents in the folder are stored both on the desktop and on the floppy disk in drive A. If you want to stop the copying process, you can click the Cancel button in the Copying dialog box.

Opening a Folder on a Floppy Disk

After copying a folder onto a floppy disk, you may wish to verify that the folder has been copied properly onto the floppy disk or, you may wish to open a document stored in the folder directly from the floppy disk. To open a folder stored on a floppy disk, complete the following steps.

The Send To Command

Commands can easily be added to and removed from the Send To submenu. To view the steps to accomplish this, launch Windows Help, click the Index tab, type Send to folder, click adding destinations to Send To folder, click the Display button.

Backups

Copying a file or folder to a floppy disk is one way to create a backup, but backing up files often is a much more elaborate process. Most backup systems use tape or portable hard disks that contain hundreds of megabytes (millions of characters) or even gigabytes (billions of characters).

 To Open a Folder Stored on a Floppy Disk

1 **Double-click the My Computer icon. Move and resize the window to resemble the My Computer window shown in Figure 2-41. Point to the 3½ Floppy (A:) icon in the My Computer window.**

The My Computer window opens and the My Computer button is recessed (Figure 2-41). Notice that the Back and Forward buttons on the Standard Buttons toolbar appear dimmed and are unavailable. When the buttons are not dimmed, you can click the buttons to display previously displayed windows.

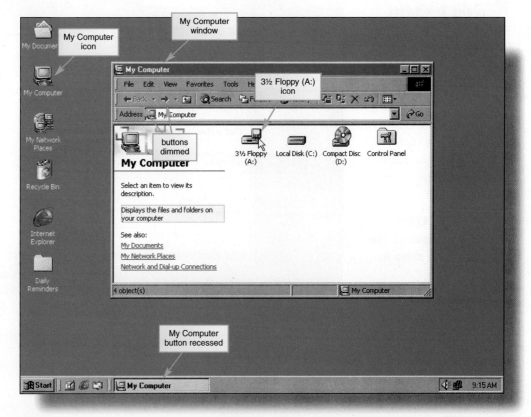

FIGURE 2-41

2 **Double-click the 3½ Floppy (A:) icon. Point to the Daily Reminders icon in the 3½ Floppy (A:) window.**

The 3½ Floppy (A:) window opens in the same window as the My Computer was displayed (Figure 2-42). The 3½ Floppy (A:) button replaces the My Computer button in the taskbar button area. Because the My Computer window was opened before opening the 3½ Floppy (A:) window, the Back button on the Standard Buttons toolbar no longer is dimmed and is available for use.

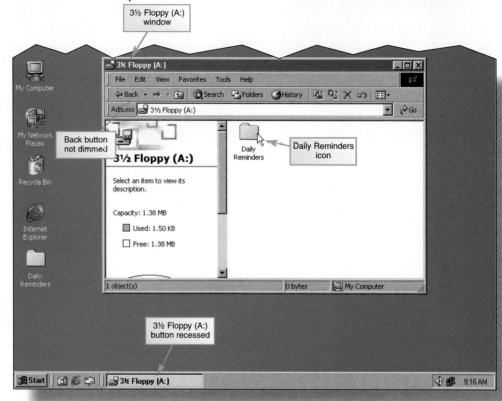

FIGURE 2-42

3 **Double-click the Daily Reminders icon. Point to the Close button on the Daily Reminders title bar.**

The Daily Reminders window opens in the same window as 3½ Floppy (A:) was displayed (Figure 2-43). The Daily Reminders button replaces the 3½ Floppy (A:) button.

4 **Click the Close button. Remove the floppy disk from drive A.**

The Daily Reminders window closes and the Daily Reminders button no longer displays in the taskbar button area.

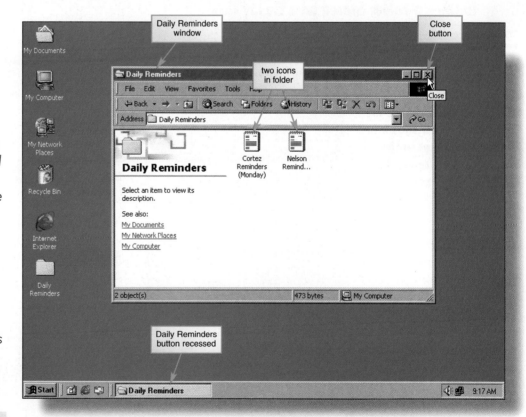

FIGURE 2-43

1. Double-click My Computer icon, double-click 3½ Floppy (A:), right-click folder icon, click Open on shortcut menu

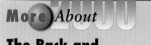

If you wish to open one of the documents in the folder stored on the floppy disk in drive A as shown in Figure 2-43, double-click the document icon.

Creating Document Shortcuts

One of Windows 2000's more powerful features is its capability of being easily customized. One way to customize Windows 2000 is to use shortcuts to launch application programs and open documents. A **shortcut** is an icon that represents a document or an application program. Placing a shortcut to represent an application or document on the Start menu or on the desktop can make it easier to launch the application or open the document.

Placing a Shortcut on the Start Menu

You can add an application shortcut or a document shortcut to the Start menu that displays when you click the Start button. You do not actually place the application or document on the menu, instead you place a shortcut to the application or document on the menu.

You want to open the Cortez Reminders (Monday) document from the Start menu. To place the Cortez Reminders (Monday) document shortcut on the Start menu, complete the following steps.

Steps To Place a Document Shortcut on the Start Menu

1 **Double-click the Daily Reminders icon to open the folder.**

The Daily Reminders window opens (Figure 2-44). The Cortez Reminders (Monday) and Nelson Reminders (Monday) document icons are contained in the folder.

> **More About**
>
> **The Back and Forward Buttons**
>
> When the Back or Forward button is not dimmed, clicking the Back button displays the last window opened and clicking the Forward button displays the next window in a previously displayed sequence of windows.

> **More About**
>
> **Shortcuts**
>
> A shortcut icon is a pointer to the location of a document or application on the hard drive. The shortcut icon is not the actual document or application. When you delete a shortcut icon, you delete the shortcut icon but do not delete the document or application. It remains on the hard drive.

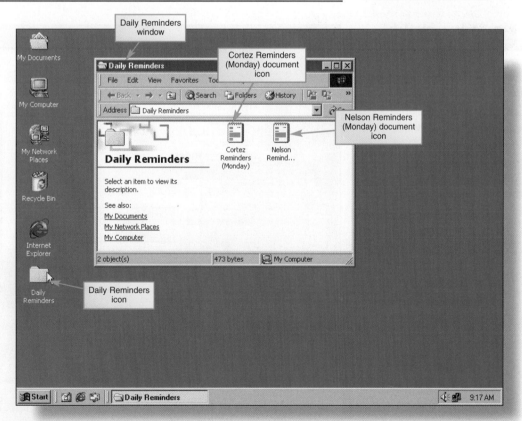

FIGURE 2-44

2 Hold down the left mouse button and drag the Cortez Reminders (Monday) icon on top of the Start button on the taskbar.

When you drag the icon on top of the Start button, the icon appears dimmed and the Start menu displays (Figure 2-45).

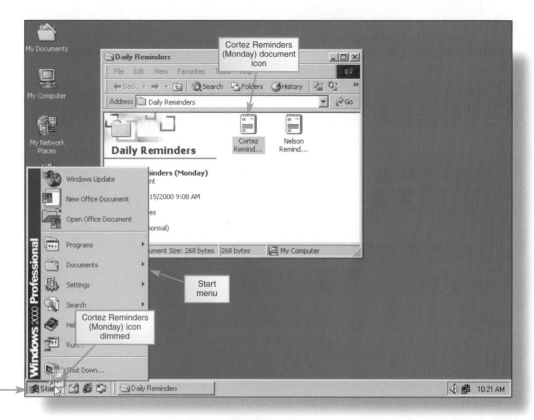

FIGURE 2-45

3 Release the left mouse button.

When you release the mouse button, the Start menu remains on the desktop and the Cortez Reminders (Monday) shortcut displays in the section above the Programs command on the Start menu (Figure 2-46).

4 Click an open area of the desktop to close the Start menu. Click the Close button in the Daily Reminders window.

Other Ways

1. Right-click the Start menu, click Open, drag document icon to Start Menu window

2. Right-click the Start menu, click Open, right-drag document icon to Start Menu window, click Copy Here

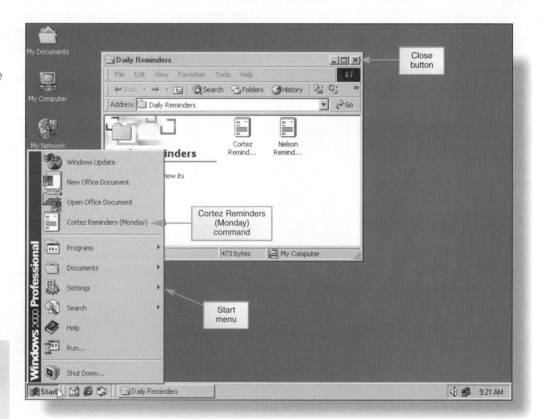

FIGURE 2-46

Opening a Document from the Start Menu

Once you have placed a document or application program shortcut on the Start menu, you can click the Start button and open the document or application program from the Start menu. To open the Cortez Reminders (Monday) document from the Start menu, complete the following steps.

 To Open a Document Using the Start Menu

1 **Click the Start button on the taskbar. Point to Cortez Reminders (Monday) on the Start menu.**

The Start menu displays (Figure 2-47).

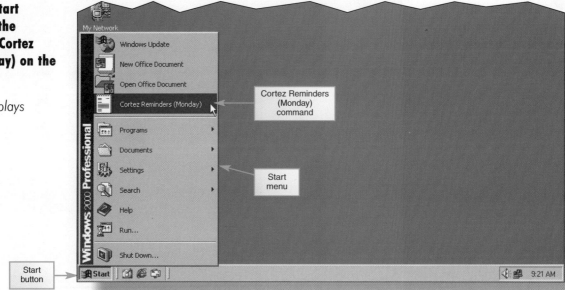

FIGURE 2-47

2 **Click Cortez Reminders (Monday).**

Notepad launches and the Cortez Reminders (Monday) document displays on the desktop (Figure 2-48).

3 **Click the Close button in the Cortez Reminders (Monday) - Notepad window.**

The window closes.

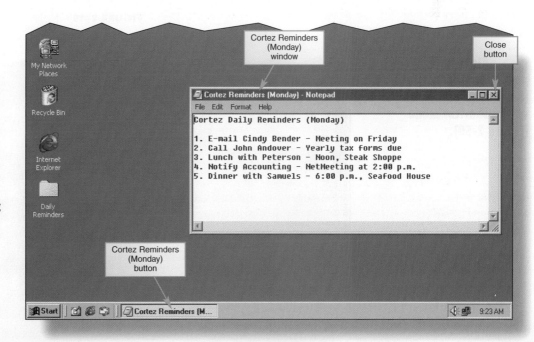

FIGURE 2-48

Removing a Shortcut from the Start Menu

Just as you can add document or application program shortcuts to the Start menu, you also can remove them. To remove the Cortez Reminders (Monday) shortcut from the Start menu, complete the following steps.

 To Remove a Shortcut from the Start Menu

1 **Click the Start button on the taskbar. Point to Cortez Reminders (Monday) on the Start menu (Figure 2-49).**

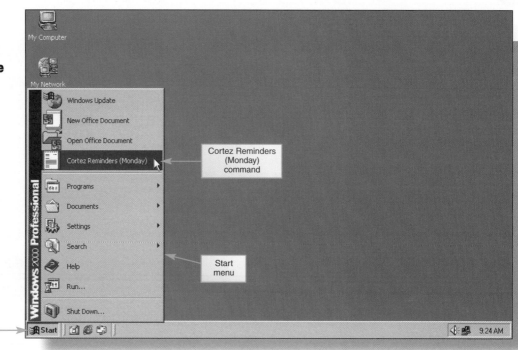

FIGURE 2-49

2 **Right-click Cortez Reminders (Monday). Point to Delete on the shortcut menu (Figure 2-50).**

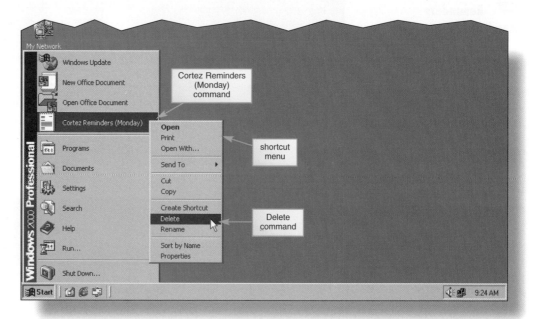

FIGURE 2-50

3 Click Delete. When the Confirm File Delete dialog box displays, point to the Yes button.

The Confirm File Delete dialog box displays (Figure 2-51).

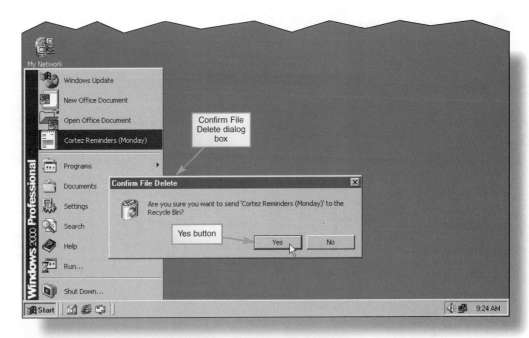

FIGURE 2-51

4 Click the Yes button.

The Cortez Reminders (Monday) shortcut no longer displays on the Start menu (Figure 2-52).

5 Click an open area of the desktop to close the Start menu.

The Start menu closes.

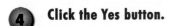

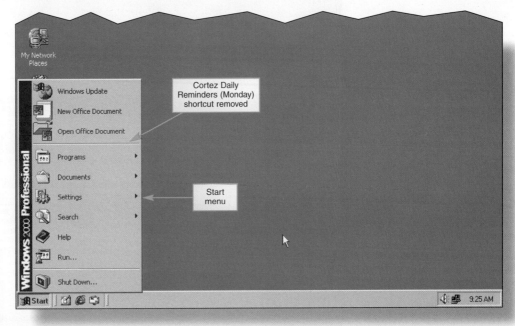

FIGURE 2-52

The capability of adding and removing shortcuts and folders on the Start menu provides great flexibility when customizing Windows 2000.

Creating a Shortcut on the Desktop

You also can create document and application program shortcuts directly on the desktop. To create a shortcut for the Nelson Reminders (Monday) document on the desktop, complete the steps on the next page.

Other **Ways**

1. Right-click the Start menu, click Open, right-click document icon, click Delete, click Yes button

2. Right-click the Start menu, click Open, right-drag document icon to Recycle Bin icon, click Move Here

To Create a Shortcut on the Desktop

1 **Double-click the Daily Reminders** icon to open the Daily Reminders window. Right-drag the Nelson Reminders (Monday) icon from the Daily Reminders window to the desktop. Point to Create Shortcut(s) Here on the shortcut menu.

The Daily Reminders window, a dimmed icon, and a short-cut menu display on the desktop (Figure 2-53).

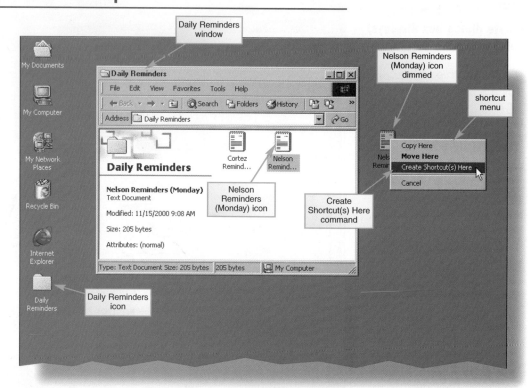

FIGURE 2-53

2 **Click Create Shortcut(s) Here.** If the shortcut does not display on the desktop, move and resize the Daily Reminders window until the shortcut is visible.

Windows 2000 creates a shortcut on the desktop (Figure 2-54). The shortcut is identified with an icon title and a small arrow in the bottom-left corner of the icon. The shortcut may display on the desktop where you dragged it or next in line in the columns of icons, depending the computer's settings.

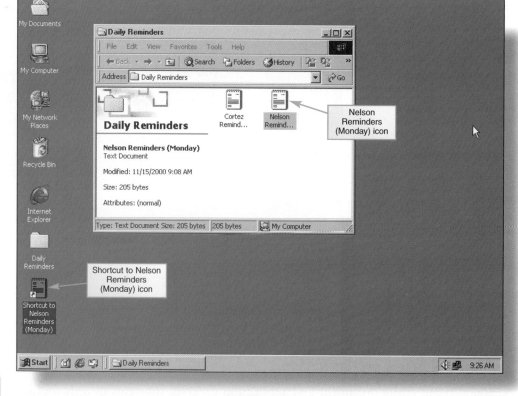

Other **Ways**

1. Press CTRL+SHIFT and drag icon to desktop

FIGURE 2-54

Opening a Document or Launching an Application Program Using a Shortcut on the Desktop

Once you have created the shortcut on the desktop, you can open the shortcut by double-clicking it. To open the Nelson Reminders (Monday) document, complete the following steps.

Steps To Open a Document Using a Shortcut on the Desktop

1 **Double-click the Shortcut to Nelson Reminders (Monday) icon.**

Notepad launches and the Nelson Reminders (Monday) document displays in the Notepad window (Figure 2-55).

2 **Click the Close button on the Nelson Reminders (Monday) - Notepad title bar to close the window. Click the Close button on the Daily Reminders title bar to close the window.**

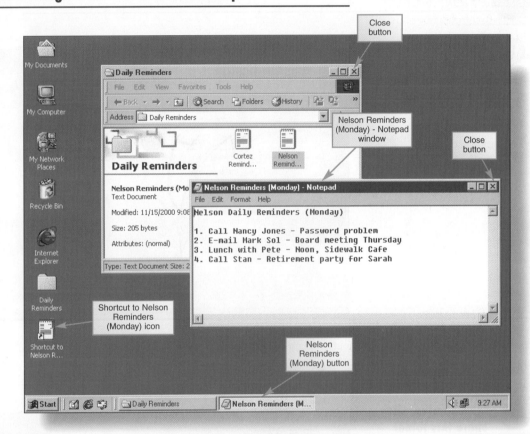

FIGURE 2-55

Shortcuts can be quite useful because they can reference application programs and documents stored on the hard disk. You can store a document in a folder on the computer's hard disk, and then create a shortcut to the folder on the desktop. In that manner, you can open the document from the desktop but the document remains stored in a folder on the computer's hard disk.

Sharing a Folder

In Project 1, a simple computer network consisting of a server, three workstations, and a printer was illustrated (see Figure 1-1 on page WIN 1.7). If your computer is connected to a network, you may want to share the computer's resources (documents, files, folders, programs, and printers) with other computer users on the network. You may want to share the Daily Reminders folder, containing the daily reminders documents for Mr. Cortez and Ms. Nelson, with the computers that Mr. Cortez and Ms. Nelson use.

When you share an object, you have the option of setting the permissions for that object. A **permission** is a rule associated with an object, such as a folder, to regulate which users gain access to the object and the manner in which they gain access. Unless changed, permission to fully control the object is given. Perform the following steps to allow all computer users on the network to fully control the Daily Reminders folder.

To Share a Folder

1 **Right-click the Daily Reminders folder icon on the desktop and then point to Sharing.**

A shortcut menu, containing the Sharing command, displays (Figure 2-56).

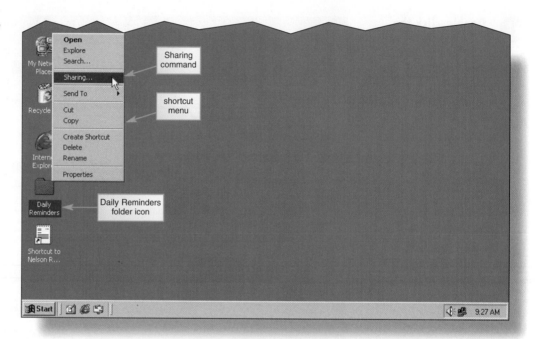

FIGURE 2-56

2 **Click Sharing, click Share this folder in the Daily Reminders Properties dialog box, and then point to the OK button.**

The Sharing sheet displays in the Daily Reminders Properties dialog box and the Share this folder option button is selected (Figure 2-57). The Daily Reminders share name, which is the name of the shared folder that other network users see on their computers, displays in the Share name text box.

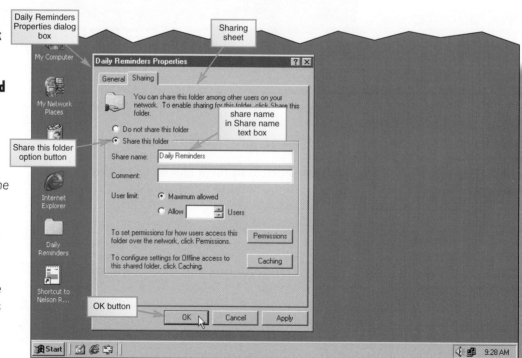

FIGURE 2-57

3 **Click the OK button.**

The Daily Reminders Properties dialog box closes and an arm and hand display on the lower edge of the Daily Reminders folder icon (Figure 2-58). The folder is accessible fully to other computers on the network.

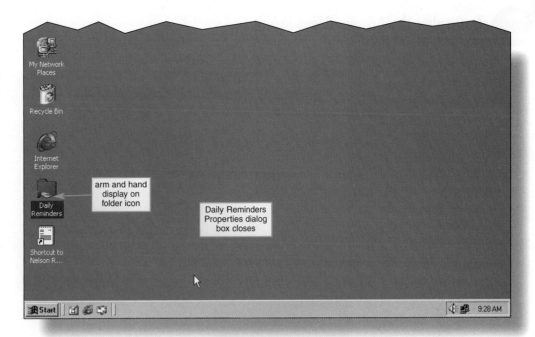

arm and hand display on folder icon

Daily Reminders Properties dialog box closes

FIGURE 2-58

Other users on the network have full control of the Daily Reminders folder. To access the folder from another computer, the user uses the My Network Places icon on the desktop to locate the folder identified by the share name, Daily Reminders, and then double-clicks the shared Daily Reminders folder icon. At this point, the user can view and change the contents of the folder and the contents of the documents in the folder. You will learn how to view computers on a network and access shared folders on those computers in Project 3 of this book.

Removing Sharing from a Folder

Return the folder to its original state by removing sharing from the folder. Perform the following steps to remove sharing from the Daily Reminders folder.

TO REMOVE SHARING FROM A FOLDER

1 Right-click the Daily Reminders icon on the desktop.

2 Click Sharing.

3 Click Do not share this folder in the Sharing sheet.

4 Click the OK button in the Daily Reminders Properties dialog box.

The arm and hand no longer display on the Daily Reminders icon on the desktop. The folder is no longer available to other computers on the network.

Arranging Icons

You may want to control the sequence and arrangement of the icons on the desktop. To arrange the icons, you can use the shortcut menu that displays when you right-click the desktop. To display the shortcut menu and arrange icons on the desktop, complete the steps on the next page.

More About

Sharing

You control the permissions for an object, such as the Daily Reminders folder, by clicking the Permissions button in the Daily Reminders Properties dialog box and clicking the appropriate Allow or Deny check boxes in the Permissions for Daily Reminders dialog box.

To Display the Arrange Icons Submenu

1 **Right-click an open area on the desktop and then point to Arrange Icons.**

A shortcut menu and the Arrange Icons submenu display (Figure 2-59). A check mark precedes the Auto Arrange command to indicate the command is selected and Windows 2000 will arrange the icons automatically on the desktop.

2 **Click an open area of the desktop.**

The shortcut menu and Arrange Icons submenu no longer display on the desktop.

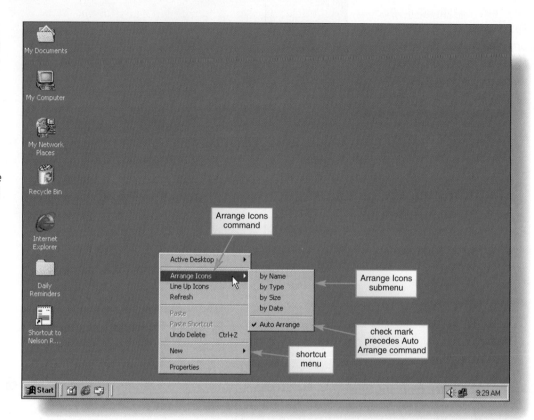

FIGURE 2-59

If the Auto Arrange command is selected, Windows 2000 will arrange all icons automatically on the desktop. If an icon is added to the desktop, Windows 2000 will place the icon where it belongs in the columns of icons that display on the left side of the desktop. If the Auto Arrange command is not selected, you can place icons anywhere on the desktop you want.

If you click the **by Name command** on the Arrange Icons submenu, the icons you have created on the desktop will be arranged in ascending alphabetical order. The **by Type command** will arrange the icons by the type of file they represent. The **by Size command** arranges the icons from the smallest to the largest file, and the **by Date command** arranges the icons from the newest to the oldest based on when the files were created. Clicking any of these commands will arrange all icons on the desktop in columns that display on the left side of the desktop.

Deleting Shortcuts, Folders, and Documents on the Desktop

In many cases after you have worked with folders and documents on the desktop, you will want to delete the folders and documents from the desktop. Windows 2000 offers three different techniques to perform this operation: (1) right-drag the object to the Recycle Bin; (2) right-click the object and then click Delete on the shortcut menu; and (3) drag the object to the Recycle Bin. The steps in this section will demonstrate all three methods.

It is important to realize what you are doing when you delete a folder or document off the desktop. Always be extremely cautious when deleting anything. When you **delete a shortcut** from the desktop, you delete only the shortcut icon and its reference to the document or application program. The document or application program itself, which is stored elsewhere on the hard disk, is not deleted. When you **delete the icon** for a folder, document, or application program on the desktop that is not a shortcut, the actual folder, document, or application program is deleted.

When you delete a folder, document, or application program from the desktop, Windows 2000 places these items in the **Recycle Bin**, which is an area on the hard disk that contains all the items you have deleted not only from the desktop but from the hard disk as well. When the Recycle Bin becomes full, empty it. Up until the time you empty the Recycle Bin, you can recover deleted files and application programs. Even though you have this safety net, you should be extremely cautious whenever deleting anything from the desktop or hard disk.

At the end of the week, you no longer have a need for the Cortez Reminders (Monday) and the Nelson Reminders (Monday) documents. You decide you can delete them safely from the desktop. To accomplish this, you must delete the shortcut to the Nelson Reminders (Monday) document, the two documents, and the folder in which the documents are stored. To delete the shortcut, complete the following steps.

 To Delete a Shortcut from the Desktop

1 **Right-drag the Shortcut to Nelson Reminders (Monday) icon to the Recycle Bin icon on the desktop. Point to Move Here on the shortcut menu.**

The Shortcut to Nelson Reminders (Monday) icon appears dimmed on top of the Recycle Bin icon, and a shortcut menu with two commands displays (Figure 2-60). The Shortcut to Nelson Reminders (Monday) icon remains on the desktop.

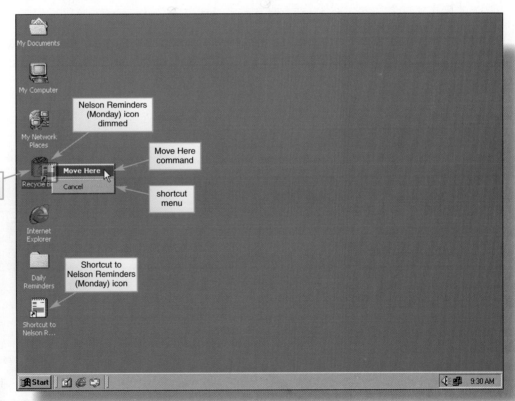

FIGURE 2-60

2 **Click Move Here.**

The Shortcut to Nelson Reminders (Monday) icon no longer displays on the desktop (Figure 2-61). The icon now is contained in the Recycle Bin.

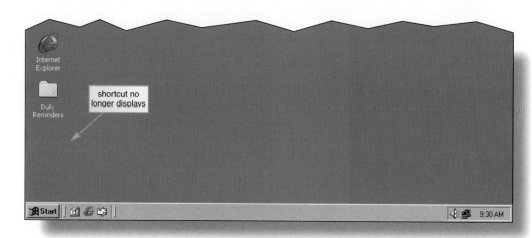

FIGURE 2-61

Other **Ways**

1. Drag shortcut icon to Recycle Bin
2. Right-click shortcut icon, click Delete, click Yes button

As noted previously, you can recover a shortcut, document, or application program you have moved to the Recycle Bin from the desktop or the hard disk. To do so, double-click the Recycle Bin icon to open the Recycle Bin window, right-click the object you want to restore to the desktop, and then click Restore on the shortcut menu.

Deleting Multiple Files

You can delete multiple files at the same time. You want to delete both the Cortez Reminders (Monday) and the Nelson Reminders (Monday) documents. To do so, complete the following steps.

Steps **To Delete Multiple Files**

1 **Double-click the Daily Reminders icon on the desktop. Place the mouse pointer below and to the right of the two document icons in the Daily Reminders window. Drag up and to the left until both icons are selected.**

The Daily Reminders window opens, a dotted line surrounds the Cortez Reminders (Monday) and Nelson Reminders (Monday) icons and the icons are selected (Figure 2-62).

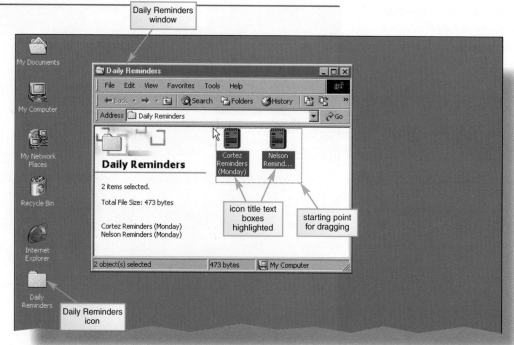

FIGURE 2-62

2 **Right-click either icon. Point to Delete on the shortcut menu.**

The Cortez Reminders (Monday) icon is right-clicked and a shortcut menu displays (Figure 2-63). Some of the commands on the shortcut menu may be different from those on your computer.

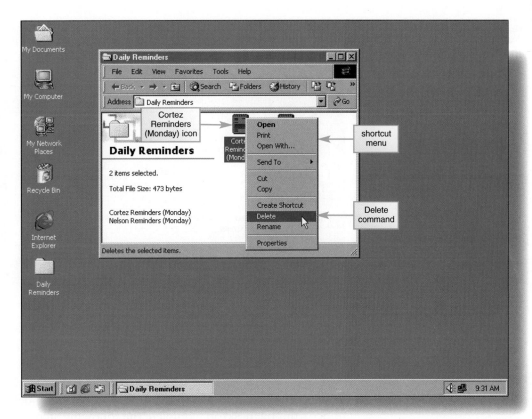

FIGURE 2-63

3 **Click Delete. Point to the Yes button in the Confirm Multiple File Delete dialog box.**

The Confirm Multiple File Delete dialog box displays (Figure 2-64). This dialog box ensures that you really want to delete the files. On some computers, this dialog box will not display because a special option has been chosen that specifies not to show this dialog box. If the dialog box does not display on your computer, the documents will be placed directly in the Recycle Bin.

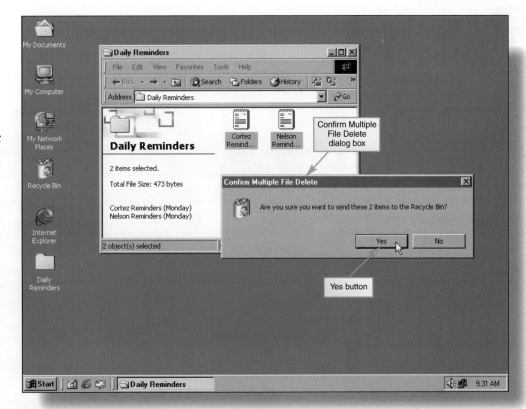

FIGURE 2-64

Microsoft Windows 2000

④ Click the Yes button.

The two files are removed from the Daily Reminders window and are placed in the Recycle Bin (Figure 2-65).

⑤ Click the Close button on the Daily Reminders title bar.

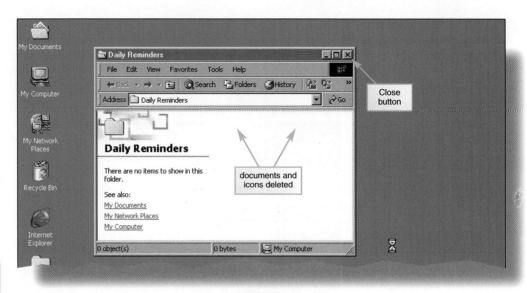

FIGURE 2-65

1. Click first document icon, hold down SHIFT key, click other icon, release SHIFT key, right-click either icon, click Delete, click Yes button
2. Select two icons, click Delete button on Standard Buttons toolbar, click Yes button

Deleting a Folder

You also can delete folders from the desktop. To delete the Daily Reminders folder from the desktop, complete the following step.

 To Delete a Folder from the Desktop

① Drag the Daily Reminders icon to the Recycle Bin icon.

When you drag the icon onto the Recycle Bin icon, a dimmed icon displays on the Recycle Bin icon (Figure 2-66). When you release the left mouse button, the dimmed icon no longer displays and the folder no longer displays on the desktop.

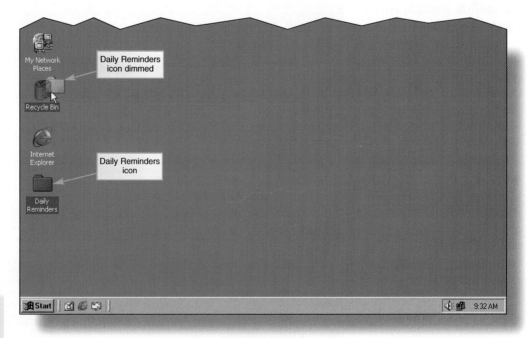

FIGURE 2-66

Other Ways

1. Right-drag folder icon to Recycle Bin, click Move Here
2. Right-click folder icon, click Delete on shortcut menu, click Yes button

In summary, you have used three different methods to delete an object from the desktop: (1) right-drag the object to the Recycle Bin; (2) right-click the object and then click Delete on the shortcut menu; and (3) drag the object to the Recycle Bin.

It is important to understand that when you delete a folder icon, you are deleting the folder and its contents from the computer. Therefore, you must be extremely cautious when deleting files.

If after deleting an icon from the desktop you want to return the icon immediately to the desktop, you can right-click the desktop and then click the Undo Delete command on the shortcut menu. For example, if you delete the Daily Reminders icon from the desktop, right-click the desktop and click Undo Delete on the shortcut menu. Windows 2000 will retrieve the deleted icon from the Recycle Bin and place it on the desktop. You also can return multiple deleted icons to the desktop in a similar fashion.

Working with the Windows 2000 Active Desktop™

Windows 2000 allows you to display Web pages from the Internet or intranet directly on the desktop and update the content of the pages automatically. Examples of this constantly changing content, referred to as **active content**, can be a weather map, a constantly updating stock market ticker of stock quotes, fast-breaking news stories from a favorite online newspaper, the latest sports scores, or a favorite Web page. When the desktop displays active content, the desktop is referred to as the **Active Desktop™**.

Turning On the Active Desktop™

Before you display active content on the desktop, you must turn on the Active Desktop so that the desktop becomes active. On some computers, the Active Desktop may already be turned on. Perform the following steps to turn on the Active Desktop.

 To Turn On the Active Desktop

① **Right-click an open area of the desktop, point to Active Desktop on the shortcut menu, and then point to Show Web Content on the Active Desktop submenu.**

A shortcut menu and the Active Desktop submenu display (Figure 2-67). The Show Web Content command on the Active Desktop submenu displays without a check mark preceding the command name to indicate the Active Desktop is turned off.

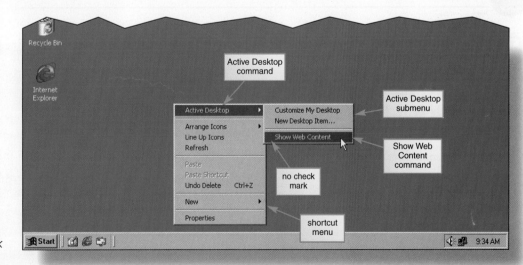

FIGURE 2-67

2 **If no check mark precedes the Show Web Content command, click the Show Web Content command.**

The Active Desktop is turned on (Figure 2-68). The shortcut menu and Active Desktop submenu no longer display on the desktop. Although not visible in Figure 2-68, a check mark precedes the Show Web Content command on the Active Desktop submenu.

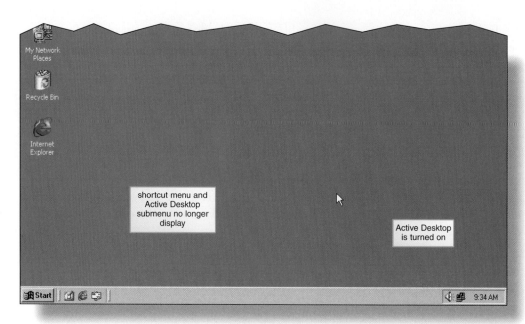

FIGURE 2-68

After turning on the Active Desktop, you can add active content to it.

Adding the Current Home Page to the Active Desktop

One method to add active content on the Active Desktop is to display a Web page on it. In Project 1, when you launched the Internet Explorer browser, Windows 2000 displayed the MSN.COM home page in the Microsoft Internet Explorer window. Because this home page displays each time you launch Internet Explorer, the page is referred to as the **current home page**, or **default home page**. Perform the following steps to add the current home page to the Active Desktop.

 To Add the Current Home Page to the Active Desktop

1 **Right-click an open area of the desktop, point to Active Desktop on the shortcut menu, and then point to My Current Home Page.**

A shortcut menu and the Active Desktop submenu display (Figure 2-69). The highlighted My Current Home Page command displays on the Active Desktop submenu. No check mark precedes the My Current Home Page command.

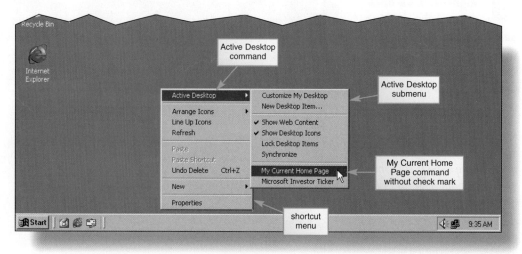

FIGURE 2-69

Click My Current Home Page.

The shortcut menu and Active Desktop submenu no longer display on the Active Desktop (Figure 2-70). The current home page (MSN.COM) displays in the open area above the taskbar and to the right of the desktop icons on the Active Desktop. Although not visible, a check mark precedes the My Current Home Page command on the Active Desktop submenu to indicate the current home page displays on the Active Desktop.

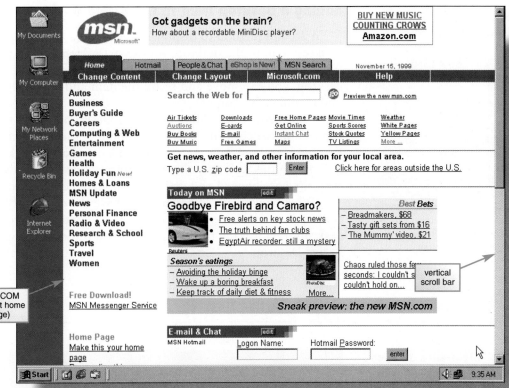

FIGURE 2-70

In Figure 2-69, check marks precede the Show Web Content and Show Desktop Icons commands to indicate the Active Desktop is turned on and the desktop icons (My Documents, My Computer, My Network Places, Recycle Bin, and Internet Explorer) display on the Active Desktop. Clicking the Show Desktop Icons command removes the icons from the desktop.

After displaying the current home page on the Active Desktop, you have access to the Internet. The vertical scroll bar along the right side of the page allows you to view hidden areas of the Web page.

Pointing to the left edge of the home page displays a gray vertical bar that you can use to resize the home page. Pointing to the top edge displays a gray bar that contains buttons to allow you to maximize the page, display the page in a separate window on the Active Desktop, and remove the home page.

When you no longer want the current home page to display on the Active Desktop, you can remove the home page. Perform the step below to remove the current home page from the desktop.

TO REMOVE THE CURRENT HOME PAGE FROM THE ACTIVE DESKTOP

 Right-click an open area of the desktop, point to Active Desktop on the shortcut menu, and then click My Current Home Page.

The current home page (MSN.COM) no longer displays on the desktop and a check mark no longer precedes the My Current Home Page command on the Active Desktop submenu.

More About 2000

The Active Desktop Submenu

Notice the difference between the Active Desktop submenu in Figure 2-67 on page WIN 2.47 and the Active Desktop submenu in Figure 2-69 on page WIN 2.48. When you turn on the Active Desktop, five additional commands display at the bottom of the Active Desktop submenu.

Active Desktop Items

After adding an Active Desktop item to the desktop, you can move the item by pointing to the desktop item name and dragging the gray bar that displays to a new position on the desktop. You also can resize the item by pointing to a corner or border until a double-headed arrow displays and then dragging the corner or border.

Adding a Desktop Item to the Active Desktop

A second method to display active content on the desktop is to add an Active Desktop item to the desktop. An **Active Desktop item** displays active content from a Web page directly on the desktop and updates the content periodically. Once on the desktop, you can move and resize the item and specify how often you want to update the active content.

In the process of adding an Active Desktop item to the desktop, you create a connection between the Web site containing the active content and the Internet Explorer browser. This connection, called a **channel**, links the Internet Explorer browser to the Web site, allowing Internet Explorer to determine if the content of the Web site has changed and deliver the updated content to the Active Desktop.

When you create a channel, you have the choice of being notified when new content is available or having the updated content delivered automatically to the desktop. Perform the following steps to add the ESPN SportsZone™ item to the Active Desktop.

To Add a Desktop Item to the Active Desktop

1 **Right-click an open area on the desktop, point to Active Desktop, and then point to New Desktop Item.**

A shortcut menu and the Active Desktop submenu display (Figure 2-71). The highlighted New Desktop Item command displays on the Active Desktop submenu.

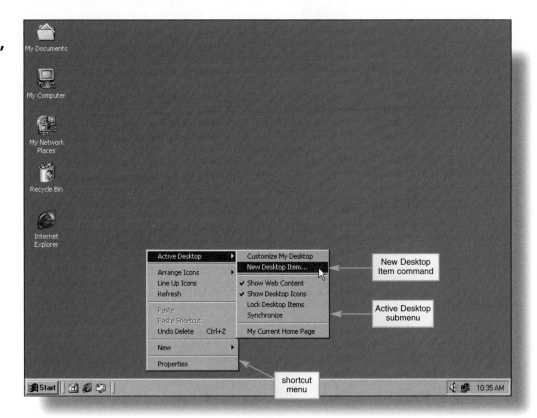

FIGURE 2-71

2 **Click New Desktop Item. Point to the Visit Gallery button in the New Active Desktop Item dialog box.**

The New Active Desktop Item dialog box displays (Figure 2-72). A message in the dialog box indicates you can add new Desktop Items, live Web content, or pictures to the Active Desktop. Clicking the Visit Gallery button allows you to visit the **Microsoft's Active Desktop Gallery** and add a new desktop item.

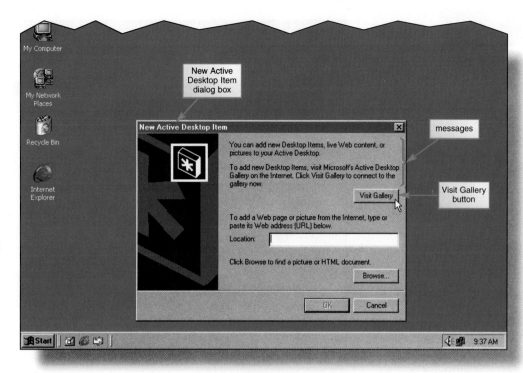

FIGURE 2-72

3 **Click the Visit Gallery button. Click the Maximize button in the Desktop Gallery – Microsoft Internet Explorer window. Point to the sports icon in the window.**

Windows 2000 launches Internet Explorer and displays the maximized Desktop Gallery window (Figure 2-73). The Gallery index contains six icons, each representing a category of desktop items. A message, the Microsoft Investor desktop item, and the Add to Active Desktop button display to the right of the icons. The mouse pointer changes to a hand icon when you point to the sports icon to indicate the icon is a hyperlink.

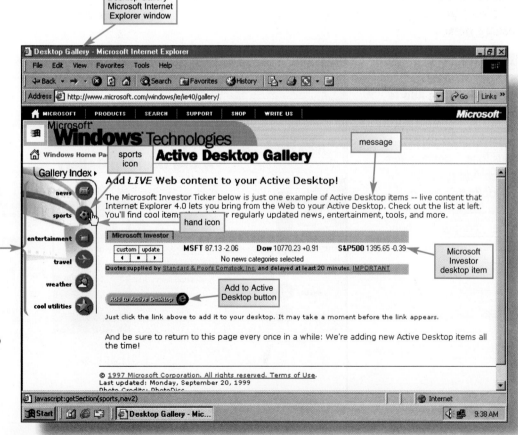

FIGURE 2-73

④ Click the sports icon and then point to ESPN SportsZone™.

The entries in the sports category (CBS Sportscenter and ESPN SportsZone™) replace the information to the right of the Gallery index (Figure 2-74). The ESPN SportsZone™ entry displays in red text and the mouse pointer changes to a hand icon.

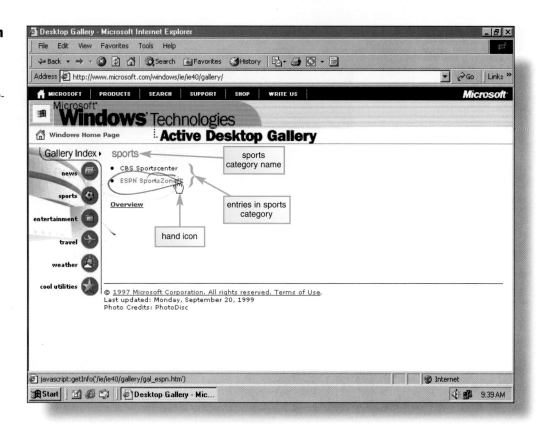

FIGURE 2-74

⑤ Click ESPN SportsZone™ and then point to the Add to Active Desktop button.

A sample of the ESPN SportsZone™ desktop item and the Add to Active Desktop button display (Figure 2-75). The mouse pointer changes to a hand icon.

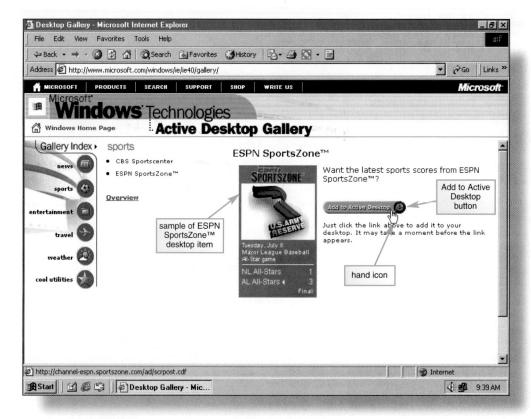

FIGURE 2-75

Click the Add to Active Desktop button. Point to the Yes button in the Internet Explorer dialog box.

The Internet Explorer dialog box displays (Figure 2-76). A question asks if you want to add an Active Desktop item to your desktop.

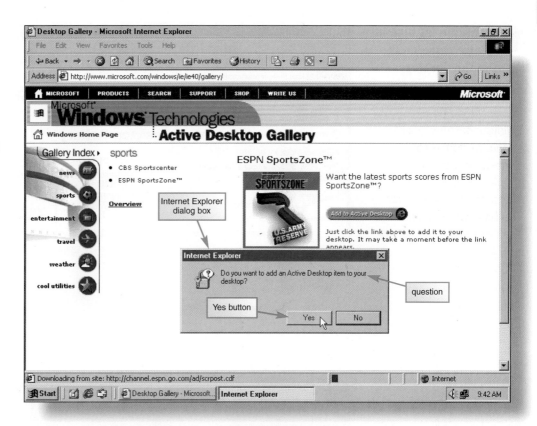

FIGURE 2-76

Click the Yes button. Point to the OK button in the Add item to the Active Desktop(TM) dialog box.

The Add item to Active Desktop(TM) dialog box displays (Figure 2-77). The dialog box contains a message that indicates you have chosen to make the ESPN SportsZone™ Web site available offline and add it to the Active Desktop.

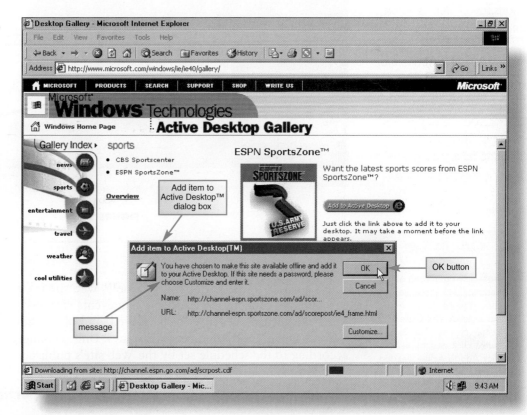

FIGURE 2-77

⑧ **Click the OK button. Point to the Close button in the Desktop Gallery window.**

The Synchronizing dialog box displays momentarily while the channel to the ESPN SportsZone™ Web site is established. After the channel is established, the Synchronizing dialog box closes and you can view the ESPN SportsZone™ desktop item by clicking the Close button in the Desktop Gallery window (Figure 2-78).

FIGURE 2-78

⑨ **Click the Close button.**

The Desktop Gallery window closes and the ESPN SportsZone™ item is visible on the desktop (Figure 2-79). The updated sports scores that display at the bottom of the item change approximately every four seconds.

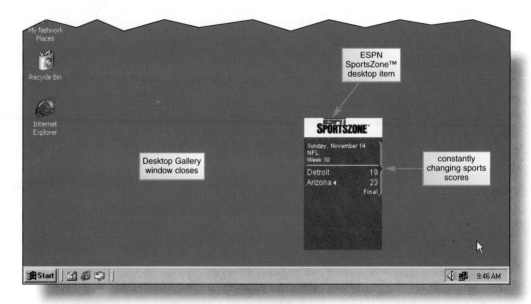

FIGURE 2-79

Other **Ways**

1. Right-click open area of desktop, click Properties, click Web tab, click New button, click Visit Gallery button, click icon in Gallery Index, click desktop item, click Add to Active Desktop button, click Yes button, click OK button

A channel to the ESPN SportsZone™ Web site is established. This allows you to view the changing scores of sporting events currently in progress, view the game times of sporting events yet to be played, and obtain additional information about the sporting event that currently displays. Unless changed, updates are performed according to the schedule set by the Web site's publisher.

Displaying Additional Information About a Sporting Event

After adding the ESPN SportsZone™ desktop item to the Active Desktop, you may want to obtain additional information about a sporting event that displays in the Active Desktop item. Perform the following steps to display additional information about a sporting event.

Steps **To Display Additional Information About a Sporting Event**

1 **Point to the score summary on the ESPN SportsZone™ desktop item.**

The mouse pointer points to the score summary of a football game (Figure 2-80).

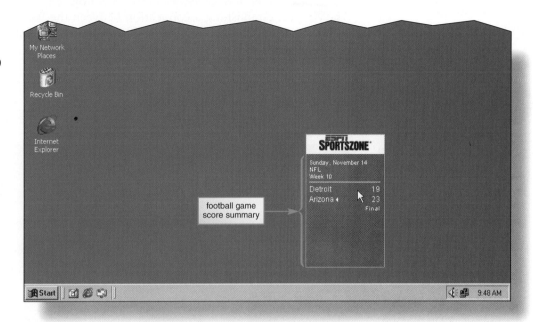

FIGURE 2-80

2 **Click the score summary. Click the Maximize button in the Microsoft Internet Explorer window.**

The maximized Microsoft Internet Explorer window displays (Figure 2-81). The window displays additional information about the sporting event.

3 **Scroll the window to read the information about the sporting event. When finished, click the Close button in the Microsoft Internet Explorer window to close the window.**

The Microsoft Internet Explorer window closes.

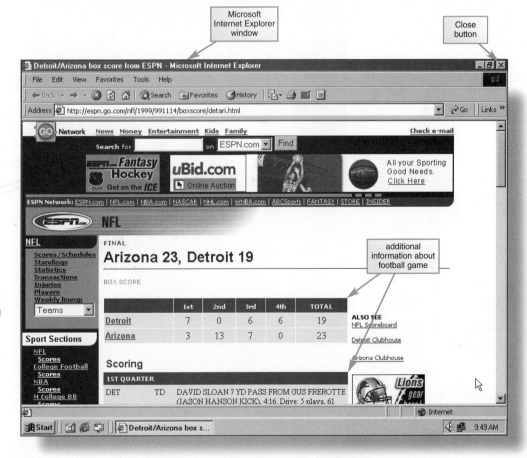

FIGURE 2-81

Removing a Desktop Item from the Active Desktop

When you no longer use a desktop item on the Active Desktop, remove the item. The channel establishing a connection between the Web site and Active Desktop will be closed. Perform the following steps to remove the ESPN SportsZone™ item and close the channel.

Steps To Remove a Desktop Item from the Active Desktop

1 Right-click an open area on the desktop, point to Active Desktop, and then point to Customize My Desktop.

A shortcut menu and the Active Desktop submenu display (Figure 2-82). The highlighted Customize My Desktop command displays on the Active Desktop submenu. A check mark preceding the ie4_frame.html entry indicates the ESPN SportsZone™ item displays on the desktop.

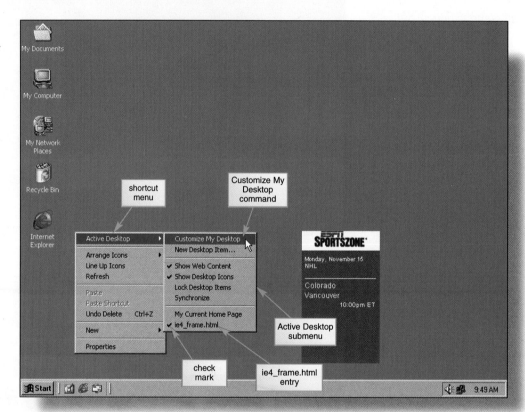

FIGURE 2-82

2 Click Customize My Desktop. If necessary, click the Web tab in the Display Properties dialog box. Point to http://channel-espn.sportszone.com/ad/scorepost/ie4_frame.html, representing the ESPN SportsZone™ desktop item.

The Display Properties dialog box displays (Figure 2-83). A check mark in the http://channel-espn.sportszone.com/ad/scorepost/ie4_frame.html check box and the light blue rectangle on the monitor indicate the ESPN SportsZone™ item displays on the desktop.

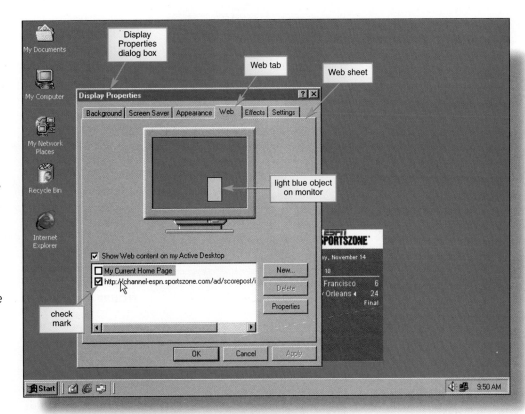

FIGURE 2-83

3 Click http://channel-espn.sportszone.com/ad/scorepost/ie4_frame.html to highlight the title. Point to the Delete button.

The http://channel-espn.sportszone.com/ad/scorepost/ie4_frame.html entry is highlighted and the color of the rectangle in the monitor changes to dark blue (Figure 2-84).

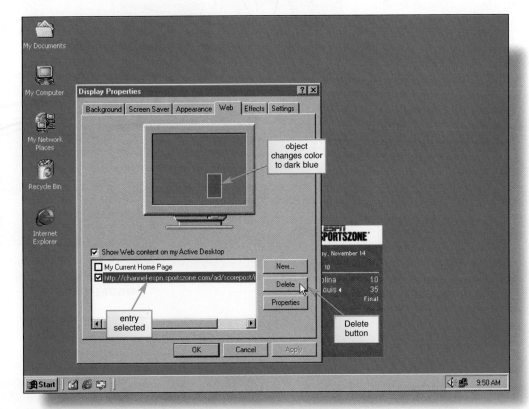

FIGURE 2-84

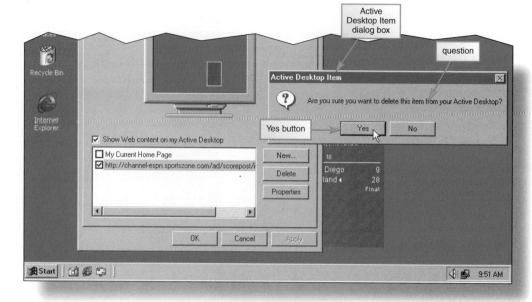

4 **Click the Delete button. Point to the Yes button in the Active Desktop Item dialog box.**

The Active Desktop Item dialog box displays (Figure 2-85). The question, Are you sure you want to delete this item from your Active Desktop?, displays in the dialog box. Clicking the Yes button will close the channel between the ESPN SportsZone™ Web site and the Active Desktop.

FIGURE 2-85

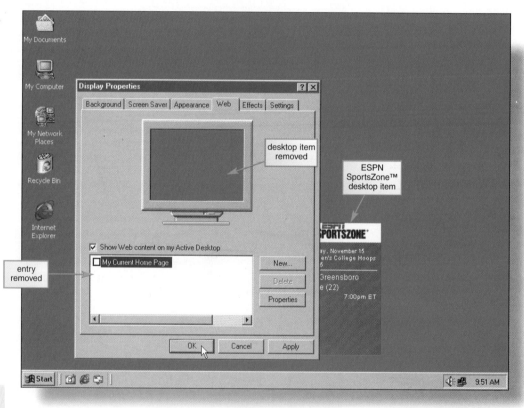

5 **Click the Yes button. Point to the OK button in the Display Properties dialog box.**

The http://channel-espn. sportszone.com/ad/ scorepost/ie4_frame.html check box, title, and the object that it represents in the monitor are deleted from the Display Properties dialog box, and the channel to the ESPN SportsZone™ Web site is closed (Figure 2-86).

6 **Click the OK button.**

The ESPN SportsZone™ item no longer displays on the desktop.

1. Point to desktop item name on Active Desktop item, click down arrow button on gray bar, click Customize My Desktop, click desktop item name, click Delete button, click Yes button, click OK button

2. Point to desktop item name on Active Desktop item, click Close button on gray bar

FIGURE 2-86

If after removing a desktop item from the Active Desktop, you wish to return the item to the desktop, follow the steps illustrated on pages WIN 2.50 through WIN 2.54 to return the item.

Turning Off the Active Desktop

When you no longer want active content on the desktop, you can turn off the Active Desktop. When you turn off the Active Desktop, all desktop items are removed and the desktop no longer is active. Perform the following steps to turn off the Active Desktop.

 ### To Turn Off the Active Desktop

 Right-click an open area of the desktop, point to Active Desktop on the shortcut menu, and then point to Show Web Content on the Active Desktop submenu.

A shortcut menu and the Active Desktop submenu display (Figure 2-87). A check mark precedes the Show Web Content command on the Active Desktop submenu to indicate the Active Desktop is turned on.

2 **Click Show Web Content.**

The Active Desktop is turned off, and the shortcut menu and Active Desktop submenu no longer display on the desktop.

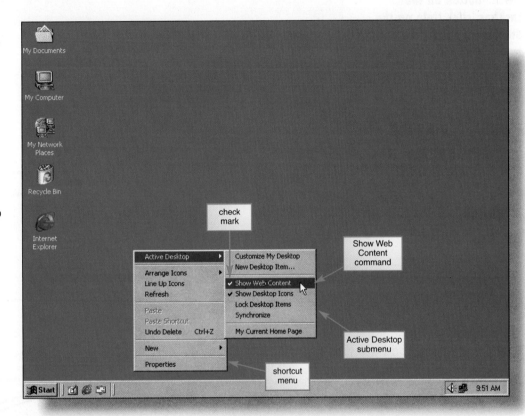

FIGURE 2-87

Using Web Help to Obtain Online Help

Windows Help provides a variety of ways to obtain information. In Project 1, you browsed through Help topics by category using the Contents sheet. Next, you found answers to questions about Windows 2000 by searching entries in the Index sheet and viewing Help screens. Last, you searched for Help topics using a keyword and the Search sheet.

Another way to obtain information about Windows 2000 is to use Web Help. **Web Help** allows you to use the Internet to obtain technical support, answers to frequently asked questions (FAQs), and tips about Windows 2000. Because Microsoft routinely updates its Help information on the Internet, the information you obtain using Web Help is more current than the information contained in the Windows Contents, Index, and Search sheets.

Other Ways

1. Click Start button, point to Settings, click Control Panel, double-click Display icon, click Web tab, click Show Web content on my Active Desktop, click OK button

2. Click Start button, point to Settings, click Control Panel, double-click Folder Options icon, click General tab, click Enable Web content on my desktop, click OK button

In this project, you will use Web Help and the Internet to access helpful information located on the Microsoft Web site. Perform the following steps to obtain help from the Microsoft Web site.

Steps **To Use Web Help to Obtain Online Help**

1 **Click the Start button on the taskbar, click Help on the Start menu, and then point to the Web Help button on the Help toolbar.**

The Windows 2000 window displays (Figure 2-88). The Web Help button is located on the Help toolbar.

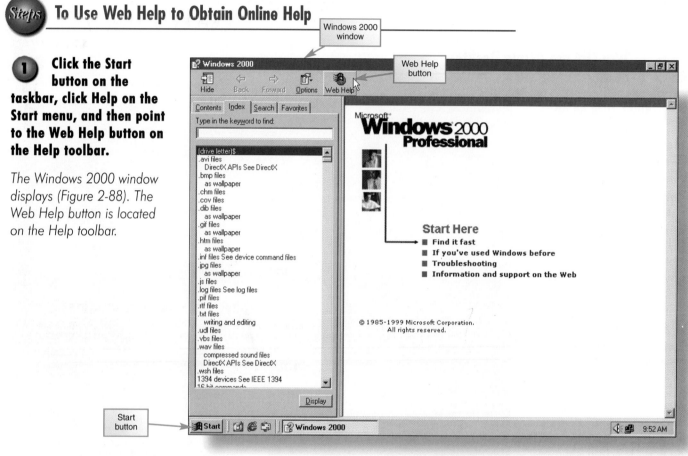

FIGURE 2-88

2 **Click the Web Help button. Point to the Windows 2000 home page hyperlink in the topics pane.**

The Online support and information sheet displays in the topics pane of the Windows 2000 window (Figure 2-89). Nine hyperlinks display in the topics pane of the window.

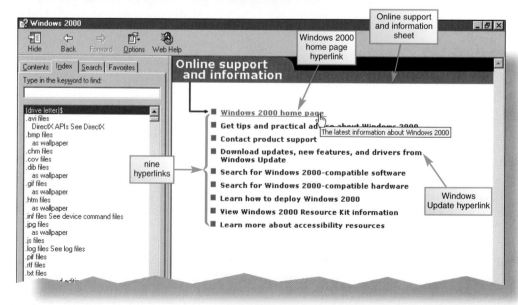

FIGURE 2-89

3 Click Windows 2000 home page. Maximize the Windows 2000 Professional Documentation - Microsoft Internet Explorer window.

The Windows 2000 Professional Documentation - Microsoft Internet Explorer window displays (Figure 2-90). The window contains a wealth of knowledge about Windows 2000 Professional.

4 Click the Close button on the Microsoft Internet Explorer title bar. Click the Close button in the Windows 2000 window.

The Windows 2000 Professional Documentation - Microsoft Internet Explorer window and Windows 2000 window close.

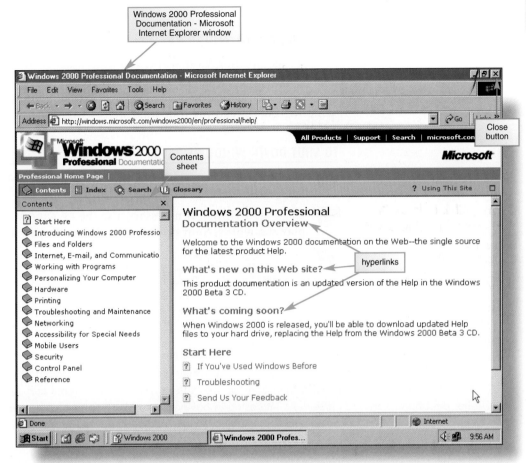

Windows 2000 Professional Documentation - Microsoft Internet Explorer window

Contents sheet

Close button

hyperlinks

FIGURE 2-90

A wealth of knowledge is available from the Microsoft home page shown in Figure 2-90. Currently, the contents of the Contents sheet displays on the home page. In addition, the page contains hyperlinks that allow you to find additional helpful information on the Microsoft Web site. Because Microsoft routinely updates its Help information on the Internet, the contents of the Contents sheet is more current than the contents of the Contents sheet in Windows Help.

More About

Windows 2000 Web Help

Microsoft Web Help replaces the need for lengthy, hard-to-understand technical manuals. Because the Help information in Microsoft Web Help can be updated quickly by Microsoft, it provides the most up-to-date technical information, answers to frequently asked questions, and late-breaking tips about working with Windows 2000.

Shutting Down Windows

After completing your work, you may wish to shut down Windows 2000 using the Shut Down command on the Start menu. If you want to shut down Windows 2000, perform the following steps. If you are not sure about shutting down Windows 2000, read the following steps without performing them.

TO SHUT DOWN WINDOWS 2000

(1) Click the Start button on the taskbar and then point to Shut Down on the Start menu.

(2) Click Shut Down. If necessary, use the UP ARROW or DOWN ARROW key to display the words, Shut down, in the What do you want the computer to do? box.

(3) Click the OK button.

Windows 2000 is shut down.

CASE PERSPECTIVE SUMMARY

After creating the Monday daily reminder documents for Mr. Cortez and Ms. Nelson, you receive an e-mail message from Mr. Cortez thanking you for the document and stating how easy it is to view and change his reminders. Ms. Nelson stopped by your office to inform you that she showed her daily reminders document to other employees in her department and they also were interested in having them. Ms. Nelson also mentioned that being able to add a reminder to another employee's list was a brilliant idea. While in your office Ms. Nelson noticed the football scores on your desktop and asked if you would show her how to display them on her computer. Your supervisor, after hearing from Mr. Cortez and Ms. Nelson, placed you in charge of developing a reminders system for the entire company.

Project Summary

In this project you used the application-centric approach and document-centric approach to create two text documents on the desktop. You then modified and printed these documents. Using a shortcut menu, you created a folder on the desktop, placed documents in the folder, copied the folder onto a floppy disk in drive A, and then shared the folder. You worked with multiple documents open at the same time. You placed a document shortcut on both the Start menu and desktop. Using various methods, you deleted shortcuts, documents, and a folder from the desktop. You learned how to turn on and add an item to the Active Desktop. Additionally, you displayed information about a sporting event, removed the item, and turned off the Active Desktop. Finally, you used Web Help to access the Microsoft Web page dedicated to Windows 2000 Professional.

What You Should Know

Having completed this project, you now should be able to perform the following tasks:

▶ Add a Desktop Item to the Active Desktop (WIN 2.50)

▶ Add the Current Home Page to the Active Desktop (WIN 2.48)

▶ Close a Document (WIN 2.12)

▶ Close and Save a Modified Document on the Desktop (WIN 2.16)

▶ Close and Save Open Windows from the Taskbar (WIN 2.26)

▶ Copy a Folder on the Desktop onto a Floppy Disk (WIN 2.30)

▶ Create a Blank Document on the Desktop (WIN 2.13)

▶ Create a Shortcut on the Desktop (WIN 2.38)

▶ Create and Name a Folder on the Desktop (WIN 2.17)

▶ Delete a Folder from the Desktop (WIN 2.46)

▶ Delete a Shortcut from the Desktop (WIN 2.43)

▶ Delete Multiple Files (WIN 2.44)

▶ Display Additional Information About a Sporting Event (WIN 2.55)

▶ Display the Arrange Icons Submenu (WIN 2.42)

▶ Enter Data into a Blank Document (WIN 2.15)

▶ Launch a Program and Create a Document (WIN 2.6)

▶ Minimize All Open Windows (WIN 2.25)

▶ Move a Document into a Folder (WIN 2.18)

▶ Name a Document on the Desktop (WIN 2.14)

▶ Open a Document on the Desktop (WIN 2.14)

▶ Open a Document Using a Shortcut on the Desktop (WIN 2.39)

▶ Open a Document Using the Start Menu (WIN 2.35)

▶ Open a Folder (WIN 2.20)

▶ Open a Folder Stored on a Floppy Disk (WIN 2.31)

▶ Open an Inactive Window (WIN 2.24)

▶ Open and Modify a Document in a Folder (WIN 2.21)

▶ Open and Modify Multiple Documents (WIN 2.22)

▶ Place a Document Shortcut on the Start Menu (WIN 2.33)

▶ Print a Document (WIN 2.11)

▶ Print Multiple Documents from Within a Folder (WIN 2.28)

▶ Remove a Desktop Item from the Active Desktop (WIN 2.56)

▶ Remove a Shortcut from the Start Menu (WIN 2.36)

▶ Remove Sharing from a Folder (WIN 2.41)

▶ Remove the Current Home Page from the Active Desktop (WIN 2.49)

▶ Save a Document on the Desktop (WIN 2.8)

▶ Share a Folder (WIN 2.40)

▶ Shut Down Windows 2000 (WIN 2.62)

▶ Turn Off the Active Desktop (WIN 2.59)

▶ Turn On the Active Desktop (WIN 2.47

▶ Use Web Help to Obtain Online Help (WIN 2.60)

P. 148

 *Test Your Knowledge*

1 True/False

Instructions: Circle T if the statement is true or F if the statement is false.

T F   1. Document-centric means a user thinks in terms of the application program used to create a document rather than the document itself.

T F   2. To create a text document directly on the desktop, right-click the desktop, point to New on the shortcut menu, and then click Text Document on the New submenu.

T F   3. To open a document stored on the desktop, click the Start button, point to Programs, and then click the document name on the Programs submenu.

T F   4. To create a folder on the desktop, right-click the desktop, and then click Folder on the shortcut menu.

T F   5. When you drag a document into a folder on the desktop, you must click Move Here on the shortcut menu to place the document in the folder.

T F   6. To open a folder stored on the desktop, click the folder icon.

T F   7. The concept of multiple programs running at the same time is called multitasking.

T F   8. You can create a shortcut on the Start menu.

T F   9. One way to view active content on your desktop is to add an Active Desktop item to your desktop.

T F   10. The Help information you obtain while using Web Help is located on the Internet.

2 Multiple Choice

Instructions: Circle the correct response.

1. A(n) _____ is a program that allows you to accomplish a specific task for which the program is designed.
   a. document
   b. operating system
   c. user interface
   d. application

2. To create a text document on the desktop, _____.
   a. click the desktop, and then click Text Document
   b. right-click the desktop, point to New, and then click Text Document
   c. click the desktop, point to Document, and then click Text Document
   d. right-click the desktop, point to New, and then click Document

3. To open an inactive window, _____.
   a. click the inactive window's button in the taskbar button area
   b. press ALT+TAB until the name of the window displays, and then release the keys
   c. click the inactive window's button on the Start menu
   d. both a and b

Test Your Knowledge

4. To select two documents within a folder, _____.
   a. right-drag any single document
   b. click File on the menu bar and then click Select All
   c. click one document icon, hold down the SHIFT key, and then click the other document icon
   d. click the folder title bar

5. A shortcut is _____.
   a. a program that makes your work easier and faster
   b. an icon that represents a document or an application program
   c. any icon found in an open window
   d. another name for a button in the taskbar button area

6. To open a document located on the Start menu, _____ on the Start menu.
   a. double-click the document name
   b. click the document name
   c. right-click the document name
   d. point to the document name

7. When you delete a shortcut from the desktop, _____.
   a. the shortcut is placed in the Recycle Bin
   b. Windows 2000 will display an error message
   c. the shortcut and the related file are placed in the Recycle Bin
   d. the shortcut is deleted permanently

8. Which of the following is not a way to delete an object from the desktop?
   a. Right-drag the object to the Recycle Bin.
   b. Drag the object to the Recycle Bin.
   c. Click the object and then click Delete on the shortcut menu.
   d. Right-click the object and then click Delete on the shortcut menu.

9. The current home page is the _____.
   a. Web page currently visible in the Microsoft Internet Explorer window
   b. last Web page displayed before quitting Internet Explorer
   c. Web page that displays when you launch Internet Explorer
   d. Microsoft home page

10. When you add a desktop item to the Active Desktop, you also _____ to a _____.
   a. create a channel, Web site
   b. add active content, window
   c. add a button, toolbar
   d. move a window, new location

3 Working with Folders and Documents

Instructions: The open Business Documents folder displays on the desktop shown in Figure 2-91 on the next page. The Address Book and Daily Appointments documents are stored in the Business Documents folder. In the spaces on the next page, write the steps to accomplish the tasks indicated.

(continued)

Test Your Knowledge

Working with Folders and Documents (*continued*)

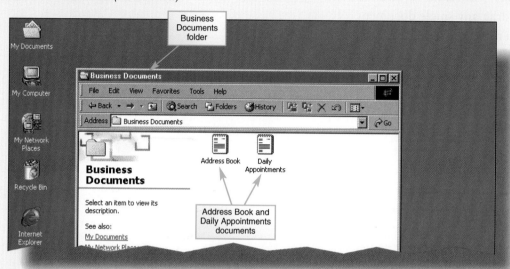

FIGURE 2-91

To Print the Address Book document

Step 1: _____

Step 2: _____

To Copy the Daily Appointments document to the desktop

Step 1: _____

Step 2: _____

To Delete the Address Book document from the Business Documents folder

Method 1:

Step 1: _____

Step 2: _____

Step 3: _____

Method 2:

Step 1: _____

Step 2: _____

Method 3:

Step 1: _____

To Delete the Business Documents folder from the desktop

Method 1:

Step 1: _____

Step 2: _____

Step 3: _____

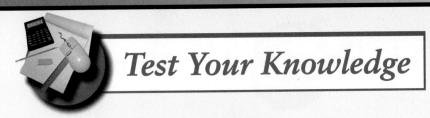

Test Your Knowledge

Method 2:

Step 1: _____

Step 2: _____

Method 3:

Step 1: _____

4 Working with Document Shortcuts

Instructions: The closed Sales Documents folder displays on the desktop. The Monthly Sales document is stored in the Sales Documents folder. In the spaces provided below, write the steps to accomplish the tasks indicated.

To place a document shortcut for the Monthly Sales document on the Start menu

Step 1: _____

Step 2: _____

To open the Monthly Sales document from the Start menu

Step 1: _____

Step 2: _____

To remove the Monthly Sales shortcut from the Start menu

Step 1: _____

Step 2: _____

Step 3: _____

Step 4: _____

5 Adding a Desktop Item to the Active Desktop

Instructions: List the steps in the spaces provided to add the ESPN SportsZone™ desktop item to the Active Desktop.

Step 1: _____

Step 2: _____

Step 3: _____

Step 4: _____

Step 5: _____

Step 6: _____

Step 7: _____

Step 8: _____

Step 9: _____

1 Using Windows 2000 Professional Online Help

Instructions: Use a computer and Windows Online Help to perform the following tasks.

Part 1: *Launching Windows 2000 Professional Online Help*

1. Start Windows 2000. If necessary, connect to the Internet.
2. Click the Start button on the taskbar, click Help on the Start menu, and then click the Web Help button in the Windows 2000 window.
3. Click the Windows 2000 home page hyperlink in the topics pane and maximize the Windows 2000 Professional Documentation - Microsoft Internet Explorer window. The maximized Windows 2000 Professional Documentation window displays (Figure 2-92). The navigation pane contains the Contents, Index, Search, and Glossary buttons. The topics pane contains the Windows 2000 Professional Documentation overview. Read the overview.

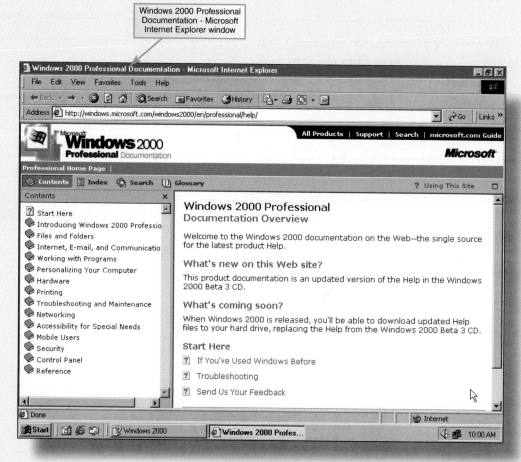

FIGURE 2-92

Part 2: *Using the Contents sheet*

1. If necessary, click the Contents button in the navigation pane of the window.
2. Click the Files and Folders closed book icon.
3. Click the Files and Folders overview Help topic and read the files and folders overview.
4. Right-click the topics pane, click Print on the shortcut menu, and then click the Print button in the Print dialog box to print the Help topic.
5. Click the Files and Folders open book icon to close the book.
6. Click the Personalizing Your Computer closed book icon.
7. Click the Add a shortcut to the Start menu Help topic.
8. Right-click the topics pane, click Print on the shortcut menu, and then click the Print button in the Print dialog box to print the Help topic.

Part 3: *Using the Index sheet*

1. Click the Index button in the navigation pane of the window.
2. Type active desktop in the Enter at least two letters text box.
3. Click the overview link in the list box below the Enter at least two letters text box.
4. Right-click the topics pane, click Print on the shortcut menu, and then click the Print button in the Print dialog box to print the Help topic.

Part 4: *Using the Search sheet*

1. Click the Search button in the navigation pane of the window.
2. Type windows update in the Enter a keyword or phrase text box.
3. Click the Go button in the Search sheet.
4. Click the Using Windows Update link in the topics pane.
5. Right-click the topics pane, click Print on the shortcut menu, and then click the Print button in the Print dialog box to print the Help topic.

Part 5: *Quitting Windows 2000 Professional Online Help*

1. Close the Windows 2000 Professional Documentation window.
2. Close the Windows 2000 window.

2 Using Windows Update

Instructions: Use a computer and Windows Online Help to perform the following tasks.

Part 1: *Launching Windows 2000 Professional Online Help*

1. Start Windows 2000. If necessary, connect to the Internet.
2. Click the Start button on the taskbar, click Help on the Start menu, and then click the Web Help button in the Windows 2000 window.
3. Click the Download updates, new features, and drivers from Windows Update link in the right pane. Maximize the Microsoft Windows Update - Microsoft Internet Explorer window.

(continued)

Using Windows Update *(continued)*

4. Read the information in the Microsoft Windows Update window (Figure 2-93).

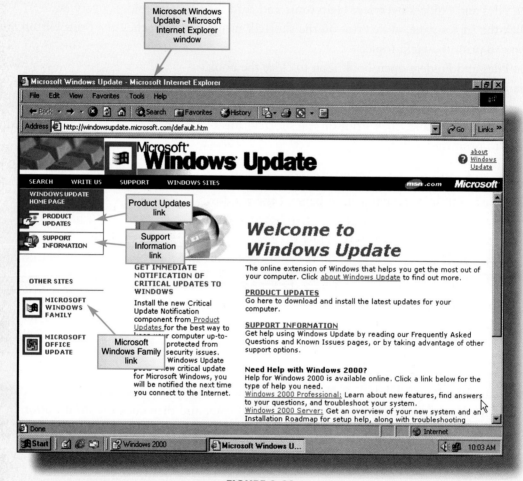

FIGURE 2-93

Part 2: Viewing Product Updates

1. Click the Product Updates link in the Microsoft Windows Update window (Figure 2-93). Information about software product updates displays in the right pane of the window. Scroll to read the information about product updates and answer the following questions in the spaces provided.

   a. List the critical updates.

   _____

   b. List the picks of the month.

   _____

   c. List the recommended updates.

   _____

Use Help

   d. List the device drivers.

_____

Part 3: *Viewing Support Information*

1. Click the Support Information link in the Microsoft Windows Update window (Figure 2-93). Support information displays in the right pane of the window.
2. Click the Frequently Asked Questions link in the right pane. Answer the following questions in the spaces provided.

   a. What is Windows Update?

_____

   b. What is Product Updates?

_____

   c. Does information about your computer get transmitted to Microsoft? Explain.

_____

Part 4: *The Microsoft Windows Family*

1. Click the Microsoft Windows Family link in the Microsoft Windows Update window (Figure 2-93). Maximize the Windows: Windows Home Page - Microsoft Internet Explorer window. Answer the following questions in the spaces provided.

   a. What versions of Windows are listed?

_____

_____

2. Point to the Windows 2000 Professional link.

   a. Summarize the information that displays when you point to the link.

_____

_____

Part 5: *Quitting Windows Update*

1. Close the Windows: Windows Home Page window.
2. Close the Microsoft Windows Update window.
3. Close the Windows 2000 window.

In the Lab

1 Launching an Application, Creating a Document, and Modifying a Document

Problem: Your boss asks you to create a list of vendor names and Web sites for company employees to use to order supplies and services. You create the vendor list shown in Figure 2-94 using the application-centric approach and Notepad.

Instructions:

Part 1: *Launching the Notepad Application*

1. If necessary, start Microsoft Windows 2000.
2. Click the Start button.
3. Point to Programs on the Start menu.
4. Point to Accessories on the Programs submenu.
5. Click Notepad on the Accessories submenu.
6. Enter the text shown in Figure 2-94.

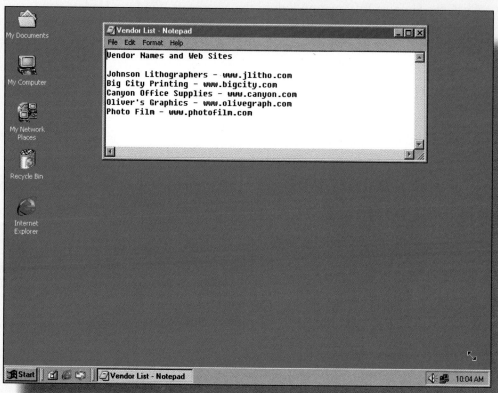

FIGURE 2-94

Part 2: *Saving the Document onto a Floppy Disk and Printing the Document*

1. Insert a formatted floppy disk in drive A of your computer.
2. Click File on the menu bar and then click Save As to display the Save As dialog box.
3. Type Vendor List in the File name text box.
4. Click the My Computer button on the Shortcut bar.
5. Click the 3½ Floppy (A:) icon in the list.
6. Click the Open button in the Save As dialog box to display the contents of the 3½ Floppy (A:) drive.
7. Click the Save button in the Save As dialog box to save the Vendor List document.
8. Click File on the menu bar, click Print on the File menu, and then click the Print button.
9. Click the Close button on the Notepad title bar.
10. If you are not completing Part 3 of this assignment, remove your floppy disk from drive A.

In the Lab

Part 3: *Modifying a Document*

1. Click the Start button, point to Programs, point to Accessories, and then click Notepad.
2. Click File on the menu bar and then click Open.
3. Click the My Computer icon on the Shortcut bar.
4. Click the 3½ Floppy (A:) icon in the list.
5. Click the Open button in the Open dialog box to display the contents of the 3½ Floppy (A:) drive.
6. Click the Vendor List file name in the text.
7. Click the Open button to open the Vendor List document.
8. Press the DOWN ARROW key seven times.
9. Type Kelly's Camera - www.kellyscamera.com and then press the ENTER key.
10. Click File on the menu bar and then click Save.
11. Click File on the menu bar, click Print on the File menu, and then click the Print button.
12. Click the Close button on the Notepad title bar.
13. Remove the floppy disk from drive A.

2 Creating, Saving, and Printing Windows 2000 Professional Seminar Announcement and Schedule Documents

Problem: A two-day Windows 2000 Professional seminar will be offered to all teachers at your school. You have been put in charge of developing two text documents for the seminar. One document announces the seminar and will be sent to all teachers. The other document contains the schedule for the seminar. You prepare the documents shown in Figures 2-95 and 2-96 on the next page using Notepad.

Instructions:

Part 1: *Creating the Windows 2000 Professional Seminar Announcement Document*

1. If necessary, start Microsoft Windows 2000.
2. Create a blank text document on the desktop. Name the document Windows 2000 Professional Seminar Announcement.
3. Enter the text shown in Figure 2-95.
4. Save the document on the desktop.
5. Print the document.

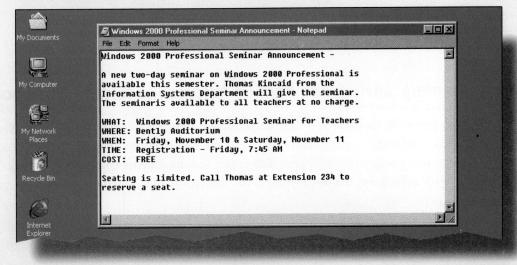

FIGURE 2-95

(continued)

In the Lab

Creating, Saving, and Printing Windows 2000 Professional Seminar Announcement and Schedule Documents *(continued)*

6. Create a folder on the desktop called Windows 2000 Seminar Documents.
7. Place the Windows 2000 Professional Seminar Announcement document in the Windows 2000 Seminar Documents folder.

Part 2: *Creating the Windows 2000 Professional Seminar Schedule Document*

1. Create a blank text document on the desktop. Name the document Windows 2000 Professional Seminar Schedule.
2. Enter the text shown in Figure 2-96.
3. Save the document on the desktop.
4. Print the document.
5. Place the Windows 2000 Professional Seminar Schedule document in the Windows 2000 Seminar Documents folder.
6. Move the Windows 2000 Seminar Documents folder to a floppy disk.

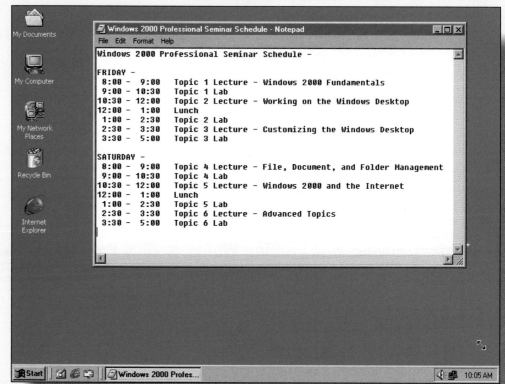

FIGURE 2-96

3 Creating, Saving, and Printing Automobile Information Documents

Problem: For eight months, you have accumulated data about your 2000 Dodge Viper automobile. Some of the information is written on pieces of paper, while the rest is in the form of receipts. You have decided to organize this information using your computer. You create the documents shown in Figures 2-97, 2-98, 2-99, and 2-100 on page WIN 2.76 using the document-centric approach and Notepad.

Instructions:

Part 1: *Creating the Automobile Information Document*

1. If necessary, start Microsoft Windows 2000.
2. Create a text document on the desktop. Name the document Automobile Information.
3. Enter the text shown in Figure 2-97.

In the Lab

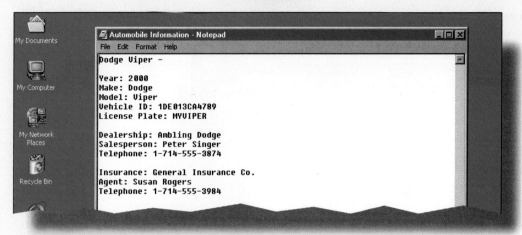

FIGURE 2-97

4. Save the document on the desktop.
5. Print the document.
6. Create a folder on the desktop called Automobile Documents.
7. Place the Automobile Information document in the Automobile Documents folder.

Part 2: *Other Automobile Documents*

1. Create the Phone Numbers document (Figure 2-98), the Automobile Gas Mileage document (Figure 2-99 on the next page), and the Automobile Maintenance document (Figure 2-100 on the next page).
2. Save each document on the desktop.
3. Print each document.
4. Place each document in the Automobile Documents folder.
5. Move the Automobile Documents folder to a floppy disk.

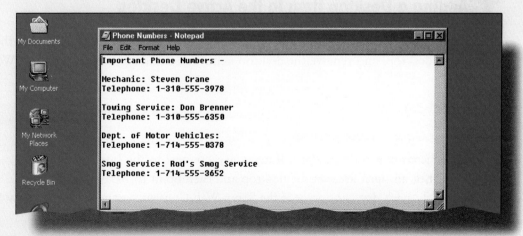

FIGURE 2-98

(continued)

In the Lab

Creating, Saving, and Printing Automobile Information Documents (continued)

FIGURE 2-99

FIGURE 2-100

4 Adding a Desktop Item to the Active Desktop

Problem: A fellow employee asks you to show him how to add a desktop item to the desktop, reposition the item on the desktop, and remove the desktop item. You decide to use the MSNBC Weather desktop item to show him.

Instructions:

Part 1: *Turn On the Active Desktop*

1. Start Microsoft Windows 2000. If necessary, connect to the Internet.
2. Right-click an open area on the desktop and then point to Active Desktop.
3. If a check mark does not precede the Show Web Content command, click Show Web Content.

Part 2: *Adding a Desktop Item to the Desktop*

1. Right-click an open area on the desktop, point to Active Desktop, and then click New Desktop Item.
2. Click the Visit Gallery button in the New Active Desktop Item dialog box.
3. Click the Maximize button in the Desktop Gallery window.
4. Click the weather icon in the Desktop Gallery window (Figure 2-101).

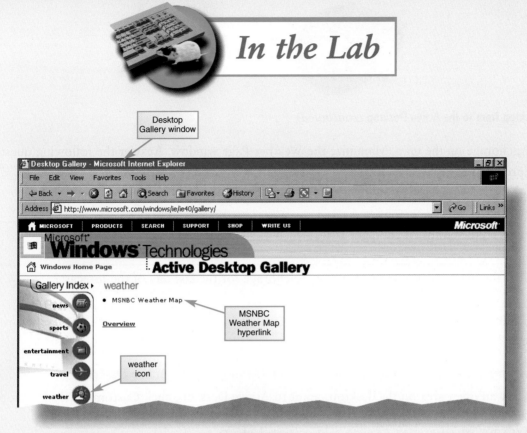

FIGURE 2-101

5. Click MSNBC Weather Map name.
6. Click the Add to Active Desktop button.
7. Click the Yes button in the Internet Explorer dialog box.
8. Click the OK button in the Add item to Active Desktop™ dialog box.
9. Click the Close button in the Desktop Gallery window.

Part 3: *Sizing the Desktop Item*

1. Size the desktop item so that the entire United States map is visible. To size the item, point to a border or corner to change the mouse pointer to a double-headed arrow and drag the border or corner.

Part 4: *Checking the Weather*

1. Click San Francisco on the map. Maximize the Weather Page window. Answer the following questions in the spaces provided.

   a. What is the current temperature, barometric pressure, and humidity in San Francisco?

   _____

   b. What is the weather forecast for the next four days in San Francisco?

   _____

   c. What is the high and low temperature for tomorrow in San Francisco?

   _____

2. Click the Print button on the Standard Buttons toolbar to print the map.
3. Close the Weather Page window.

(continued)

In the Lab

Adding a Desktop Item to the Active Desktop *(continued)*

4. Click Anchorage on the map. Maximize the Weather Page window. Answer the following questions in the spaces provided.
    a. What is the wind speed and direction in Anchorage?

    _____

    b. Is snow predicted for Anchorage? If so, which day(s) might it snow?

    _____

    c. What is the high and low temperature in Anchorage for the last day of the forecast?

    _____

5. Click the Print button on the Standard Buttons toolbar to print the map.
6. Close the Weather Page window.

Part 5: *Removing a Desktop Item on the Desktop and Turning Off the Active Desktop*

1. Right-click an open area on the desktop, point to Active Desktop, click Customize My Desktop.
2. Click the Web tab in the Display Properties dialog box.
3. Click MSNBC Weather to highlight it and then click the Delete button.
4. Click the Yes button in the Active Desktop Item dialog box.
5. Click the OK button in the Display Properties dialog box.
6. Right-click an open area on the desktop, point to Active Desktop, and then click Show Web Content.

Cases and Places

The difficulty of these case studies varies:
▌ are the least difficult; ▌▌ are more difficult; and ▌▌▌ are the most difficult.

1 ▌ A friend of yours, who owns a chain of fast food restaurants, approaches you with questions about installing the new Windows 2000 Professional operating system on several computers. Because the current operating system on each computer is not the same, your friend asks you to prepare a list of operating systems from which you can and cannot upgrade to Windows 2000 Professional. You prepare the list shown in Figure 2-102. Use Notepad to prepare the list. Use the concepts and techniques presented in this project to start Notepad and create, save, and print the document.

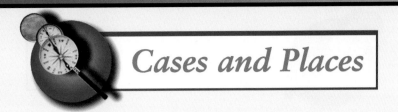

Cases and Places

Supported Upgrade Paths to Windows 2000 Professional

You can upgrade to Windows 2000 Professional from these operating systems:
    Windows 95
    Windows 98
    Windows NT 3.51 Workstation
    Windows NT 4.0 Workstation

You cannot upgrade to Windows 2000 Professional from these operating systems:
    Windows 3.x, including Windows for Workgroups
    Versions of Windows NT prior to version 3.51
    BackOffice Small Business Server
    Non-Microsoft operating systems

FIGURE 2-102

2 ▶ Your employer is concerned that some people in the company are not thoroughly researching office supplies purchases. She has prepared a list of steps she would like everyone to follow when purchasing office supplies (Figure 2-103). Your employer asks you to use WordPad to prepare a copy of this list and post it in every department. Use the concepts and techniques presented in this project to create a WordPad document on the desktop. Save and print the document. After you have printed one copy of the document, try experimenting with different WordPad features to make the list more eye-catching. If you like your changes, save and print a revised copy of the document. If WordPad is not available on your computer, use Notepad.

Requests for Office Supplies

1. Determine your department's office supplies needs
2. Identify at least two Internet sites that sell the office supplies you need
3. Obtain prices for the office supplies from their Web site
4. Submit your results to Nancy Bradford for review

FIGURE 2-103

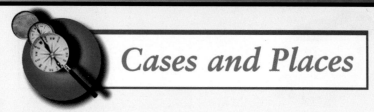

Cases and Places

3 ▶▶ Prepare a brief report on the document-centric approach versus the application-centric approach. Explain what each approach means to the computer user, summarize the advantages and disadvantages of each approach, and indicate which is the better approach for you and why. Do you think one approach will be more popular in the future? Will future operating systems emphasize one approach over the other? Support your opinions with information from computer magazines, articles on the Internet, and other resources.

4 ▶▶ Retraining employees can be an expensive task for any size business. Many Windows 2000 users believe the Windows 2000 operating system is an intuitive operating system and is easy to learn and reduces retraining costs. Using the Internet, current computer magazines, or other resources, research this topic and write a brief report summarizing your findings. Include and explain those features that you think make the Windows 2000 operating system an easy-to-use operating system.

5 ▶▶▶ Microsoft Corporation offers many ways to obtain information about its software products. The Microsoft Web site (www.microsoft.com) contains helpful information about Microsoft products. Products include operating systems (Windows 95, Windows 98, and Windows 2000), application software (Office, Word, Excel, Access, PowerPoint, NetMeeting, Encarta, and Outlook Express), and an online service (MSN). Using any two operating systems, any four application programs, and the online service just mentioned, write a brief report summarizing each product's function. Write a single paragraph about each product.

6 ▶▶▶ Choosing an operating system is an important decision for most businesses. Locate three local businesses: one that uses Windows 98, one that uses Windows NT, and one that uses Windows 2000. Interview a person at each business about their operating system. Based on your interviews, write a brief report on why each business chose that operating system, how satisfied they are with it, and under what circumstances they might consider switching to a different operating system.

7 ▶▶▶ Registering for classes can be a daunting task for incoming college freshmen. As someone who has gone through the process, prepare a guide for students who are about to register for the first time next semester. Your guide should be two or more documents, include a calendar and/or schedule of key dates and times, a description of the registration procedure, and suggestions for how students can make registration easier. Give the documents suitable names and save them in a folder on the Windows 2000 desktop. Print each document.

Microsoft **Windows 2000**

Microsoft Windows 2000

P R O J E C T

File, Document, and Folder Management and Windows 2000 Explorer

3

You will have mastered the material in this project when you can:

O B J E C T I V E S

- Display icons in various views in a window
- View the contents of a drive and folder
- Open a document and application program from a window
- Cascade and tile open windows on the desktop
- Copy, move, and delete files from open windows
- Launch Windows 2000 Explorer
- Display files and folders in Explorer
- Expand drives and folders in Explorer
- View the contents of drives and folders in Explorer
- Launch an application program from Explorer
- Close folder expansions
- Copy, move, rename, and delete files and folders in Explorer
- Close Explorer
- Display drive and folder properties
- Find files and folders using Search on the Start menu
- Use the Run command
- View computers and computer resources on a network
- Search for a computer on a network
- Map and access a network drive

Desktop Explorer

Navigating Resources and Networks

The great explorers from Portugal, Spain, Italy, France, and England ventured farther with each voyage, spanning the globe in the face of great peril. It is only through the expanse of time that the great undertakings of the seafarers and their everyday woes can be understood completely. In the fifteenth and sixteenth centuries, northern voyagers such as Jacques Cartier and John Davis endured great hardship in contrast to the mild winds Columbus experienced in the southerly passages. From the navigators' perspective, an Atlantic crossing was simple.

In rough seas, anything might happen to mariners in the North Atlantic. Gales from the west hurled giant waves against vessels; easterly gusts soaked the sailors with freezing rain; brutal northerly winds cracked masts and split sails. Many died on these northern journeys.

After Christopher Columbus's return to Spain from the famous 1492 voyage across the Atlantic, other European explorers began navigating to North America. In 1497, John Cabot explored the coasts of Labrador, Newfoundland, and New England. Juan Ponce de León discovered Florida and part of the Yucatán Peninsula in the early 1500s. Hernán Cortés invaded Mexico in 1519 and then conquered the Aztecs.

Every age has produced those who have an insatiable thirst for knowing what lies over the next hill: Sir Edmund Hillary, Junípero Serra, Louis Joliet, Amelia Earhart, Vasco Nuñez de Balboa, Sir Walter Raleigh, and Leif Ericsson. The list of familiar names seems endless. In the latter half of the twentieth century, Neil Armstrong and Buzz Aldrin led the way to the Moon, Jacques Cousteau explored the wonders beneath the sea, and Robert Ballard discovered the resting place of the Titanic.

The names of the crafts in the trek toward the stars are legendary in themselves: *Apollo, Sputnik, Explorer, Voyager, Mir,* the *Mars Pathfinder.* These and many others have spun the first fibers of a golden rope that may lift humankind to Mars and beyond in the twenty-first century.

The increasing power and versatility of modern personal computers have given people the means to embark on these and other grand individual adventures.

Yet, the progressive complexity of these systems can dissuade many from achieving the necessary skills to manage their work effectively. In this project, you will examine documents, files, and folders on your computer in a variety of ways. The application program provided with the operating system, Windows 2000 Explorer, and the My Computer window offer two major ways for you to work with files and documents. It allows you to view hardware components on the computer and computer resources on a network, as well as search for computers on a network and map and access network drives. Whether setting up on the desktop or in the most demanding Web server environment, Windows 2000 provides significant performance advantages over previous releases.

As a desktop explorer of the twenty-first century, you have the tools to navigate computer and network resources at the click of a mouse button using the best of the Windows operating systems developed to date.

Microsoft Windows 2000

File, Document, and Folder Management and Windows 2000 Explorer

P R O J E C T

3

C A S E   P E R S P E C T I V E

Your organization has installed a Windows 2000 network and has decided to connect all computers to the network. In the process, the organization will upgrade the operating system on each computer to Windows 2000 Professional. The new network administrator believes that to use Windows 2000 effectively, users must be able to control and manage windows on the Windows 2000 desktop and locate computers and computer resources on the network. An understanding of these skills will be critical for the successful implementation of Windows 2000. Everyone is excited about the change, but those who have little computer experience are apprehensive about the new network and operating system. Your boss asks you to teach a class with an emphasis on managing windows, using Windows 2000 Explorer, and locating objects on the network for employees who are not experienced Windows users. Your goal in this project is to become competent using these features of Windows 2000 so that you can teach the class.

Introduction

In Project 2, you used Windows 2000 to create documents and store them on both a floppy disk and the desktop, you created folders in which to place the documents, and shared folders on a network. Windows 2000 also allows you to examine the documents, files, and folders on your computer in a variety of ways, depending on the easiest and most accessible manner during your work on the computer. The My Computer window and Windows 2000 Explorer, which is an application program provided with Windows 2000, are the two major ways for you to work with files and documents. In addition, Windows 2000 allows you to view computers and computer resources on a network, search for computers on a network, and map and access network drives. This project will illustrate how to accomplish these tasks using the tools supplied by Windows 2000.

My Computer Window

As noted in previous projects, the My Computer icon displays on the Windows 2000 desktop. The **My Computer icon** represents a window that contains all the hardware components on the computer (i.e., disk drives, CD-ROM drives, and DVD drives) and the Control Panel folder. To open and maximize the My Computer window and view the components of the computer, complete the following steps.

The Standard Buttons toolbar shown in Figure 3-2 contains buttons you will use in this project to navigate between windows (Back and Forward), delete files (Delete), and change the appearance of the icons in a window (Views button).

To Open and Maximize the My Computer Window

1 **Double-click the My Computer icon on the desktop and then point to the Maximize button in the My Computer window.**

The My Computer window displays (Figure 3-1).

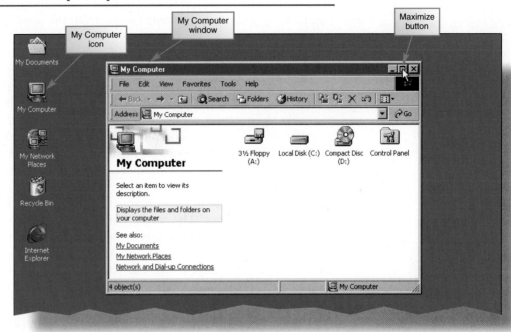

FIGURE 3-1

2 **Click the Maximize button.**

Windows 2000 maximizes the My Computer window (Figure 3-2).

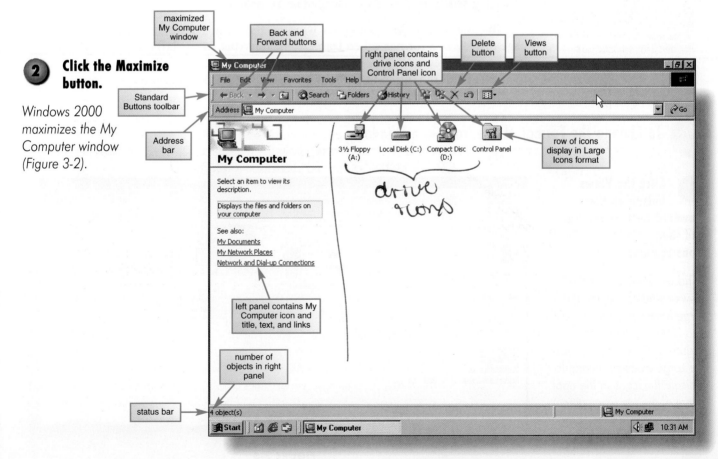

FIGURE 3-2

Other Ways

1. Right-click My Computer icon, click Open
2. Click My Computer icon, press ENTER
3. Press WINDOWS+E (WINDOWS key on Microsoft Natural keyboard)

More About

Viewing Icons

You can display icons in any window as large icons, as small icons, in a list, or with details. You also can increase the size of the icons on the desktop and decrease the size of the icons on the Start menu. For detailed instructions for making these changes, consult Windows 2000 Help.

The area below the Address bar is divided into two panels. The **left panel** contains the My Computer icon and title, text, and three links. The **right panel** contains a row of icons. The row contains three drive icons (3½ Floppy (A:), Local Disk (C:), and Compact Disc (D:)) and the Control Panel folder icon. The icons on your computer may display in a different format from the ones shown in Figure 3-2 on the previous page.

The **Local Disk (C:) icon** shown in Figure 3-2 represents the hard disk on the computer. The **hard disk** is where you can store files, documents, and folders. Storing data on a hard disk often is more convenient than storing it on a floppy disk in drive A because using a hard disk is faster, and generally more storage room is available. A computer always will have at least one hard disk drive, normally designated as drive C. On the computer represented by the My Computer window in Figure 3-2 on the previous page, the hard disk has been given a **disk label**, or title (*Local Disk*). The label is not required. Later in this project, you will see how to give a drive a name.

The **Compact Disc (D:) icon** represents a CD-ROM drive and the label for the drive is Compact Disc. The icon consists of an image of a CD-ROM disc on top of an image of a CD-ROM drive because the drive does not contain a CD-ROM. If you insert a CD-ROM in the drive, such as an **audio CD** containing music, then Windows 2000 removes the image of the CD-ROM drive from the icon, adds musical notes to the compact disc icon, and changes the label to Audio CD (D:).

The status bar at the bottom of the My Computer window indicates the right panel of the window contains four objects.

Viewing Icons in the My Computer Window

The icons in the My Computer window shown in Figure 3-2 on the previous page display in a format called **Large Icons**, referring to the large size of icons. The icons can, however, display in other formats. Complete the following steps to display the icons in all the different formats available in the My Computer window.

Steps **To Change the Format of the Icons in a Window**

1 **Click the Views button on the Standard Buttons toolbar and then point to the Small Icons command.**

Windows 2000 opens the Views menu containing the Large Icons, Small Icons, List, and Details commands (Figure 3-3). A dot precedes the Large Icons command to indicate the icons in the right panel of the My Computer window display in the Large Icons format.

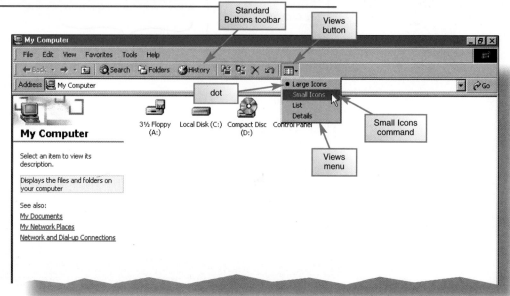

FIGURE 3-3

Click Small Icons.

The icons display in Small Icons format with the icon title adjacent to the icon (Figure 3-4).

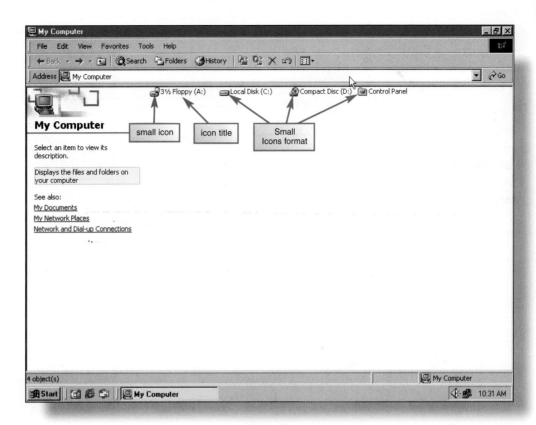

FIGURE 3-4

3 **Click the Views button on the Standard Buttons toolbar and then click List.**

The icons display in List view using the Small Icons format (Figure 3-5). The List view places the drive and folder icons in a list.

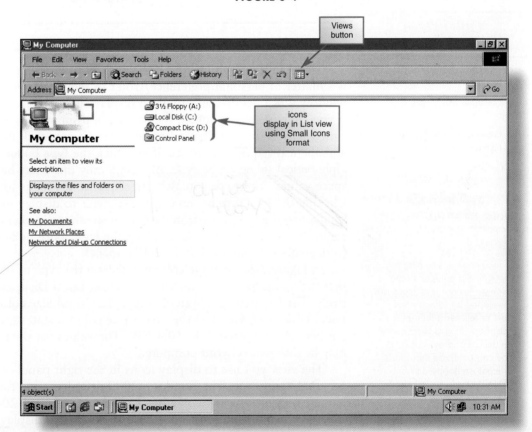

FIGURE 3-5

4 **Click the Views button on the Standard Buttons toolbar and then click Details.**

The icons display in a list in Details view using the Small Icons format (Figure 3-6). The **Details view** *provides detailed information about each drive or folder.*

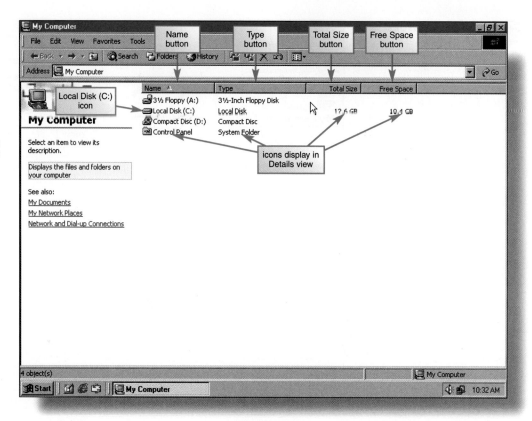

FIGURE 3-6

The manner in which you display folder contents in the My Computer window is a matter of personal preference. You can sequence the icons in the My Computer window when detailed information displays using the buttons below the Address bar. If you click the **Name button**, the items will display in alphabetical sequence by name either in ascending or descending sequence. If you click the Name button again, the alphabetical sequence reverses. If you click the **Type button**, the items will display in alphabetical sequence by type. Although only one entry has the total size and free space values displayed, you also can sequence the icons by total size and free space. Clicking the **Total Size button** causes the items to display in size sequence, from the smallest to the largest or from largest to smallest. By clicking the Total Size button again, the sequence reverses. Clicking the **Free Space button** causes items to display from smallest to largest based on free space.

In Figure 3-6, the Type column tells you the type of object for each icon. The first three objects are 3½-Inch Floppy Disk, Local Disk, and Compact Disc, respectively. The last item is a System Folder. The Total Size column states the size of the Local Disk (12.6 GB) and the Free Space column states the amount of space that is not being used on the disk (10.4 GB). The values for the total size and free space may be different on your computer.

The view you use to display icons in the right panel of a window is a matter of personal preference. The Windows 2000 default setting for viewing the icons is the Large Icons view. When you close a window, Windows 2000 remembers the format of the icons in the window and uses that format to display the icons the next time you open the window. For example, if you close the My Computer window displaying in the Details view shown in Figure 3-6 and then open the window, the icons in the window will display in Details view.

Viewing the Contents of Drives and Folders

In addition to the contents of My Computer, you also can view the contents of drives and folders. In previous projects, you have seen both windows for folders and windows for floppy drive A. In fact, the contents of any folder or drive on a computer can display in a window.

The default option for opening drive and folder windows, called the **Open each folder in the same window option**, uses the same window to display the contents of a newly opened drive or folder. Because only one window displays on the desktop at a time, this option eliminates the clutter of multiple windows on the desktop. To illustrate the Open each folder in the same window option and view the contents of drive C, complete the following step.

Steps **To View the Contents of a Drive**

1 **Double-click the Local Disk (C:) icon in the My Computer window.**

The maximized Local Disk (C:) window opens in the same window as My Computer was displayed (Figure 3-7). The left panel changes to contain the Local Disk (C:) icon and title, disk capacity, pie chart, and hyperlinks. The button in the taskbar button area is now for the Local Disk (C:) window, not for the My Computer window.

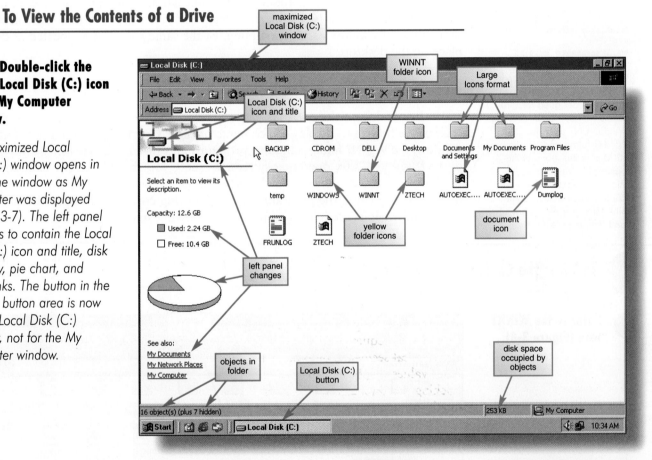

FIGURE 3-7

A yellow folder icon represents each folder in the Local Disk (C:) window. Application programs and documents are represented by icons unique to the application program or to the documents the application program opens.

The contents of the Local Disk (C:) window you display on your computer can differ from the contents shown in Figure 3-7 because each computer has its own folders, application programs, and documents. The manner in which you interact with and control the programs and documents in Windows 2000 is the same, however, regardless of the actual programs or documents.

Other **Ways**

1. Right-click Local Disk (C:), click Open
2. Click Local Disk (C:), press ENTER

Hidden Files

The status bar may or may not indicate that a folder contains a hidden file. Hidden files usually are placed on your hard disk by software vendors such as Microsoft and often are critical to the operation of the software. Rarely will you designate a file as hidden. You should almost never delete a hidden file.

The WINNT Folder

WINNT is an abbreviation for Windows NT, an older operating system designed for businesses with networks. Because Windows NT used the WINNT folder and Windows 2000 contains many of the features of Windows NT, Microsoft decided to use the WINNT folder name. Some think Microsoft should have used Windows 2000.

The status bar shown in Figure 3-7 on the previous page contains information about the folders, programs, and documents displaying in the window. Sixteen objects (folders, programs, and documents) display in the window. Seven hidden objects do not display in the window. Storing a file as a **hidden file**, meaning the name of the file does not display when you use My Computer or Windows Explorer and cannot be found using the Search command, prevents the file from being deleted accidentally.

The designation, 253 KB, on the status bar in Figure 3-7 on the previous page indicates the objects in the window consume 253 kilobytes on the hard drive. This number does not include the contents of any of the folders displayed in Figure 3-7. Recall from Figure 3-6 on page WIN 3.8 that the entire drive C, which is 12.6 gigabytes in size, has only 10.4 gigabytes free. Therefore, more storage space is used on drive C than 253 kilobytes.

If you did not maximize the My Computer window in Figure 3-7 before double-clicking the Local Disk (C:) icon, the Local Disk (C:) window will display in the same physical window as My Computer, be the same size, and be located at the same place on the desktop.

Viewing the Contents of a Folder

In Figure 3-7 on the previous page, eleven folder icons display. You can open each of the folders to display the contents of each. One folder in the Local Disk (C:) window, the **WINNT folder**, contains programs and files necessary for the operation of the Windows 2000 operating system. As such, you should exercise caution when working with the contents of the WINNT folder because changing the contents of the folder may cause the programs to stop working correctly. To open the WINNT folder and view its contents, complete the following steps.

 To View the Contents of a Folder

 Point to the WINNT icon (Figure 3-8).

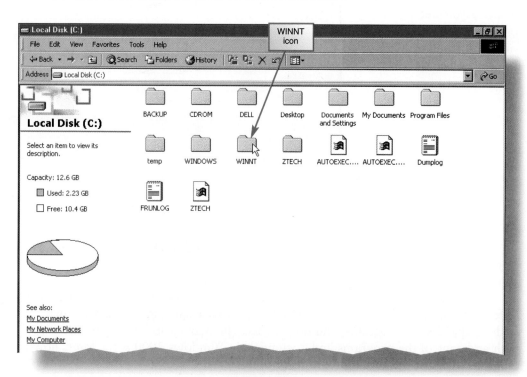

FIGURE 3-8

2 **Double-click the WINNT icon and then point to the Show Files hyperlink.**

The maximized WINNT window opens in the same window that contained the Local Disk (C:) window, and the WINNT button replaces the Local Disk (C:) button in the taskbar button area (Figure 3-9). The contents of the left panel change to reflect information about the WINNT folder. The right panel contains a graphics image and the WINNT entry displays in the Address bar.

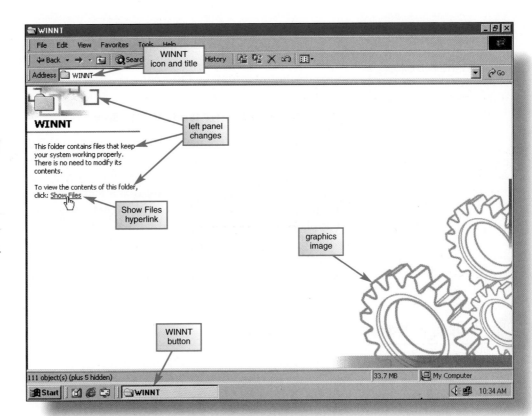

FIGURE 3-9

3 **Click Show Files.**

The files and folders in the WINNT folder display in the right panel and the message in the left panel changes (Figure 3-10). The status bar indicates the objects in the window consume 33.7 megabytes.

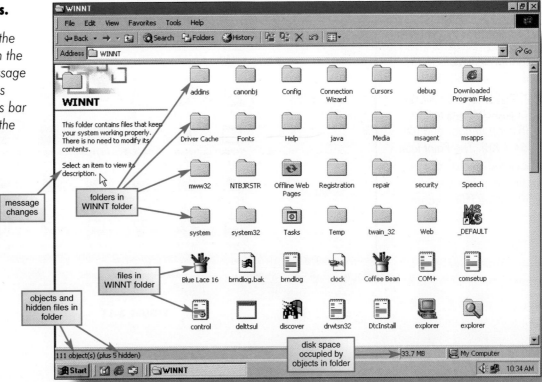

FIGURE 3-10

Other Ways

1. Right-click WINNT icon, click Open, click Show Files
2. Click WINNT icon, press ENTER, click Show Files

The majority of objects shown in Figure 3-10 on the previous page are folder icons. As you can see, folder icons always display first in the window. As with every window you will see in the steps illustrated in this book, the contents of the windows on your computer may be different.

Opening a Document from a Window

In Project 2, you created a text document on the desktop and then opened the document by double-clicking the document icon on the desktop. In addition to opening a text document on the desktop, you can open a Paint document located in a folder in a similar fashion. A Paint document contains a graphics image, called a **bitmap image**, and is created using the **Paint program** (called MSPAINT), which is an application program supplied with Windows 2000. Several Paint documents are included with Windows 2000 and stored in the WINNT folder on the hard drive. A Paint icon identifies each Paint document. To open a Paint document located in the WINNT folder, complete the following steps.

Steps To Open a Document from a Window

1 **Scroll down the right panel until the Soap Bubbles icon displays. Point to the Soap Bubbles icon. If the computer does not contain the Soap Bubbles icon, find and point to another Paint icon.**

The right panel scrolls to display the Soap Bubbles icon and a ToolTip (Figure 3-11). The ToolTip contains the file type (Bitmap Image) and file size (64.4 KB). The **Paint icon** *is associated with all document files that can be opened by the Paint program.*

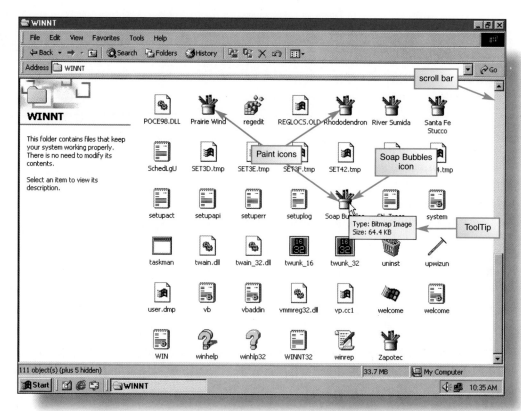

FIGURE 3-11

2 Double-click the Soap Bubbles icon. If the Soap Bubbles - Paint window is maximized, click the Restore button and then size the window to the size shown in Figure 3-12.

Windows 2000 launches the Paint program, the Paint window displays on top of the WINNT window, the recessed Soap Bubbles - Paint button displays in the taskbar button area, and the left panel of the WINNT window contains information about the Soap Bubbles file (Figure 3-12).

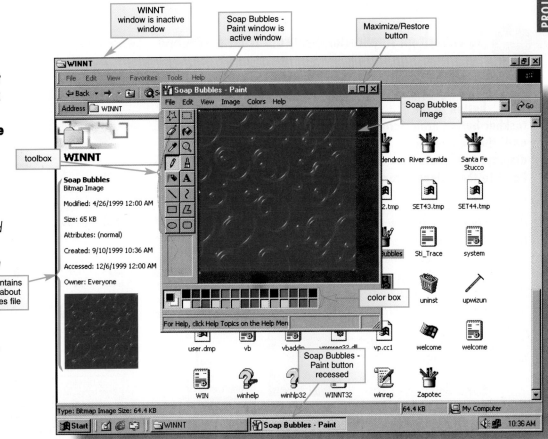

FIGURE 3-12

The Soap Bubbles - Paint window displays on top of the WINNT window. The Soap Bubbles - Paint window consists of a title bar and menu bar. On the left of the window is the **toolbox**, which contains tools used to create or alter images. At the bottom of the window is the **color box**, where you can select colors for an image. The Soap Bubbles - Paint window is the active window and the WINNT window is the inactive window. Currently, a folder window and a document window are open on the desktop.

Launching an Application Program from a Window

In addition to opening a document from a window, you also can launch an application program from a window. To launch the Notepad application program, complete the steps on the next page.

Other Ways

1. Right-click document icon, click Open
2. Click document icon, press ENTER

More *About*
2000

The Paint Program

An image with color usually has more impact than one without color. The Paint program allows you to create color images. To learn about the Paint program, click Help on the menu bar in the Paint window, click Help Topics, and use the Contents or Index sheet to read about the features of Paint.

Microsoft **Windows 2000**

 Steps To Launch an Application Program from a Window

1 Click the WINNT button in the taskbar button area. Scroll until the notepad icon displays in the window. Point to the notepad icon.

The active WINNT window displays on top of the Soap Bubbles - Paint window and its button is recessed in the taskbar button area (Figure 3-13). The notepad icon and ToolTip display in the right panel. The ToolTip contains the file type (Application) and file size (49.7 KB) of the notepad file.

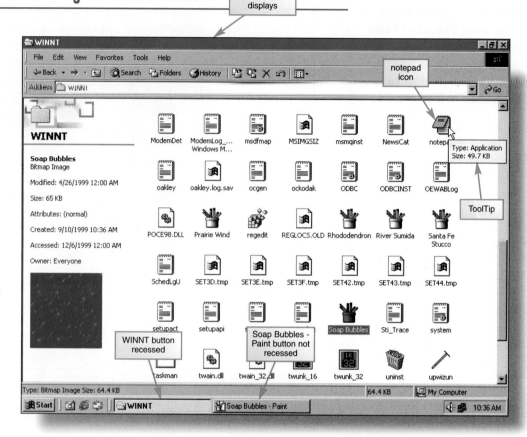

FIGURE 3-13

2 Double-click the notepad icon.

Windows 2000 launches the Notepad application program (Figure 3-14). The Untitled - Notepad button in the taskbar button area is recessed, indicating the window is active. Three windows now are open on the desktop. Although the Soap Bubbles - Paint window is not visible on the desktop, its button displays in the taskbar button area. The left panel of the WINNT window contains information about the notepad program.

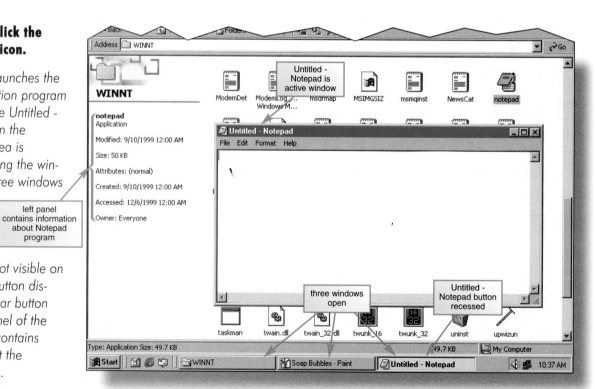

FIGURE 3-14

As shown in Figure 3-13, whenever you click a button for an open window in the taskbar button area, the window displays and becomes the active window. Windows 2000 also provides another method to switch between windows. If you press and hold down the ALT key and then press the TAB key, a box showing an icon for each open window displays on the screen, together with the name of an open window. If you continue to hold down the ALT key, each time you press the TAB key, the name of the next open window will display and the associated icon in the box will be highlighted by a colored square. When you release the TAB key, the window associated with the highlighted icon will become the active window.

In this section, you have opened the My Computer window, the Local Disk (C:) window, a folder window (WINNT), a document window (Soap Bubbles - Paint), and an application program window (Notepad).

Managing Open Windows

In Figure 3-14, three windows are open. Windows 2000 allows you to open many more windows, depending on the amount of RAM you have on the computer. As you can see in Figure 3-14, however, many open windows on the desktop can cause clutter and become difficult to use. Therefore, Windows 2000 provides some tools with which to manage open windows. You already have used one tool — maximizing a window. When you maximize a window, it occupies the entire screen and cannot be confused with other open windows.

In some cases, however, it is important that multiple windows display on the desktop. Windows 2000 allows you to arrange the windows in specific ways. The following sections describe the ways in which you can manage open windows.

Cascading Windows

One way to organize windows on the desktop is to **cascade** them, which means they display on top of each other in an organized manner. To cascade the open windows on the desktop shown in Figure 3-14, complete the following steps.

Other Ways

1. Click WINNT button in taskbar button area or press ALT+TAB until WINNT displays in box on screen, right-click notepad icon, click Open

2. Click WINNT button in taskbar button area or press ALT+TAB until WINNT displays in box on screen, click notepad icon, press ENTER

More About 2000

ALT+TAB

In Windows 3.1, an older version of Windows, the most convenient way to switch between open windows was pressing the ALT+TAB keys. Microsoft discovered that most users did not know about this method. Microsoft solved the problem by placing the buttons of open windows on the taskbar.

Steps: To Cascade Open Windows

1 **Right-click an open area on the taskbar. Point to Cascade Windows on the shortcut menu.**

A shortcut menu displays (Figure 3-15). The commands on the menu apply to the open windows on the desktop. Right-clicking the taskbar causes the Notepad window to no longer be the active window.

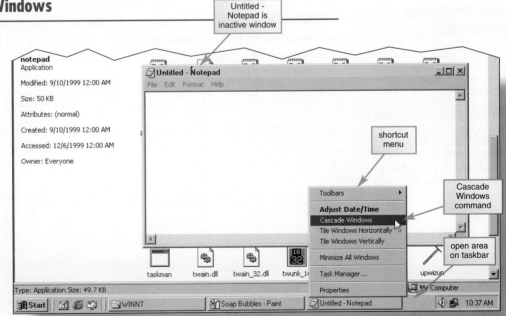

FIGURE 3-15

2 **Click Cascade Windows.**

The open windows display cascaded on the desktop (Figure 3-16). You can see the title bar of each window and the top two windows move slightly to the right. None of the windows is the active window (all light blue title bars and no recessed buttons).

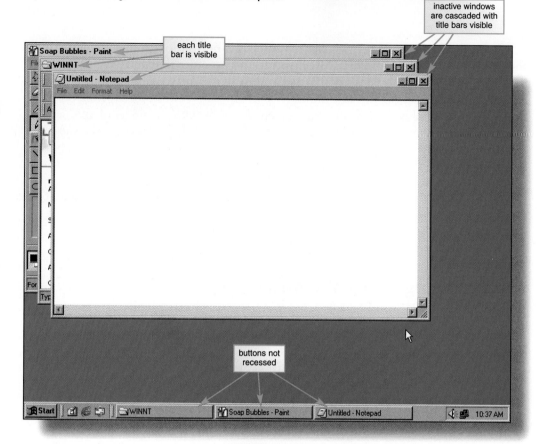

FIGURE 3-16

The Cascading Windows

When you cascade windows, you must right-click an open area of the taskbar. Sometimes it is difficult to find an open area on the taskbar. If so, try right-clicking the area to the left or right of the taskbar buttons, the area to the left of the first icon on the Quick Launch toolbar, or a blank area in the status area.

Windows 2000 cascades only windows that are open. Windows that are minimized or closed will not be cascaded on the desktop. When you cascade the open windows, the windows are resized for cascading. In Figure 3-16, all windows have been resized to be the same size.

Making a Window the Active Window

When windows are cascaded as shown in Figure 3-16, they are arranged so you see them easily, but you must make one of the windows the active window in order to work in the window. To make the Soap Bubbles - Paint window the active window, complete the following step.

To Make a Window the Active Window

Steps

1 Click the Soap Bubbles - Paint window title bar.

The Soap Bubbles - Paint window moves to the top of the desktop indicating it is active (dark blue title bar) and the Soap Bubbles - Paint button is recessed in the taskbar button area (Figure 3-17).

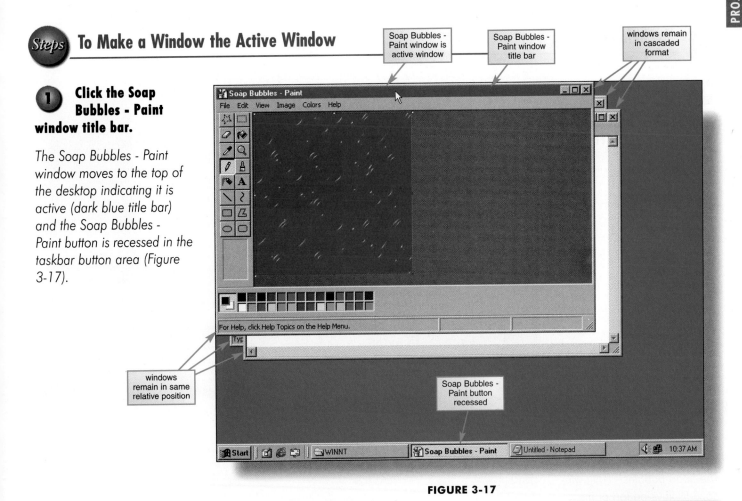

Soap Bubbles - Paint window is active window

Soap Bubbles - Paint window title bar

windows remain in cascaded format

windows remain in same relative position

Soap Bubbles - Paint button recessed

FIGURE 3-17

Other Ways

1. Click Soap Bubbles – Paint button in taskbar button area
2. Press ALT+TAB until Soap Bubbles – Paint displays in box, release ALT key
3. Click anywhere in window to make it active

The size of the Soap Bubbles - Paint window shown in Figure 3-17 does not change and the other windows remain in a cascaded format. The Soap Bubbles - Paint window title bar remains just above the WINNT title bar, which is in the same relative position as it was when it was not the active window (see Figure 3-16).

To make a window the active window, you clicked the title bar of the window. You also can click the button of the window you want to make active in the taskbar button area, or you can click anywhere in the window that you want to be active. You do not necessarily have to click the title bar of the window.

Undo Cascade

Sometimes after you have cascaded the windows, you may want to undo the cascade operation and return the windows to their size and location before cascading. To undo the previous cascading, complete the steps on the next page.

To Undo Cascading

1 **Right-click an open area on the taskbar. Point to Undo Cascade on the shortcut menu (Figure 3-18).**

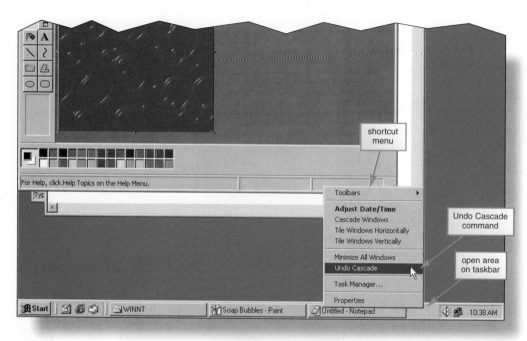

FIGURE 3-18

2 **Click Undo Cascade.**

The Soap Bubbles - Paint window displays on top of the other windows on the desktop (Figure 3-19). Although not visible, the windows on the desktop display as if they had never been cascaded. The only difference is the Soap Bubbles - Paint window remains on top instead of placing Notepad on top as it was before the windows were cascaded (see Figure 3-14 on page WIN 3.14 for the desktop prior to cascading).

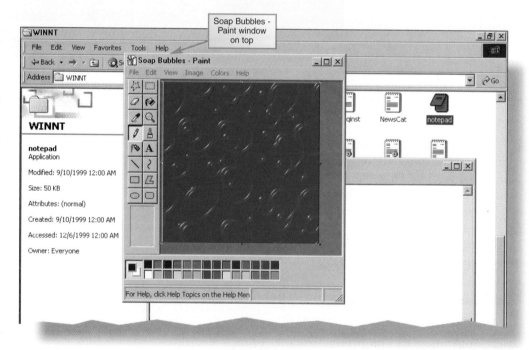

FIGURE 3-19

 Ways

1. Right-click open area on taskbar, press U
2. Press CTRL+Z

Tiling Open Windows

While cascading arranges the windows on the desktop so each of the title bars in the windows is visible, it is impossible to see the contents of each window. Windows 2000 can **tile** the open windows, which allows you to see partial contents of each window. To tile the open windows shown in Figure 3-19, complete the following steps.

To Tile Open Windows

1 **Right-click an open area on the taskbar and then point to Tile Windows Vertically on the shortcut menu (Figure 3-20).**

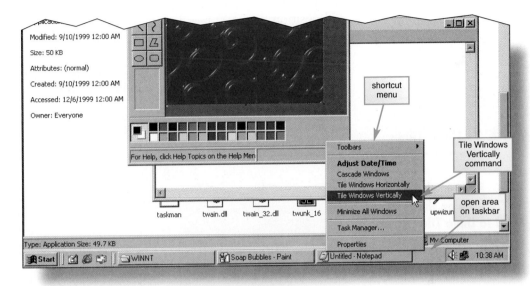

FIGURE 3-20

2 **Click Tile Windows Vertically.**

Windows 2000 arranges the three open windows in a tile format (Figure 3-21). The Paint window takes a slightly larger portion of the space in the middle because of the color box and overlaps the title bar of the Notepad window. The left and right panels in the WINNT window combine to fit in the smaller tiled window. None of the windows is active.

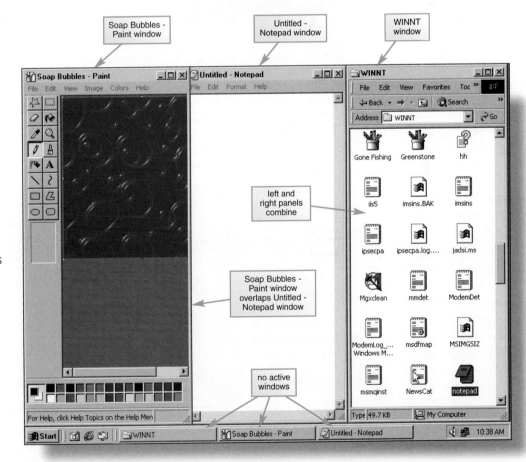

FIGURE 3-21

1. Right-click open area on taskbar, press E

While the windows shown in Figure 3-21 on the previous page are arranged so you can view all of them, it is likely that the size of each one is not useful to work in. You can undo the tiling operation if you want to return the windows to the size and position they occupied before tiling. If you want to work in a particular window, you may want to click the Maximize button in that window to maximize the window.

To undo the tiling operation and return the windows to the format shown in Figure 3-19 on page WIN 3.18, complete the following steps.

To Undo Tiling

1 **Right-click an open area on the taskbar. Point to Undo Tile (Figure 3-22).**

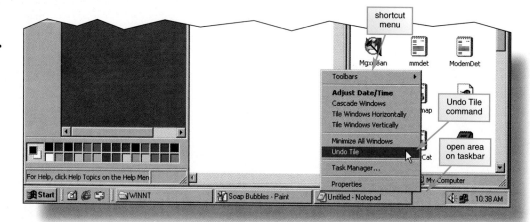

FIGURE 3-22

2 **Click Undo Tile.**

The windows no longer are tiled and display as if they had never been tiled (Figure 3-23).

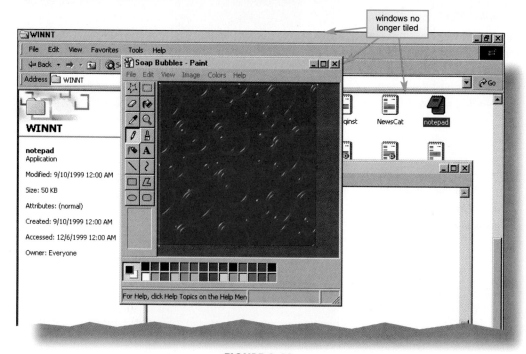

FIGURE 3-23

Other Ways

1. Right-click open area on taskbar, press U
2. Press CTRL+Z

Closing Windows

When you have finished working with windows, normally you should close the windows so the desktop remains uncluttered. To close the three open windows, complete the following steps.

TO CLOSE OPEN WINDOWS

1 Click the Close button in the Soap Bubbles - Paint window.

2 Click the Close button in the Untitled - Notepad window.

3 Click the Close button in the WINNT window.

All the windows are closed and the buttons no longer display in the taskbar button area (Figure 3-24).

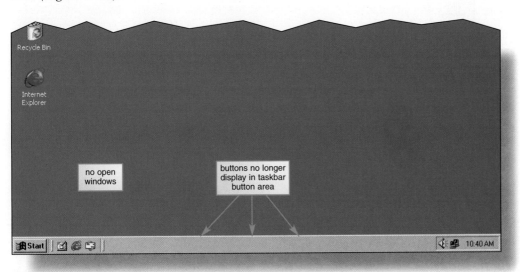

no open windows

buttons no longer display in taskbar button area

FIGURE 3-24

Copying, Moving, and Deleting Files in Windows

In Project 2, you learned how to move and copy document files on the desktop to a folder on the desktop, how to copy a folder from the desktop onto a floppy disk, and how to delete files from the floppy disk. Another method you can use to copy a file or folder is the **copy and paste method**. To copy a file from a folder to another folder or drive, open the window containing the file, right-click the file to copy, and click the Copy command on the shortcut menu to place a copy of the file in a storage area of the computer called the **Clipboard**. Then, open the folder or drive window that you want the file to be copied to, right-click an open area of the window, and click Paste on the shortcut menu to copy the file from the Clipboard to the window. The following section explains in detail how to perform these tasks.

Copying Files from a Folder to a Drive

Assume you want to copy three files, Coffee Bean, Gone Fishing, and Greenstone, from the WINNT folder onto the floppy disk in drive A. To copy from a folder, the folder window must be open on the desktop. To open the WINNT folder window and display in the window the icons for the files you want to copy, complete the steps on the next page.

TO OPEN A FOLDER WINDOW

1 Double-click the My Computer icon on the desktop.

2 Double-click the Local Disk (C:) icon in the My Computer window.

3 Double-click the WINNT icon in the Local Disk (C:) window.

4 Scroll down in the right panel of the WINNT window until the icons for the Coffee Bean, Gone Fishing, and Greenstone files are visible in the right panel. If one or more of these icons is not available in the WINNT window on your computer, display any other icons.

The Coffee Bean, Gone Fishing, and Greenstone icons are visible in the WINNT window (Figure 3-25).

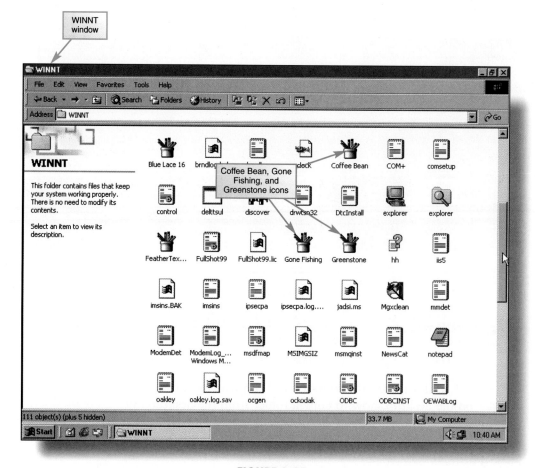

FIGURE 3-25

Once you have opened the folder window and the icons for the files to be copied are visible, you can select the files and then copy them. To copy the Coffee Bean, Gone Fishing, and Greenstone files from the WINNT folder to the floppy disk in drive A, complete the following steps.

To Copy Files from a Folder onto a Floppy Disk

1 Insert a formatted floppy disk in drive A of the computer.

2 Press and hold the CTRL key and then click the Coffee Bean, Gone Fishing, and Greenstone icons. Release the CTRL key. Right-click any highlighted icon and then point to the Copy command on the shortcut menu.

The selected Coffee Bean, Gone Fishing, and Greenstone icons and a shortcut menu display (Figure 3-26). The left panel changes to contain information about the selected icons (number of items selected, total size of files, and file names).

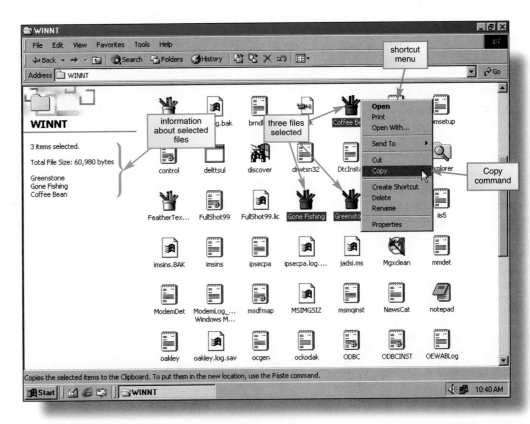

FIGURE 3-26

3 Click Copy. Point to the Back button arrow on the Standard Buttons toolbar.

Windows 2000 copies the three files to the Clipboard. The Back button and arrow become three-dimensional (Figure 3-27). The ToolTip (Back to Local Disk (C:)) indicates clicking the Back button will display the Local Disk (C:) window.

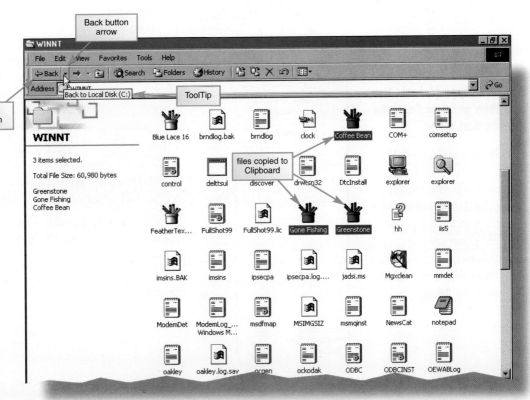

FIGURE 3-27

(4) **Click the Back button arrow and then point to My Computer.**

The Back button menu displays containing the names of the previously opened windows (Local Disk (C:) and My Computer) (Figure 3-28).

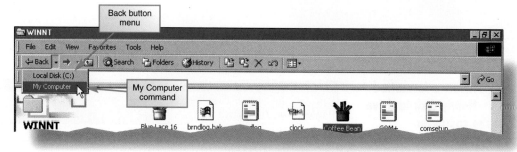

FIGURE 3-28

(5) **Click My Computer. Point to the 3½ Floppy (A:) icon in the My Computer window.**

The My Computer window displays and the My Computer icon and title display in the Address bar (Figure 3-29). The Back button appears dimmed indicating the My Computer window was the first window opened. The Forward button no longer appears dimmed.

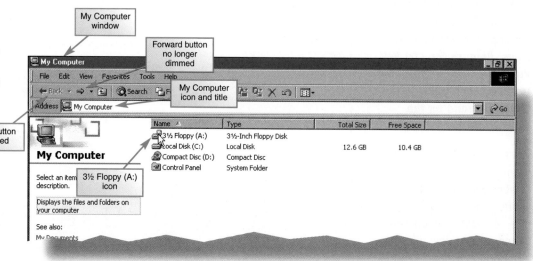

FIGURE 3-29

(6) **Double-click the 3½ Floppy (A:) icon. Right-click an open area of the 3½ Floppy (A:) window and then point to Paste on the shortcut menu.**

The 3½ Floppy (A:) window and a shortcut menu display (Figure 3-30). Information about the floppy disk in drive A displays in the left panel, the right panel contains no files or folders, and the 3½ Floppy (A:) icon and title display in the Address bar.

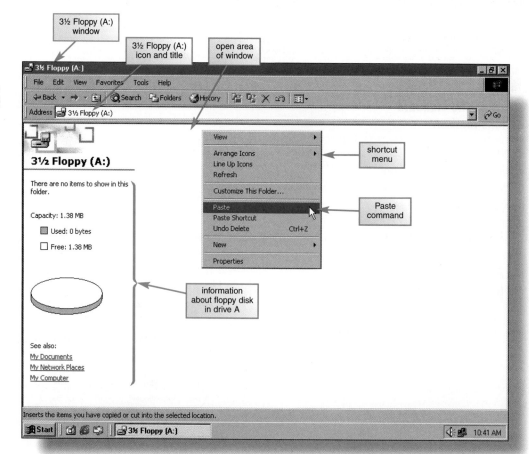

FIGURE 3-30

Click Paste.

While the files are being copied, the Copying dialog box displays indicating the files are being copied from the WINNT folder to the disk in drive A (Figure 3-31). The dialog box contains the name of the file being copied, where the file is from, and to where the file is being copied. If you wish to terminate the copying process before it is complete, you can click the Cancel button.

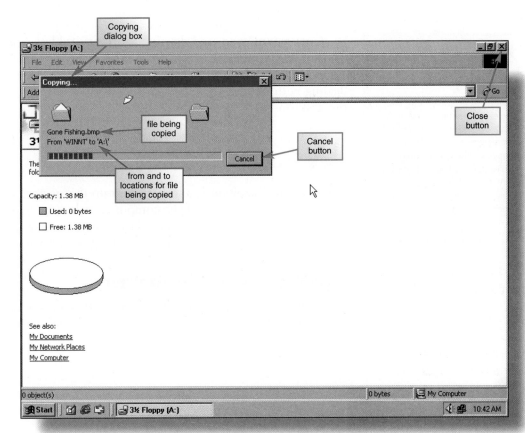

 Click the Close button to close the 3½ Floppy (A:) window.

FIGURE 3-31

After copying the three files onto the floppy disk, the files are stored on both the floppy disk and in the WINNT folder on drive C. If you want to move a file instead of copying a file, use the Cut command on the shortcut menu to move the file to the clipboard and the Paste command to copy the file from the Clipboard to the new location. When the move is complete, the files are moved onto the floppy disk and are no longer stored in the WINNT folder.

Moving and copying files is a common occurrence when working in Windows 2000. Later in this project, you will see how to accomplish these same tasks using Windows 2000 Explorer.

Deleting Files in Windows

In Project 2, you saw how to delete shortcuts, folders, and files from the desktop. You can use the same techniques when deleting shortcuts, folders, and files from an open window. To review, the methods are: (1) right-drag the object (shortcut, folder, or file icons) to the Recycle Bin, click Move Here on the shortcut menu, and then click the Yes button in the Confirm File Delete dialog box; (2) right-click the object, click Delete on the shortcut menu, and then click the Yes button in the Confirm File Delete dialog box; and (3) drag the object to the Recycle Bin and then click the Yes button in the Confirm File Delete dialog box.

Two additional methods are available when deleting shortcuts, folders, or files from an open window: (4) click the object to be deleted, click File on the menu bar, click Delete, and then click the Yes button in the Confirm File Delete dialog box; and (5) click the object to be deleted, click the Delete button on the Standard Buttons toolbar, and then click the Yes button in the Confirm File Delete dialog box.

Other Ways

1. Select icons of file(s) to be copied, on Edit menu click Copy, display window to contain file(s), on Edit menu, click Paste
2. Select icons of file(s) to be copied, on Edit menu click Copy To Folder, click plus sign to left of My Computer, click 3½ Floppy (A:) icon, click OK button
3. Select icons of file(s) to be copied, right-click an icon, click Copy, click the Address box arrow, click 3½ Floppy (A:) icon, right-click open area in 3½ Floppy (A:) window, click Paste
4. Select icons of file(s) to be copied, press CTRL+C, display window to contain file(s), press CTRL+V

More About

Deleting Files

Someone proposed that the Delete command be removed from operating systems after an employee, who thought he knew what he was doing, deleted an entire database, which cost the company millions of dollars. You should consider the Delete command a dangerous weapon.

Copying, moving, and deleting shortcuts, folders, and files is an important part of using Windows 2000. In addition, the ability to manage windows on the Windows 2000 desktop can make the difference between an organized approach to dealing with multiple windows and a disorganized, confusing mess of windows on the desktop.

Windows 2000 Explorer

Windows 2000 Explorer is another program that is part of Windows 2000. It allows you to view the contents of the computer, including drives, folders, and files, in a hierarchical format. In Explorer, you also can move, copy, and delete files in much the same manner as you can when working with open windows.

Launching Windows 2000 Explorer

As with many operations, Windows 2000 offers a variety of ways to launch Explorer. To launch Explorer using the My Computer icon, complete the following steps.

Steps **To Launch Explorer**

---

1 **Right-click the My Computer icon and then point to Explore on the shortcut menu.**

A shortcut menu displays (Figure 3-32). The Explore command will launch Windows 2000 Explorer.

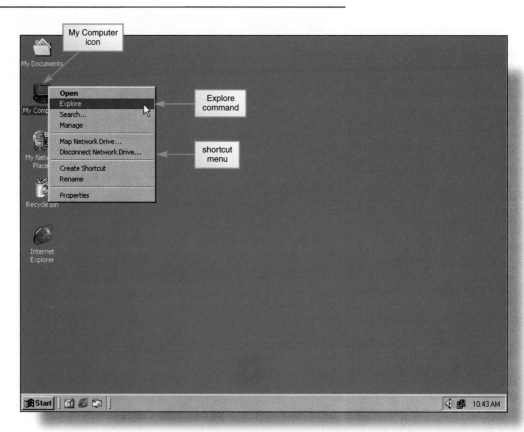

FIGURE 3-32

2 Click Explore. Maximize the My Computer window. Click the Views button on the Standard Buttons toolbar and then click Large Icons.

The maximized My Computer window displays and the icons in the right panel in the Contents pane display in Large Icons format (Figure 3-33).

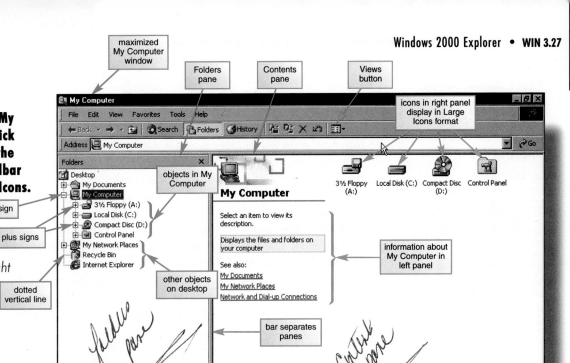

FIGURE 3-33

Exploring Window

The Exploring window (My Computer window) shown in Figure 3-33 contains a number of elements: some that should be familiar and some that are new. The title bar in the window is the same as seen in other windows, and the menu bar contains the File, Edit, View, Favorites, Tools, and Help menu names. The Standard Buttons toolbar and Address bar display respectively below the menu bar.

The main window consists of two panes – the Folders pane on the left and the Contents pane on the right. A bar separates the panes. You can drag the bar left or right to change the size of the two panes.

In the **Folders pane** (or **Folders bar**), Explorer displays, in a **hierarchical structure**, the icons and titles on the computer. The top level in the hierarchy is the Desktop. Connected by a dotted vertical line below the Desktop are the My Documents, My Computer, My Network Places, Recycle Bin, and Internet Explorer icons. These icons display on the desktop. Your computer may have other icons.

To the left of the My Computer icon and title is a minus sign in a small box. The **minus sign** indicates that the drive or folder represented by the icon next to it, in this case My Computer, contains additional folders or drives and these folders or drives display below the icon. Thus, below the My Computer icon, again connected by a dotted vertical line, are the 3½ Floppy (A:), Local Disk (C:), Compact Disc (D:), and Control Panel icons. These drives and folders are contained within the My Computer window, as seen in previous examples.

The My Computer Window

The title of the window in Figure 3-33 on the previous page is My Computer. In Windows 98, the title was Exploring - My Computer. In fact, if you click the Folders button on the Standard Buttons toolbar, the Folder bar is removed from the window, making it identical to the My Computer window in Figure 3-2 on page WIN 3.5.

A Hierarchy

One definition of hierarchy in *Merriam Webster's Collegiate Dictionary* is, a division of angels. While no one would argue angels have anything to do with Windows 2000, some preach that working with a hierarchical structure is less secular (of or relating to the worldly) and more spiritual (of or relating to supernatural phenomena) than the straightforward showing of files in windows. What do you think?

The 3½ Floppy (A:), Local Disk (C:), Compact Disc (D:), and Control Panel icons each have a small box with a plus sign next to it. The **plus sign** indicates that the drive or folder represented by the icon has more folders within it but the folders do not display in the Folders pane of the My Computer window. As you will see shortly, clicking the box with the plus sign will display the folders within the drive or folder represented by the icon. If an item contains no folders, such as Recycle Bin and Internet Explorer, no hierarchy exists to display and no small box displays next to the icons.

The **Contents pane** is identical to the My Computer window (see Figure 3-2 on page WIN 3.5). The left panel in the Contents pane contains information about My Computer. The right panel in the Contents pane contains the 3½ Floppy (A:), Local Disk (C:), Compact Disc (D:), and Control Panel icons. These icons may be different and display in a different format on your computer. A message on the left of the status bar located at the bottom of the window indicates the right panel of the Contents pane contains four objects.

Windows 2000 Explorer displays the drives and folders on the computer in hierarchical structure. This arrangement allows you to move and copy files and folders using only the Folders pane and Contents pane.

Displaying Files and Folders in Windows 2000 Explorer

You can display files and folders in the right panel of the Contents pane as large icons, small icons, a list, or with details. Currently, the files and folder display in Large Icons format. The manner in which you display folder contents in the right panel of the Contents pane is a matter of personal preference.

Displaying Drive and Folder Contents

Explorer displays both the hierarchy of items in the Folders pane of the window and the contents of drives and folders in the Contents pane of the window. To display the contents of a drive or folder, click the drive or folder icon in the Folders pane of the window. To display the contents of the Local Disk (C:) drive, complete the following step.

To Display the Contents of a Drive

① Click the Local Disk (C:) icon in the Folders pane.

The selected Local Disk (C:) title displays in the Folders pane (Figure 3-34). The left panel of the Contents pane contains information about Local Disk (C:) and the right panel contains the contents of Local Disk (C:). Notice that all the folder icons display first and then the file icons display.

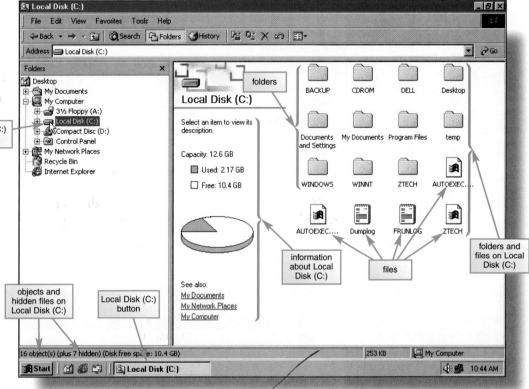

FIGURE 3-34

The status bar shown in Figure 3-34 contains information about the folders and files displaying in the right panel of the Contents pane. Sixteen objects display in the window plus seven hidden files do not display in the window.

Expanding a Selected Drive or Folder

When a plus sign in a small box displays to the left of a drive or folder icon in the Folders pane of the window, you can expand the drive or folder to show all the folders it contains. To expand drive C and view the folders, complete the steps on the next page.

Other Ways

1. Double-click Local Disk (C:) icon in Contents pane
2. Press DOWN ARROW to select Local Disk (C:) icon in Folders pane
3. Press TAB to select any drive icon in Contents pane, press LEFT ARROW or RIGHT ARROW to select Local Disk (C:) icon in Contents pane, press ENTER

Steps To Expand a Drive

1 Point to the plus sign in the small box to the left of the Local Disk (C:) icon (Figure 3-35).

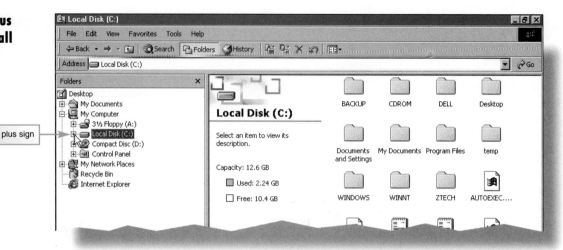

FIGURE 3-35

2 Click the plus sign.

The hierarchy below the Local Disk (C:) icon expands to display folders contained on Local Disk (C:) (Figure 3-36). A dotted vertical line connects these folders. A folder with a minus sign to the left of it contains no more folders. A folder with a plus sign contains more folders. The minus sign to the left of the Local Disk (C:) icon indicates the drive has been expanded.

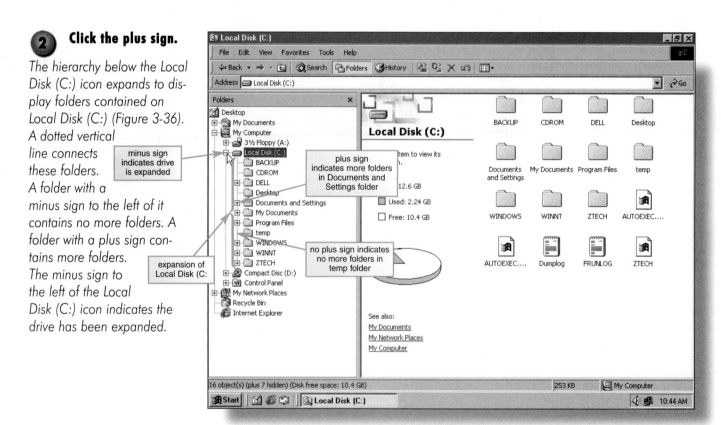

FIGURE 3-36

Other Ways

1. Double-click drive icon in Folders pane
2. Select drive to expand, press PLUS on numeric keyboard
3. Select drive to expand, press RIGHT ARROW

With a drive or folder expanded, folders contained within the expanded drive or folder display in the Folders pane of the window. You can continue this expansion to view further levels of the hierarchy. The **Documents and Settings folder** contains a separate set of folders for each computer user. To expand the Documents and Settings folder, complete the following steps.

Steps To Expand a Folder

1 Point to the plus sign in the small box to the left of the Documents and Settings icon (Figure 3-37).

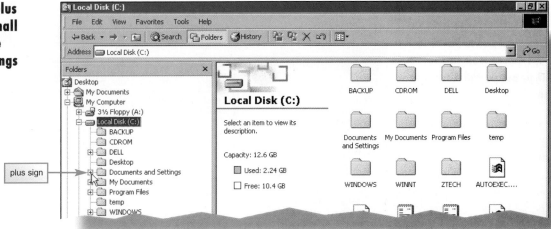

plus sign

FIGURE 3-37

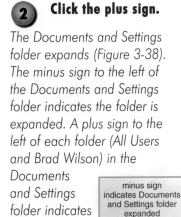

2 Click the plus sign.

The Documents and Settings folder expands (Figure 3-38). The minus sign to the left of the Documents and Settings folder indicates the folder is expanded. A plus sign to the left of each folder (All Users and Brad Wilson) in the Documents and Settings folder indicates these folders contain additional folders.

minus sign indicates Documents and Settings folder expanded

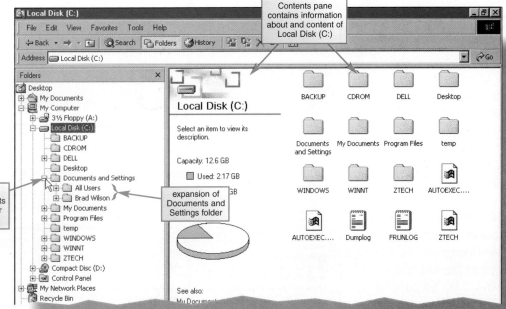

Contents pane contains information about and content of Local Disk (C:)

expansion of Documents and Settings folder

FIGURE 3-38

In Figure 3-38, the Documents and Settings folder is expanded but the Contents pane still contains information about Local Disk (C:) and the contents of the drive because the Documents and Settings folder was not opened. It was only expanded, but not opened, by clicking the plus sign next to the Documents and Settings icon.

Viewing the Contents of a Folder

Whenever folders and files display in the right panel of the Contents pane, you can display the contents of any folder or file in the right panel by double-clicking its icon. To display the contents of the All Users folder, complete the steps on the next page.

Other Ways

1. Double-click folder icon in Folders pane
2. Select folder to expand, press PLUS
3. Select folder to expand, press RIGHT ARROW

Microsoft **Windows 2000**

Steps ### To View the Contents of a Folder

1 **Click the Documents and Settings icon in the Folders pane. Point to the All Users icon in the right panel of the Contents pane.**

The Documents and Settings entry is selected in the Folders pane, information about the Documents and Settings folder displays in the left panel of the Contents pane and the contents of the Documents and Settings folder (All Users and Brad Wilson folders) display in the right panel (Figure 3-39).

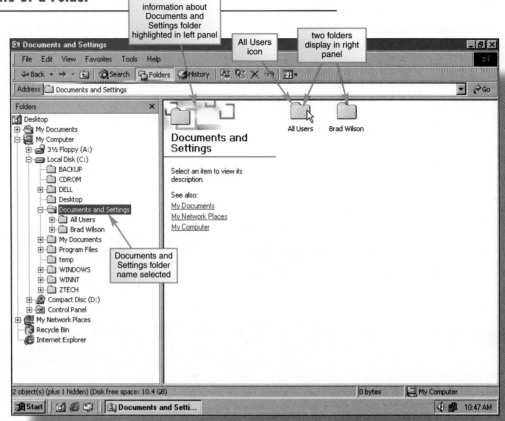

FIGURE 3-39

2 **Double-click the All Users icon.**

The Contents pane changes to contain information about the All Users folder. Information about the All Users folder displays in the left panel of the Contents pane and the contents of the All Users folder displays in the right panel (Figure 3-40). The All Users folder contains four folders (Desktop, Documents, Favorites, and Start Menu). The folders may be different on your computer.

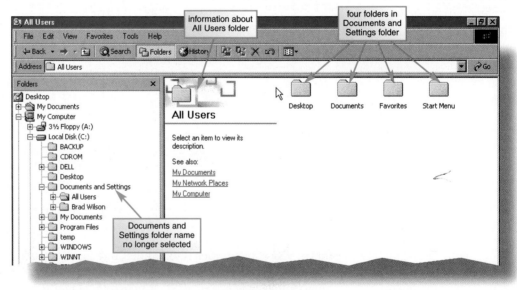

FIGURE 3-40

Other **Ways**

1. Right-click All Users icon, click Open
2. Right-click All Users icon, click Explore

In Figure 3-39, the Documents and Settings folder contains the All Users folder and a folder for each computer user. Only one computer user folder, the folder for Brad Wilson, displays in addition to the All Users folder. The **All Users folder** contains the default settings assigned to each new computer user. The **Brad Wilson folder** contains personalized settings for the user, Brad Wilson. The settings in the Brad Wilson folder control which icons display on the user's desktop, which folders and documents are contained in the user's My Documents folder, which favorite Web pages have been saved by the user, and which entries display on the user's Start Menu. The folders in the Documents and Settings folder may be different on your computer.

Launching an Application Program from Explorer

You can launch an application program from the right panel of the Contents pane using the same techniques you used for launching an application program from an open window earlier in this project (see Figures 3-13 and 3-14 on page WIN 3.14). To launch the Internet Explorer program stored in the Program Files folder, complete the following steps.

More About 2000

Launching Programs in Explorer

Usually, people find starting application programs from the Start menu or from a window easier and more intuitive than starting programs from Explorer. In most cases, you will not be launching programs from Explorer.

 To Launch an Application Program from Explorer

1 **Click the plus sign to the left of the Program Files icon in the Folders pane. Click the Internet Explorer icon in the Folders pane. Point to the IEXPLORE (Internet Explorer) icon in the right panel of the Contents pane.**

The Program Files folder is expanded, information about the Internet Explorer folder and the contents of the Internet Explorer folder display in the Contents pane (Figure 3-41).

FIGURE 3-41

2 Double-click the IEXPLORE shortcut icon.

Windows 2000 launches the Internet Explorer program. The Welcome to MSN.com - Microsoft Internet Explorer window, containing the MSN page, displays (Figure 3-42). Because Web pages are modified frequently, the Web page that displays on your desktop may be different from the Web page shown in Figure 3-42. The URL for the Web page displays in the Address bar.

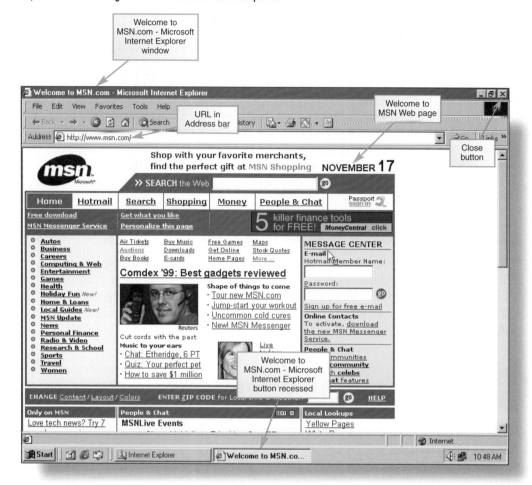

FIGURE 3-42

You can use the Internet Explorer program for any purpose you want, just as if you had launched it from the desktop or Quick Launch toolbar. When you are finished with the Internet Explorer program, you should quit the program. To quit the Internet Explorer program, complete the following step.

TO QUIT AN APPLICATION PROGRAM

1 Click the Close button on the Welcome to MSN.com - Microsoft Internet Explorer title bar.

Closing Folder Expansions

Sometimes, after you have completed work with expanded folders, you will want to close the expansions while still leaving the Explorer window open. To close the open folders shown in Figure 3-41 on the previous page, complete the following steps.

To Close Expanded Folders

1 **Click the minus sign to the left of the Program Files icon.**

The expansion of the Program Files folder closes and the minus sign changes to a plus sign (Figure 3-43). Information about the Program Files folder displays in the left panel and a graphics image displays in the right panel

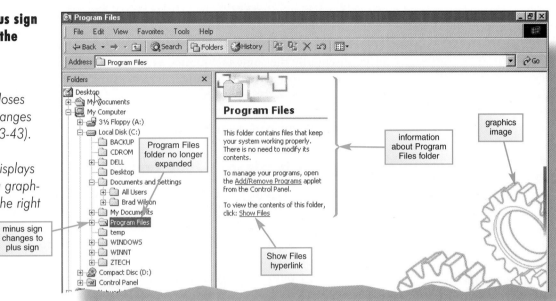

FIGURE 3-43

2 **Click the minus sign to the left of the Documents and Settings icon.**

The expansion of the Documents and Settings folder closes and the minus sign to the left of the Documents and Settings icon changes to a plus sign (Figure 3-44). The Contents pane does not change.

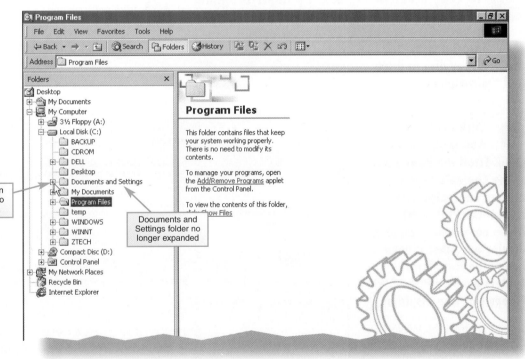

FIGURE 3-44

Moving through the Folders and Contents panes is an important skill because you will find that you use Explorer to perform a significant amount of file maintenance on the computer.

Other **Ways**

1. Click expanded folder icon, press MINUS SIGN
2. Click expanded folder icon, press LEFT ARROW
3. Double-click folder icon

Copying, Moving, Renaming, and Deleting Files and Folders in Windows 2000 Explorer

You can copy, move, rename, and delete files and folders in Windows 2000 Explorer using essentially the same techniques as when working in folder windows. Whether you perform these activities in folder windows, in Explorer, or in a combination of the two is a personal preference. It is important for you to understand the techniques used in both cases so you can make an informed decision about how you want to perform file maintenance when using Windows 2000.

Copying Files in Windows 2000 Explorer

In previous examples of copying files, you used the copy and paste method to copy a document file from a folder to a drive. Although you could use the copy and paste method to copy files in Windows 2000 Explorer, another method of copying a file is to right-drag a file (or folder) icon from the Contents pane to a folder or drive icon in the Folders pane. To copy the Prairie Wind bitmap image file from the WINNT folder onto a floppy disk in drive A of the computer, complete the following steps.

 To Copy a File in Explorer by Right-Dragging

1 Insert a formatted floppy disk in drive A of the computer.

2 Click the WINNT icon in the Folders pane. Scroll the right panel of the Contents pane to display the Prairie Wind icon. If the Prairie Wind file is not on the computer, display any other bitmap image file icon. Scroll the Folders pane until the 3½ Floppy (A:) icon displays.

The contents of the WINNT folder, including the Prairie Wind icon, display in the right panel, and the 3½ Floppy (A:) icon displays in the Folders pane (Figure 3-45).

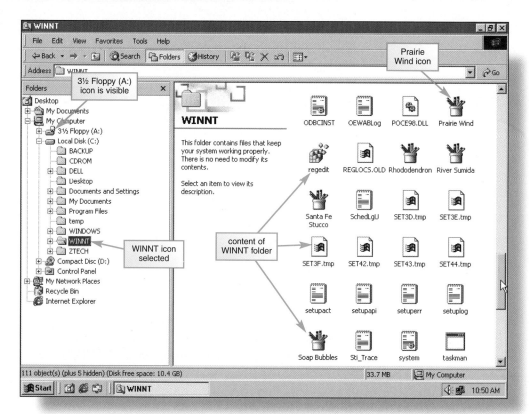

FIGURE 3-45

3 **Right-drag the Prairie Wind icon on top of the 3½ Floppy (A:) icon. Point to Copy Here on the shortcut menu.**

The dimmed image of the Prairie Wind icon displays on top of the 3½ Floppy (A:) icon, a shortcut menu displays, and information about the Prairie Wind file and a graphic image of the file display in the left panel of the Contents pane (Figure 3-46).

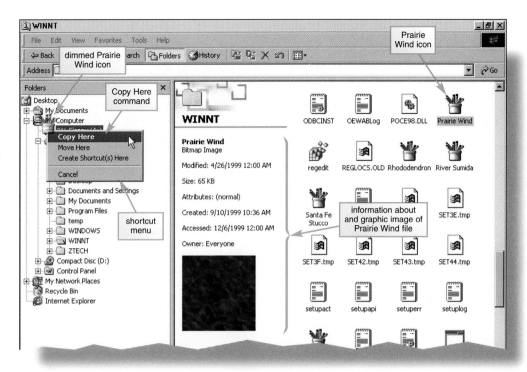

FIGURE 3-46

4 **Click Copy Here.**

The Copying dialog box displays while the file is being copied (Figure 3-47). The file being copied (Prairie Wind.bmp) and the from (WINNT) and to (A:\) locations are identified in the dialog box. After the file is copied, it is stored on the floppy disk in drive A.

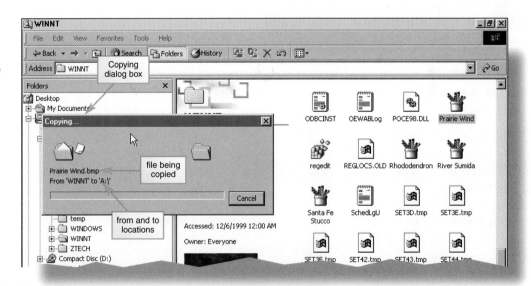

FIGURE 3-47

You can move files using the same techniques just discussed except that you click **Move Here** instead of Copy Here on the shortcut menu (see Figure 3-46). The difference between a move and a copy, as mentioned previously, is that when you move a file, it is placed on the destination drive or in the destination folder and is permanently removed from its current location. When a file is copied, it is placed on the destination drive or in the destination folder as well as remaining stored in its current location.

Other Ways

1. Right-click file to copy, click Copy, right-click 3½ Floppy (A:) icon, click Paste
2. Drag file to copy on top of 3½ Floppy (A:) icon
3. Click file to copy, on Edit menu click Copy, click 3½ Floppy (A:) icon, on Edit menu click Paste
4. Select file to copy, press CTRL+C, select 3½ Floppy (A:) icon, press CTRL+V

In general, you should right-drag or use the copy and paste method to copy or move a file instead of dragging a file. If you drag a file from one folder to another on the same drive, Windows 2000 moves the file. If you drag a file from one folder to another folder on a different drive, Windows 2000 copies the file. Because of the different ways this is handled, it is strongly suggested you right-drag or use copy and paste when moving or copying files.

Displaying the Contents of a Floppy Disk

After copying a file, you might want to examine the folder or drive where the file was copied to ensure it was copied properly. To see the contents of the floppy disk in drive A, complete the following step.

 To Display the Contents of a Floppy Disk

1 **Click the 3½ Floppy (A:) icon in the Folders pane.**

The contents of 3½ Floppy (A:) display in the right panel of the Contents pane (Figure 3-48). The Prairie Wind file is stored on the floppy disk. If you have additional files and/or folders on the floppy disk you are using, their icons and titles also display.

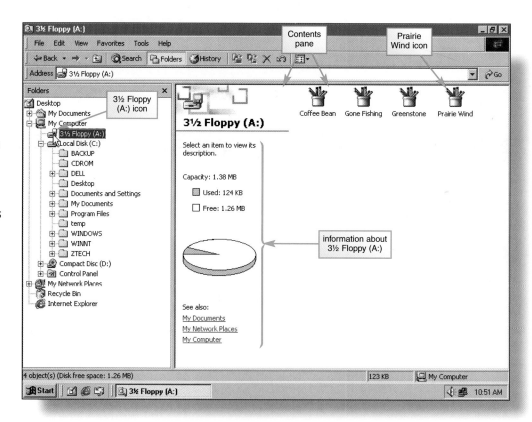

FIGURE 3-48

Renaming Files and Folders

In some circumstances, you may want to **rename** a file or a folder. This could occur when you want to distinguish a file in one folder or drive from a copy, or if you decide you need a better name to identify a file. To change the name of the Prairie Wind file on the floppy disk to Blue Prairie Wind, complete the following steps.

Steps To Rename a File

1 **Right-click the Prairie Wind icon in the right panel of the Contents pane and then point to Rename on the shortcut menu.**

The selected Prairie Wind icon and a shortcut menu display (Figure 3-49).

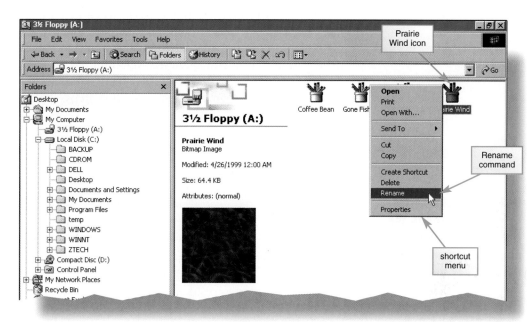

FIGURE 3-49

2 **Click Rename. Type** Blue Prairie Wind **and then press the ENTER key.**

The file is renamed Blue Prairie Wind (Figure 3-50). Note that the file in the 3½ Floppy (A:) is renamed, but the original file in the WINNT folder in drive C is not renamed.

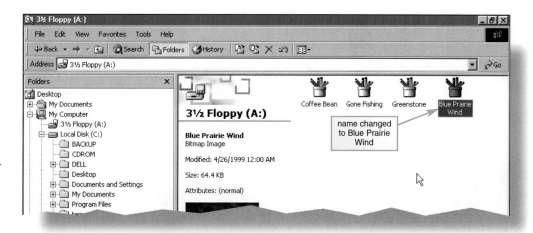

FIGURE 3-50

Renaming files in the manner shown above also can be achieved in other windows. For example, if you open the My Computer window and then open the 3½ Floppy (A:) window, you can rename any file stored on the floppy disk using the technique just shown.

You also can rename files on a hard disk using the techniques shown, but you should use caution when doing so. If you inadvertently rename a file that is associated with certain programs, the programs may not be able to find the file and, therefore, may not execute properly.

If you change a file name for which a shortcut exists on a menu, in a folder, or on the desktop, Windows 2000 will update the shortcut link so the shortcut points to the renamed file. The name of the shortcut, however, does not change to reflect the name change of the linked file.

Other Ways

1. Right-click icon, press M, type name, press ENTER
2. Click icon, press F2, type name, press ENTER
3. Click icon, on File menu click Rename, type name, press ENTER
4. Select icon, press ALT+F, press M, type name, press ENTER

Deleting Files in Windows 2000 Explorer

A final function that you may want to use in Windows 2000 Explorer is to delete a file. Exercise extreme caution when deleting a file or files. When you delete a file from a floppy disk, the file is gone permanently once you delete it. If you delete a file from a hard disk, the deleted file is stored in the Recycle Bin where you can recover it until you empty the Recycle Bin.

Assume you have decided to delete all four files from the floppy disk in drive A. To delete the files, complete the following steps.

 To Delete Files on a Floppy Disk

1 **Click the Coffee Bean icon in the right panel of the Contents pane. Press and hold down the SHIFT key and then click the Blue Prairie Wind icon. Point to the Delete button on the Standard Buttons toolbar.**

The four icons are selected (Figure 3-51). Holding the SHIFT key and then pointing to a second icon selects all the icons between the two you have clicked.

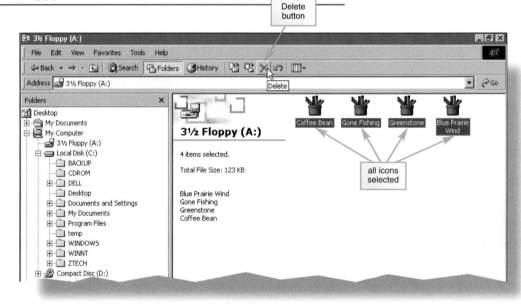

FIGURE 3-51

2 **Click the Delete button. Point to the Yes button in the Confirm Multiple File Delete dialog box.**

The Confirm Multiple File Delete dialog box displays (Figure 3-52). The dialog box asks if you are sure you want to delete the four items.

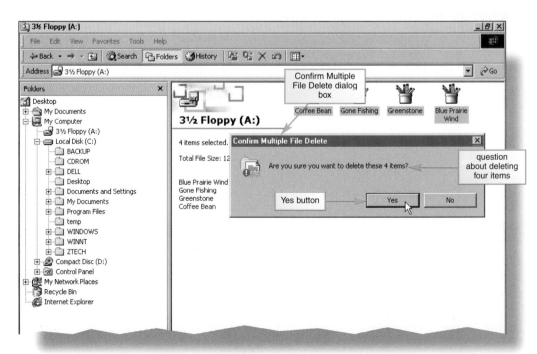

FIGURE 3-52

Click the Yes button.

A Deleting dialog box displays while the four files are being deleted (Figure 3-53). The Deleting dialog box indicates the file being deleted (Coffee Bean.bmp) and where the file is being deleted from (A:\). If you wish to terminate the deleting process before it is complete, you can click the Cancel button.

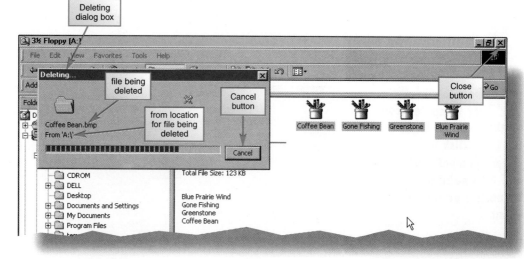

FIGURE 3-51

You can use the same methods just specified to delete folders on a floppy disk or a hard disk. Again, you should use extreme caution when deleting files and folders to ensure you do not delete something you may not be able to recover.

Closing Windows 2000 Explorer

When you are finished with file maintenance, normally you will close the Exploring window. To close the Exploring window, complete the step below.

TO CLOSE THE EXPLORING WINDOW

 Click the Close button on the 3½ Floppy (A:) window title bar.

Windows 2000 closes the Exploring window.

Summary of Windows 2000 Explorer

Windows 2000 Explorer gives you the capability of performing file maintenance in a single window without displaying additional windows or worrying about windows management on the desktop. In addition, it provides a hierarchical view of all drives, folders, and files on the computer. Whether you choose to use Explorer or the My Computer window to perform file maintenance is a personal choice. You may find that some tasks are easier using Explorer and others are easier using the My Computer window.

Properties of Objects

Every object in Windows 2000 has **properties**, which describe the object. In some cases, you can change the properties of an object. Each drive, folder, file, and program in Windows 2000 is an object. In the following section, the properties of objects will be shown.

Drive Properties

Each drive on the computer has properties. To display the properties for the hard disk, complete the steps on the next page.

Other **Ways**

1. Right-drag icon to Recycle Bin, click Move Here, click Yes button
2. Drag icon to Recycle Bin, click Yes button
3. Right-click icon, click Delete, click Yes button
4. Click icon, on File menu click Delete, click Yes button
5. Select icon, press ALT+F, press D, press Y

 *About*

Deleting Files

This is your last warning! Be EXTREMELY careful when deleting files. Hours of work can be lost with one click of a button. If you are going to delete files or folders from your hard disk, make a backup of those files to ensure that if you inadvertently delete something you need, you will be able to recover.

To Display Hard Disk Properties

1 **Double-click the My Computer icon on the desktop. Right-click the Local Disk (C:) icon in the My Computer window and then point to Properties on the shortcut menu.**

Windows 2000 opens the My Computer window and displays a shortcut menu (Figure 3-54).

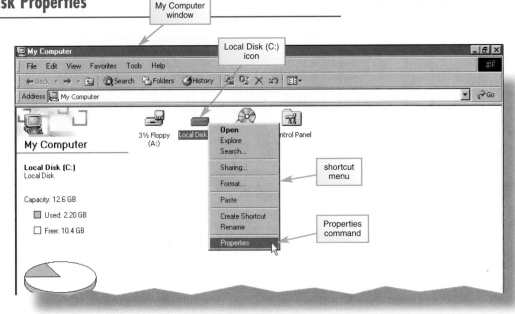

FIGURE 3-54

2 **Click Properties and then point to the Cancel button.**

The Local Disk (C:) Properties dialog box displays (Figure 3-55). The Label text box allows you to type a new hard drive label, and the drive type (Local Disk) and File system (FAT32) display. The used space on the drive (dark blue box) and free space (magenta box) display. The total capacity of the disk is specified along with a pie chart.

3 **Click the Cancel button.**

The Local Disk (C:) Properties dialog box closes.

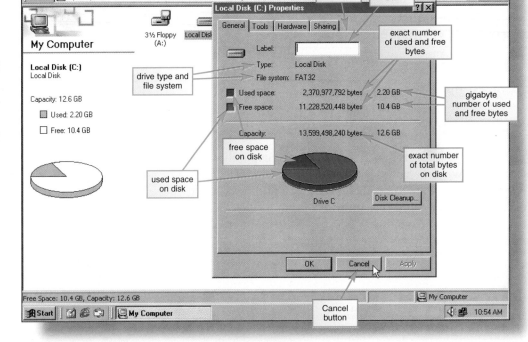

FIGURE 3-55

Other Ways

1. Click drive icon, on File menu click Properties, click Cancel button
2. Select drive icon, press ALT+ENTER, press ESC

The **Tools sheet** in the Local Disk (C:) Properties dialog box shown in Figure 3-55, accessible by clicking the Tools tab, allows you to check errors, back up, or defragment the hard drive. The **Hardware sheet**, accessible by clicking the Hardware tab, allows you to view a list of all disk drives, troubleshoot disk drives that are not working properly, and display the properties of each disk drive. The **Sharing sheet**, accessible by clicking the Sharing tab, allows you to share the contents of a hard disk with other users on the network.

In Figure 3-55, you might think the number of bytes specified for used space and for free space do not correspond with the gigabyte specification shown, but in fact they do. A **gigabyte of RAM** or disk space is not exactly one billion characters, or bytes. Because addresses are calculated on a computer using the binary number system, a gigabyte of RAM or disk space actually is 1,073,741,824 bytes, which is equal to 2^{30}. In Figure 3-55, if you multiply 2.20 times 1,073,741,824, the answer is just less than 2,370,977,792, which is shown as the total number of bytes of used space on the hard drive. Therefore, 2.20 GB is the closest estimate, expressed as gigabytes, for the total amount of unused space on the hard drive.

Properties of a Folder

Folders also have properties. To display the properties of the WINNT folder, complete the following steps.

Steps: To Display Folder Properties

1 **Double-click the Local Disk (C:) icon in the My Computer window. Right-click the WINNT icon and then point to Properties on the shortcut menu.**

Windows 2000 opens the Local Disk (C:) window and displays a shortcut menu (Figure 3-56).

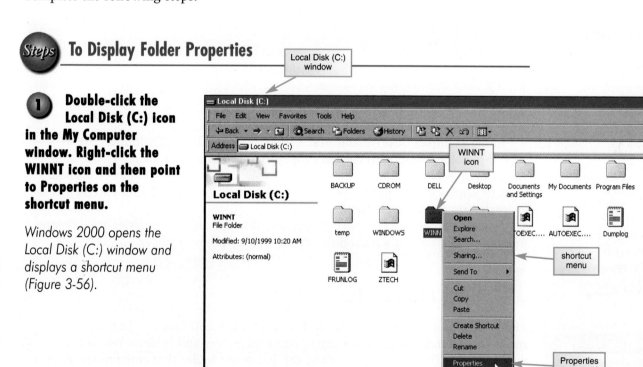

FIGURE 3-56

2 Click Properties. Point to the Cancel button.

The WINNT Properties dialog box displays (Figure 3-57). The WINNT folder name displays in a text box. The type, File Folder, is specified. The location of the folder (C:\) is shown. The size in megabytes and actual bytes displays. The WINNT folder contains 6,260 files and 128 folders. The date the file was created and the file attributes display. These values may be different on your computer.

3 Click the Cancel button. Close the Local Disk (C:) window.

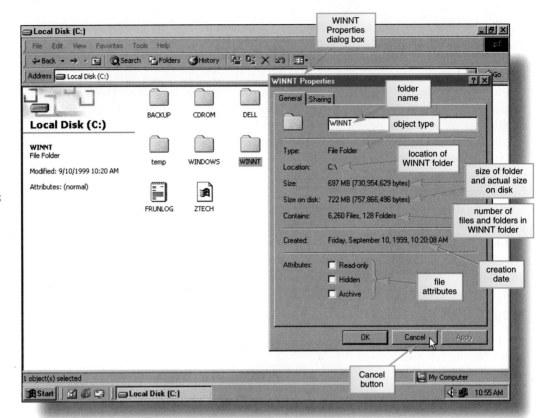

FIGURE 3-57

In the examples of drive and folder properties, you opened windows, right-clicked the object, and then clicked Properties on the shortcut menu. These same steps can be performed in Windows 2000 Explorer. If you have Explorer open and want to display the properties of drive C, right-click the drive C icon and then click Properties on the shortcut menu.

Files and programs also have properties, although these properties are different from the properties for a hard disk and the properties for a folder.

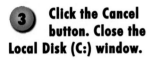

Finding Files or Folders

The WINNT folder shown in Figure 3-57 contains 6,260 files in 128 folders. The entire computer, however, will contain many more files and folders. You will know the location of files you use often and can locate the folder that contains them. In some cases, you might know you have a certain file on the computer but you have no idea in what folder it is located. To search every folder manually on the computer to find the file would be time consuming and almost impossible. Fortunately, Windows 2000 provides a **Search command** that allows you to find the location of a file if you know its name or even if you know some text that is included in the file.

Finding a File by Name

If you know the name or partial name of a file, you can use Search to locate the file. For example, you know a wallpaper bitmap image file named coffee bean exists somewhere on the computer. You want to open the file to see what the image looks like. To find the file, complete the following steps.

 To Find a File by Name

1 **Click the Start button on the taskbar. Point to Search on the Start menu. Point to For Files or Folders on the Search submenu.**

The Start menu and Search submenu display (Figure 3-58).

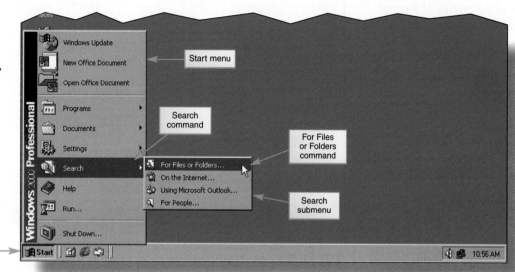

FIGURE 3-58

2 **Click For Files or Folders. Maximize the Search Results window. Type** coffee bean **in the Search for files or folders named text box and then point to the Search Now button.**

*The Search Results window, containing the **Search pane** (or **Search bar**), displays (Figure 3-59). The words you typed display in the text box. The Look in box specifies all of Local Disk (C:) will be searched. The Search Results pane contains six buttons and a message.*

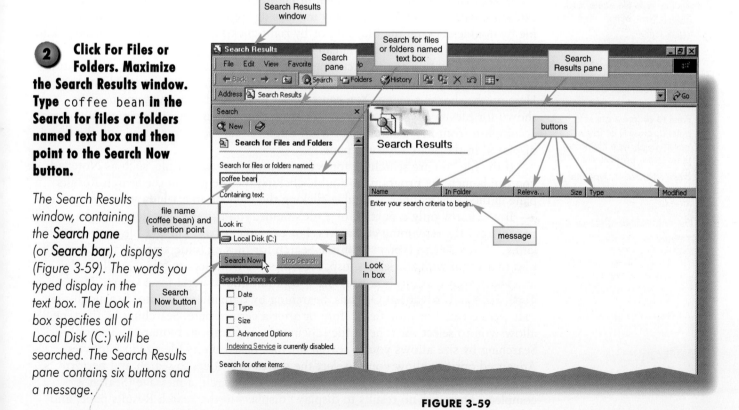

FIGURE 3-59

3 **Click the Search Now button.**

Windows 2000 searches drive C for files with the term, coffee, or the term, bean, in their names. The three files found display in the Search Results pane (Figure 3-60). The Search Results pane displays the names of the files, folders where the files are located, sizes of the files, types of files, and the dates and times the files were last modified.

4 **Click the Close button on the Search Results window title bar.**

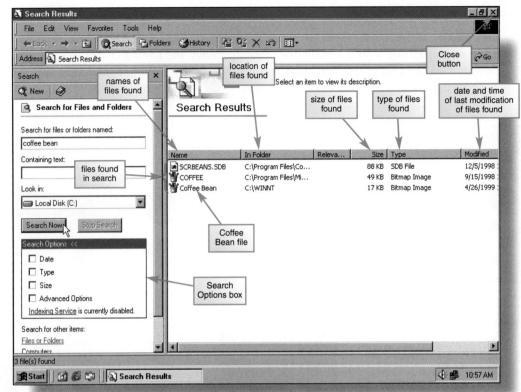

FIGURE 3-60

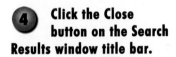

Other Ways

1. Right-click Start button, click Search, type file name, click Search Now button, click Close button

2. Right-click drive icon in Folders pane, click Search, type file name, click Search Now button, click Close button

3. Press F3 or (press CTRL+ESC, press C, press F) or (press WINDOWS+F), type file name, press ENTER, press ALT+F4

4. Press WINDOWS+F, type file name, press ENTER, press ALT+F4

In the Search Results pane shown in Figure 3-60, after the search is complete you can work with the files found in any manner desired. For example, you can open the file by double-clicking the file icon, or by right-clicking the file icon and then clicking Open on the shortcut menu. You can print the file by right-clicking the file icon and then clicking Print on the shortcut menu. You can create a shortcut on the desktop by right-dragging the file icon to the desktop and then clicking Create Shortcut(s) Here on the shortcut menu. You can copy or move the file in the same manner shown for files in My Computer or in Explorer. In summary, any operation you can accomplish from My Computer or from Explorer can be accomplished on the files displayed in the Search Results pane.

If the file you are searching for is an executable program file, such as Notepad, you can launch the program by double-clicking the file icon in the Search Results pane in the same manner as double-clicking the file icon in a window on the desktop.

If you know only a portion of a file's name, you can use an asterisk in the name to represent the remaining characters. For example, if you know a file starts with the letters MSP, you can type msp* in the Search for files or folders named text box. All files that begin with the letters msp, regardless of what letters follow, will display.

The Search Options box provides four additional criteria for a search: Date, Type, Size, and Advanced Options. Searching by date allows you to display all files that were created or modified before or after a certain date. Searching by file type allows you to select the type of file (document, application, bitmap, and so on). Searching by size allows you to search for files based on its file size in kilobytes. Advanced options allow you to select the drives or folders to search and perform case-sensitive searches. If no files are found in the search, a message (Search is complete. There are no results to display.) displays in the Search Results pane, and

another message (0 file(s) found) displays on the status bar. In this case, you may want to check the file name you entered or examine a different drive to continue the search.

The Search capability of Windows 2000 can save time when you need to locate a file on the computer.

Run Command

You have seen how to launch programs by double-clicking the program icons in a window or on the desktop, and by clicking the shortcut icons on the Programs submenu or other submenus. Windows 2000 also offers the **Run command**, located on the Start menu, to launch programs. The Run command is useful when you want to launch an application program quickly. To use the Run command to launch the Paint program (the actual name of the program is MSPAINT), complete the following steps.

 To Launch a Program Using the Run Command

1 **Click the Start button on the taskbar and then point to Run.**

Windows 2000 displays the Start menu (Figure 3-61).

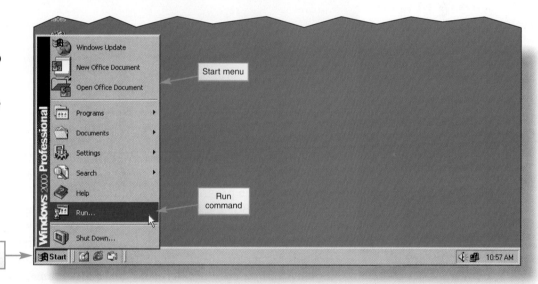

FIGURE 3-61

2 **Click Run. Type** mspaint **in the Open box in the Run dialog box and then point to the OK button.**

The Run dialog box displays (Figure 3-62). The entry, mspaint, displays in the Open box.

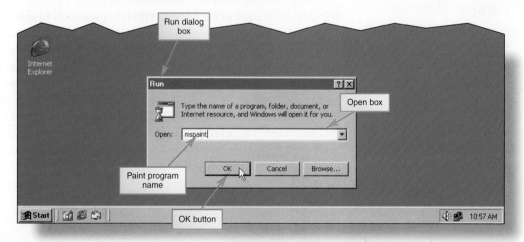

FIGURE 3-62

3 **Click the OK button.**

Windows 2000 launches the MSPAINT program (Figure 3-63). You can now use the Paint program.

4 **Click the Close button on the untitled - Paint window title bar.**

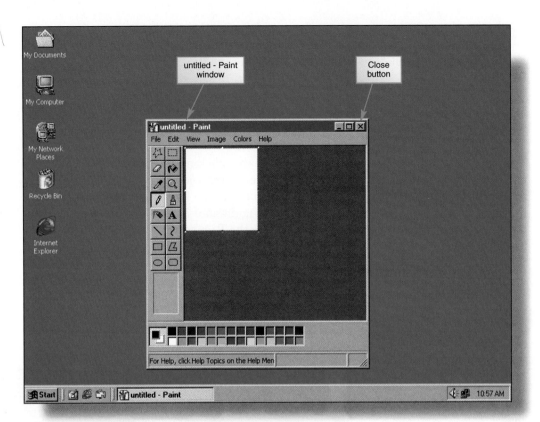

FIGURE 3-63

Paths

Paths are left over from MS-DOS and the manner in which you had to identify where a file was stored for access. To access a file on your hard drive, you merely need to open a window or, in Explorer, open the folder to access the file. However, you will have to understand and use paths to locate computers on a network.

You can use the Run command to open folders and files as well as executable programs. If the program, file, or folder is located in the WINNT folder, you simply type the name of the program, file, or folder. If the file is located elsewhere, you must type the path for the file. A **path** is the means of navigation to a specific location on a computer or network. To specify a path, you must type the drive letter, followed by a colon (:) and a backslash (\). Then type the name of the folders and subfolders that contain the file. A backslash should precede each folder name. After all the folder names have been typed, type the file name. The file name should be preceded by a backslash.

For example, the path name for the Gone Fishing bitmap image file stored in the WINNT folder on drive C is: C:\WINNT\GONE FISHING.BMP. The file extension (.bmp) identifies the file as a bitmap image file. File extensions must be specified in a path name. Using the Run command and this path name, you can launch the Paint program and display the Gone Fishing image in the Paint window.

Although the Run command is extremely useful when launching programs and opening files or folders, you also can use the Run command to display a Web page in your Web browser window. For example, using the Run command and typing the URL (uniform resource locator) for the Federal Bureau of Investigation (www.fbi.gov) will launch the Internet Explorer program and display the Federal Bureau of Investigation home page in the Internet Explorer window.

Viewing Computers and Computer Resources on a Network

If the computer is connected to a network, you have many services and computer resources available to you. One method of viewing shared computer resources on other computers on the network is to use the My Network Places icon on the desktop. A second method of locating a computer on the network involves knowing the name of the computer and using the Search For Computers command to search for the computer on the network.

The following section illustrates how to use the My Network Places icon on the desktop to view the computers in the Editorial domain on the network. A **domain** is a collection of computers defined by the administrator of the network. The **administrator** is the person or persons responsible for setting up and managing the computers and users on the network. The following sections assume the network consists of a single domain named Editorial, that consists of three computers (Brad-wilson, Patty-smith, and Server), and you have logged on to the network from the Brad-wilson computer. If the Editorial domain and three computers are not available on your network, read the steps in the following sections without performing them.

Viewing Computers and Shared Computer Resources on a Network

My Network Places allows you to view the domains on a network, computers in a domain, and shared computer resources on a computer. Perform the following steps to view the computers in the Editorial domain and the shared folders on the Patty-smith computer.

Viewing Computers on a Network

When a computer on a network is turned on, it may take a few minutes for the computer icon to display in the My Network Places window on the other computers on the network. To check for the icon without closing the window, click the Refresh command on the View menu.

Steps: To View the Computers in a Domain and the Shared Resources on a Computer

1 **Double-click the My Network Places icon on the desktop. Point to the Entire Network icon in the My Network Places window.**

The My Network Places window displays (Figure 3-64). The left panel of the window contains information about My Network Places and the right panel contains the Add Network Place and Entire Network icons.

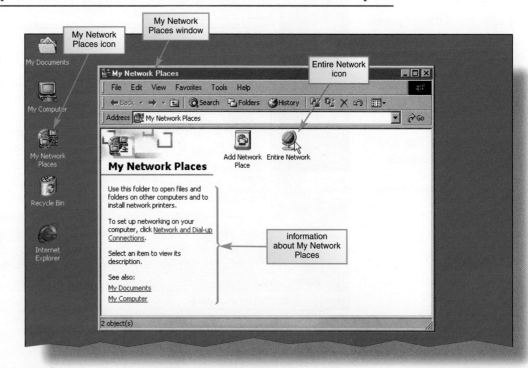

FIGURE 3-64

2 **Double-click Entire Network icon and then point to the entire contents hyperlink.**

The Entire Network window displays in the same window as the My Network Places window (Figure 3-65). The entire contents hyperlink displays in the left panel of the window along with hyperlinks for searching for a computer (Search for computers) and searching for files or folders (Search for files or folders). The right panel contains an image of a computer network.

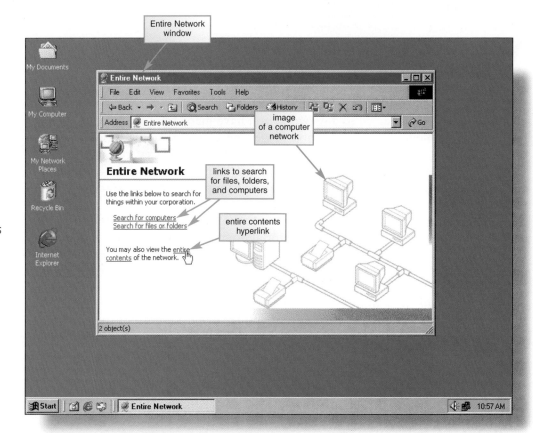

FIGURE 3-65

3 **Click entire contents and then point to the Microsoft Windows Network icon.**

The contents of the left panel change (Figure 3-66). The left panel includes hyperlinks to set up networking and dial-up Internet connections, display the My Documents window, and display the My Computer window. The right panel contains the Microsoft Windows Network icon, representing the Windows 2000 network.

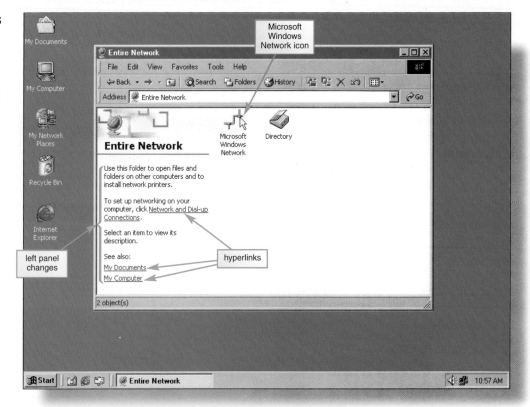

FIGURE 3-66

4 **Double-click the Microsoft Windows Network icon and then point to the Editorial icon.**

The Microsoft Windows Network window displays in the same window as the Entire Network window (Figure 3-67). The Editorial icon, representing the Editorial domain, displays in the right panel of the window.

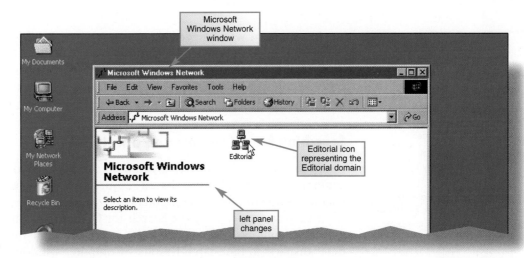

FIGURE 3-67

5 **Double-click the Editorial icon and then point to the Patty-smith icon.**

The Editorial window displays in the same window as the Microsoft Windows Network window (Figure 3-68). The contents of the left panel change and the Brad-wilson, Patty-smith, and Server icons display in the right panel, representing the computers in the Editorial domain.

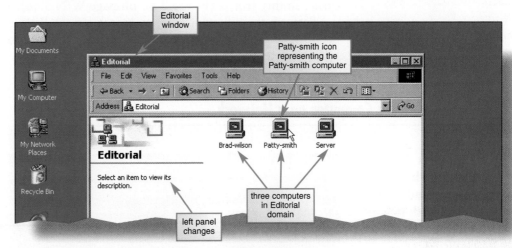

FIGURE 3-68

6 **Double-click the Patty-smith icon.**

The Patty-smith window displays in the same window as the Editorial window (Figure 3-69). The right panel contains three shared folders (W2000-PROJ1, W2000-PROJ2, and W2000-PROJ3) located on the Patty-smith computer. View the contents of a shared folder by double-clicking its icon.

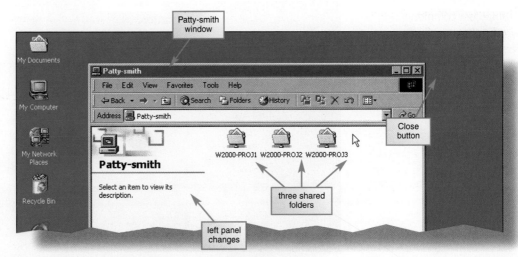

FIGURE 3-69

7 **Click the Close button in the Patty-smith window.**

The Patty-smith window closes.

Other Ways

1. Right-click My Network Places icon, click Explore
2. Right-click My Computer icon, click Explore, click My Network Places
3. Right-click Start button, click Explore, click My Network Places
4. Right-click My Network Places icon, click Search for Computers, type computer name, click Search Now button

In summary, while logged on to a computer (Brad-wilson) in the Editorial domain, you viewed the icons for the three computers (Brad-wilson, Server, and Patty-smith) and the three shared folders on the Patty-smith computer. The capability of locating other computers on a network and share resources with those computers is a basic, yet powerful, feature of a computer network.

Searching for a Computer on a Network

In the previous set of steps, you used the My Network Places icon to view the computers in a domain and shared resources on a computer. When a network consists of a large number of computers and you know the name of the computer you want to view, you can use the Search for Computers command to search for that particular computer. When a computer is located, the information about the computer displays in the Search Results - Computer window. This window is similar to the Search Results window that displayed when you searched for the coffee bean file earlier in this project (Figure 3-60 on page WIN 3.46).

Perform the following steps to search for the Patty-smith computer on the network. If the Patty-smith computer is not available on your network, read the following steps without performing them.

 To Search for a Computer on a Network

1 **Right-click the My Network Places icon on the desktop and then point to the Search for Computers command.**

A shortcut menu, containing the highlighted Search for Computers command, displays (Figure 3-70).

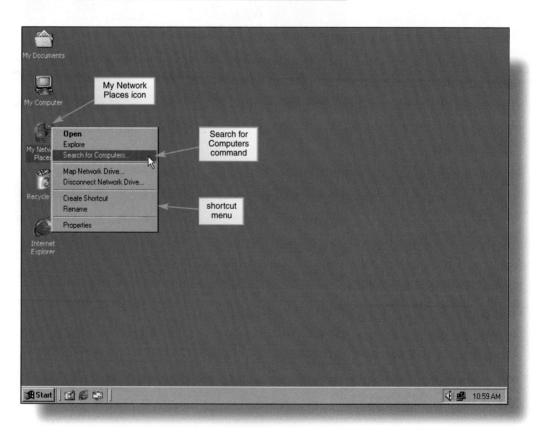

FIGURE 3-70

2 Click Search for Computers. Type patty-smith in the Computer Name text box in the Search Results - Computers window. Point to the Search Now button.

The Search Results - Computers window, containing the Search pane and Search Results - Computers pane, displays (Figure 3-71). The Search pane contains the Computer Name text box containing the Patty-smith computer name and hyperlinks to search for files and folders, computers, people, and the Internet. The Search Results - Computers pane contains three buttons (Name, Location, and Comment).

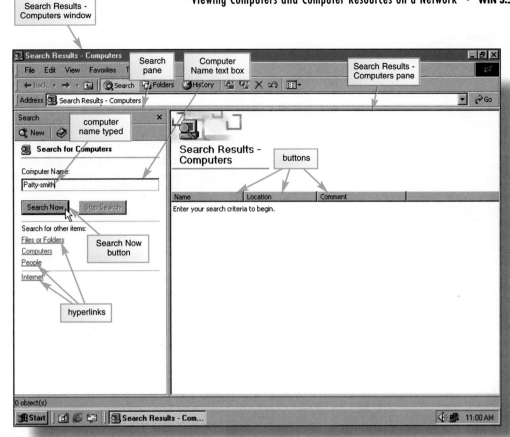

FIGURE 3-71

3 Click the Search Now button.

Windows 2000 searches the network and displays the computer name (Patty-smith), domain name (Editorial), and comment (Patty Smith's computer) in the Search Results - Computers pane (Figure 3-72). The comment contains identifying information entered by the computer user when the computer initially was connected to the network.

4 Click the Close button in the Search Results - Computers window.

The Search Results - Computers window closes.

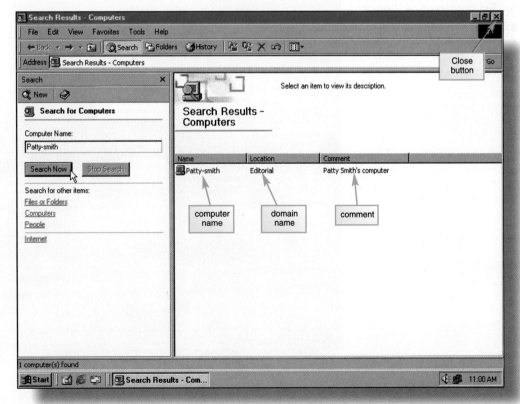

FIGURE 3-72

Other **Ways**

1. Click Start button, point to Search, click For Files or Folders, click Computers hyperlink, type computer name, click Search Now button
2. Right-click My Computer icon (or My Documents icon), click Search, click Computers hyperlink, type computer name, click Search Now button
3. Right-click Start button, click Search, click Computers hyperlink, type computer name, click Search Now button
4. Press CTRL+WINDOWS+F, type computer name, click Search Now button

Mapping a Drive Letter to a Network Resource

If you use a shared computer resource on a network computer frequently, you may want to assign an unused drive letter, such as drive E or drive F, to the resource. The process of assigning a drive letter to a shared computer resource is called **mapping a drive letter**. After mapping a drive letter to a computer resource, you can double-click the drive icon in the My Computer or Windows Explorer window to access the mapped drive.

Mapping a Drive Letter

To map a drive letter to a shared resource, you must know the path of the shared resource. The path (consisting of the computer name, location of the resource, and resource name) gives the operating system directions to find the resource on the network. For example, to map a drive letter to the W2000-PROJ1 folder on the Patty-smith computer, the path would be \\Patty-smith\W2000-PROJ1. Perform the following steps to map a drive letter (E) to the W2000-PROJ1 folder on the Patty-smith computer.

 To Map a Drive Letter

1 **Right-click the My Network Places icon and then point to the Map Network Drive command.**

A shortcut menu, containing the highlighted Map Network Drive command, displays (Figure 3-73).

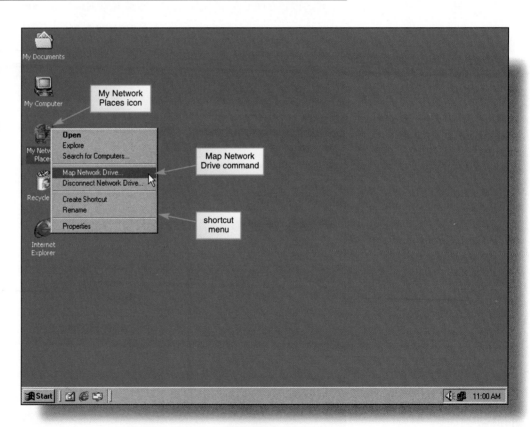

FIGURE 3-73

Step 2

Click Map Network Drive. Click the Folder box in the Map Network Drive dialog box and then type \\Patty-smith\W2000-PROJ1 **as the path. Point to the Finish button.**

The Map Network Drive dialog box displays, the next available drive letter (E:) displays in the Drive box, and the path to the W2000-PROJ1 folder (\\Patty-smith\W2000-PROJ1) is partially visible in the Folder box (Figure 3-74). The drive letter in the Drive box may be different on your computer.

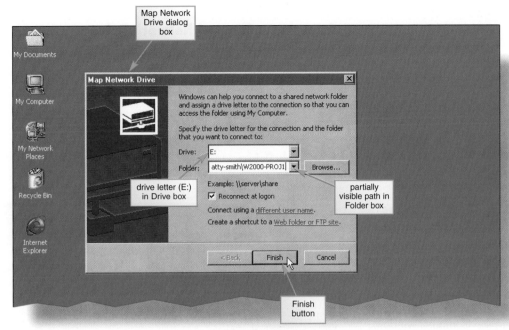

FIGURE 3-74

Step 3

Click the Finish button.

The Map Network Drive dialog box closes, the W2000-PROJ1 folder is mapped to network drive E, and the W2000-proj1 on 'Patty-smith' (E:) window displays (Figure 3-75). The left panel contains information about the W2000-proj1 on 'Patty-smith' (E:) folder. The right pane contains icons for the folder (Project 1 - Graphics Files) and two Microsoft Word documents (Project 1 - Assignments and Project 1 - Manuscript) stored in the W2000-proj1 folder on the Patty-smith computer.

Step 4

Click the Close button in the W2000-proj1 on 'Patty-smith' (E:) window.

The W2000-proj1 on 'Patty-smith' (E:) window closes.

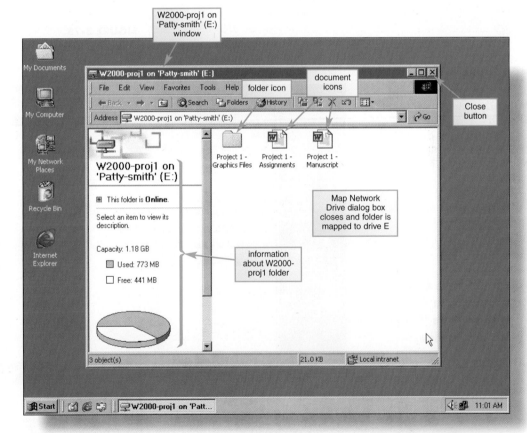

FIGURE 3-75

Other Ways

1. Right-click My Computer icon, click Map Network Drive, type path, click Finish button

Accessing a Mapped Network Drive

After mapping a network drive to the W2000-PROJ1 folder on the Patty-smith computer, you access the mapped folder by double-clicking the drive E icon in the My Computer or Windows Exploring window. Perform the following steps to access the mapped network drive E.

Steps **To Access a Mapped Network Drive**

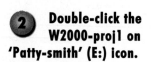 **Double-click the My Computer icon on the desktop. Point to the W2000-proj1 on 'Patty-smith' (E:) icon in the My Computer window.**

The My Computer window, containing the W2000-proj1 on 'Patty-smith' (E:) icon, displays (Figure 3-76).

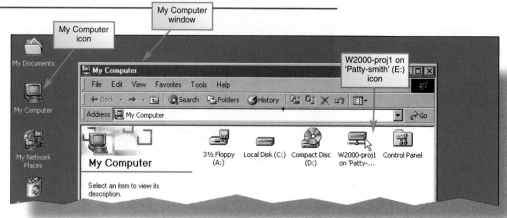

FIGURE 3-76

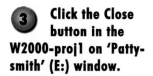 **Double-click the W2000-proj1 on 'Patty-smith' (E:) icon.**

The W2000-proj1 on 'Patty-smith' (E:) window displays (Figure 3-77). The folder and two document icons in the W2000-proj1 folder display in the right panel of the window.

 Click the Close button in the W2000-proj1 on 'Patty-smith' (E:) window.

The W2000-proj1 on 'Patty-smith' (E:) window closes.

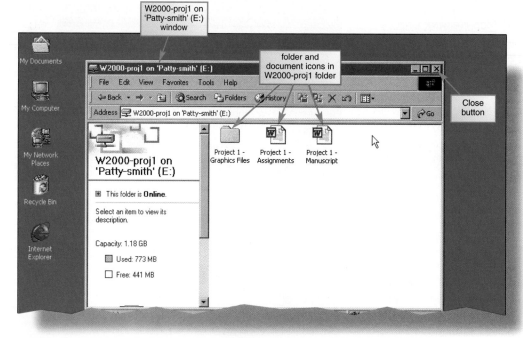

FIGURE 3-77

Other Ways

1. Right-click My Computer icon, click Open, double-click mapped drive icon
2. Right-click My Computer icon, click Explore, double-click mapped drive icon

Disconnecting a Mapped Network Drive

After mapping a network letter to the W2000-proj1 folder on the Patty-smith computer, return the network drive letters to their original configuration by disconnecting the network drive E. Perform the following steps to disconnect the network drive E.

To Disconnect a Mapped Network Drive

1 **Right-click the My Network Places icon and then point to the Disconnect Network Drive command.**

A shortcut menu, containing the highlighted Disconnect Network Drive command, displays (Figure 3-78).

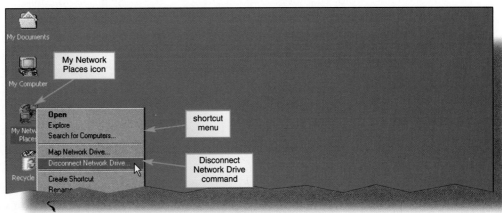

FIGURE 3-78

2 **Click Disconnect Network Drive and point to the OK button.**

The Disconnect Network Drive dialog box, containing the Select the drive(s) you want to disconnect list box, displays (Figure 3-79). The highlighted drive E icon and path display in the list box.

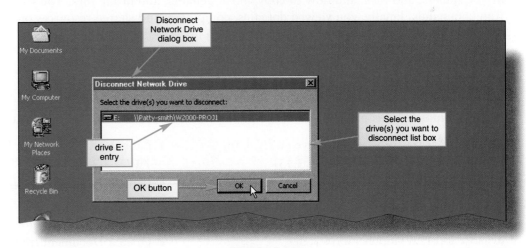

3 **Click the OK button.**

FIGURE 3-79

Windows 2000 disconnects the network drive E from the W2000-proj1 folder on the Patty-smith computer.

Shutting Down Windows 2000

After completing work with Windows 2000, you may wish to shut down Windows 2000 using the Shut Down command on the Start menu. If you are sure you want to shut down Windows 2000, perform the following steps. If you do not want to shut down Windows 2000 at this time, read the steps without actually performing them.

TO SHUT DOWN WINDOWS 2000

1 Click the Start button on the taskbar and then point to Shut Down on the Start menu.

2 Click Shut Down. Use the UP ARROW or DOWN ARROW key to display the words, Shut down, in the What do you want the computer to do? box.

3 Click the OK button.

Windows 2000 is shut down.

C A S E   P E R S P E C T I V E   S U M M A R Y

The network administrator emphasized the importance of users being able to control and manage windows on the Windows 2000 desktop, their effective use of Windows 2000 Explorer, and their ability to locate computers and computer resources on the network. With those words in mind, you developed a one-hour class for employees with little computer experience and offered the classes during normal business hours, on alternating weeknights, and on Saturday mornings. The network administrator was pleased with the results and recommended you for a newly developed networking position in his department.

Project Summary

In this project, you viewed icons in windows in different formats. After opening a document and launching an application program, you learned to manage windows on the desktop. Next, you saw how to copy, move, and delete files from an open window. You gained knowledge of Windows 2000 Explorer, both in how to display drives, folders, and files, and how to copy, move, rename, and delete files. You learned about the Search and Run commands. Finally, you viewed domains, computers, and shared resources on a network, searched for a computer on a network, mapped a drive letter to a network resource, and accessed the mapped network drive.

What You Should Know

Having completed this project, you now should be able to perform the following tasks:

- Access a Mapped Network Drive *(WIN 3.56)*
- Cascade Open Windows *(WIN 3.15)*
- Change the Format of the Icons in a Window *(WIN 3.6)*
- Close Expanded Folders *(WIN 3.35)*
- Close Open Windows *(WIN 3.21)*
- Close the Exploring Window *(WIN 3.41)*
- Copy a File in Explorer by Right-Dragging *(WIN 3.36)*
- Copy Files from a Folder onto a Floppy Disk *(WIN 3.23)*
- Delete Files on a Floppy Disk *(WIN 3.40)*
- Disconnect a Mapped Network Drive *(WIN 3.57)*
- Display Folder Properties *(WIN 3.43)*
- Display Hard Disk Properties *(WIN 3.42)*
- Display the Contents of a Drive *(WIN 3.29)*
- Display the Contents of a Floppy Disk *(WIN 3.38)*
- Expand a Drive *(WIN 3.30)*
- Expand a Folder *(WIN 3.31)*
- Find a File by Name *(WIN 3.45)*
- Launch a Program Using the Run Command *(WIN 3.47)*
- Launch an Application Program from a Window *(WIN 3.14)*
- Launch an Application Program from Explorer *(WIN 3.33)*
- Launch Explorer *(WIN 3.26)*
- Make a Window the Active Window *(WIN 3.17)*
- Map a Drive Letter *(WIN 3.54)*
- Open a Document from a Window *(WIN 3.12)*
- Open a Folder Window *(WIN 3.22)*
- Open and Maximize the My Computer Window *(WIN 3.5)*
- Quit an Application Program *(WIN 3.34)*
- Rename a File *(WIN 3.39)*
- Search for a Computer on a Network *(WIN 3.52)*
- Shut Down Windows 2000 *(WIN 3.57)*
- Tile Open Windows *(WIN 3.19)*
- Undo Cascading *(WIN 3.18)*
- Undo Tiling *(WIN 3.20)*
- View the Computers in a Domain and the Shared Resources on a Computer *(WIN 3.49)*
- View the Contents of a Drive *(WIN 3.9)*
- View the Contents of a Folder *(WIN 3.10, WIN3.32)*

P. 150

Test Your Knowledge

1 True/False

Instructions: Circle T if the statement is true or F if the statement is false.

T F 1. A hard disk is generally faster and has more storage capacity than the floppy disk on a computer.

T F 2. To open a folder, double-click the folder icon.

T F 3. You can open documents from a window, but to launch an application program you must click the Start button and use the Programs submenu.

T F 4. After you cascade or tile windows, you must restart Windows 2000 in order for the windows to display as they did before you cascaded or tiled them.

T F 5. Copying and moving files is a common occurrence in Windows 2000.

T F 6. One way to launch Windows 2000 Explorer is to right-click the My Computer icon and then click Explore.

T F 7. To display the contents of drive C on your computer in the right panel of the Contents pane of the Exploring window, click the plus sign in the small box next to the drive C icon.

T F 8. After you expand a drive or folder, the information displayed in the right panel of the Contents pane of the Exploring window is the same as the information displayed below the drive or folder icon in the Folders pane.

T F 9. To find a file by its name, you can use the Search command on the Start menu.

T F 10. My Network Places allows you to enter a computer name and search the network for that computer.

2 Multiple Choice

Instructions: Circle the correct response.

1. To display the details of the files found in the folder within a folder window, _____ .
   a. click Views on the menu bar and then click List
   b. click Edit on the menu bar and then click Details
   c. right-click the folder, point to Views, and then click Details
   d. click the Views button on the Standard Buttons toolbar and then click Details

2. To cascade all the open windows on the desktop, _____ .
   a. click File on the menu bar and then click Cascade Windows
   b. right-click the taskbar and then click Cascade Windows on the shortcut menu
   c. right-click the Start button, click Properties, and then click Cascade Windows
   d. right-click the desktop and then click Cascade Windows on the shortcut menu

3. When using the Open each folder in the same window option to browse windows, _____ .
   a. clicking the BACK button will display one window back from the window you currently are viewing
   b. you increase the probability of window clutter on your desktop
   c. you cannot use the copy and paste method
   d. the window size changes depending on the number of files and folders you want to display

(continued)

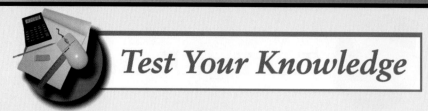

Test Your Knowledge

Test Your Knowledge *(continued)*

4. To select multiple icons in a folder at one time, _____ .
   a. right-click each icon
   b. press and hold down the SHIFT key and then point to each icon you want to select
   c. press and hold down the CTRL key and then double-click each icon you want to select
   d. press and hold down the CTRL key and then click each icon you want to select

5. When you right-click an icon and a shortcut menu displays, the command in bold means _____ .
   a. this command cannot be used at the current time
   b. this command will be executed if you double-click the icon
   c. this is the only command you can use at this time
   d. this is the preferred command to use and if you decide to click another command, Windows 2000 may not be able to carry out the command successfully

6. To display the contents of a folder in the Exploring window, _____ .
   a. click the plus sign next to the folder icon
   b. right-click the folder icon in the Folders pane of the window
   c. point to the folder icon in the Contents pane of the window
   d. click the folder icon in the Folders pane of the window

7. Before you can copy a file from one folder to another folder in Explorer by right-dragging, you must _____ .
   a. display the icon for the file you want to copy in the right panel of the Contents pane of the Exploring window
   b. display the icon for the file you want to copy in the Folders pane of the Exploring window
   c. open the My Computer window to display the folder where you want to copy the file
   d. display the folder where you want to copy the file in the right panel of the Contents pane

8. The Run command on the Start menu _____ .
   a. can be used only when no other way to launch a program is available
   b. is most useful when you are not sure of the actual name of the program
   c. is useful when you need to launch an application program quickly
   d. must be used if the program is stored with a specific path on your hard drive

9. You view the computers on a network using _____ .
   a. My Network Places
   b. The Microsoft Network
   c. the Internet
   d. the Search command

10. A _____ is a name assigned to a group of computers.
   a. computer name
   b. user name
   c. domain
   d. password

Test Your Knowledge

3 Understanding the Exploring Window

Instructions: In Figure 3-80, arrows point to several items in the WINNT window. Identify the items or objects in the spaces provided.

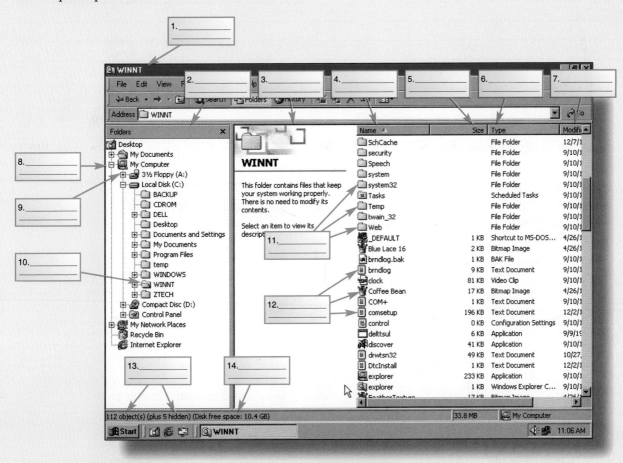

FIGURE 3-80

4 Copying Files

Instructions: Copy the Blue Lace 16 file from the WINNT folder shown in Figure 3-81 on the next page onto a floppy disk in drive A. In the space below and on the next page, write the steps to copy the file using the copy and paste method and Windows 2000 Explorer.

Copy and Paste method

right click Blue Lace to highlight
click copy
go to A drive
right click paste

(continued)

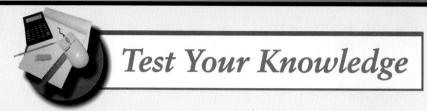

Test Your Knowledge

Copying Files *(continued)*

Windows 2000 Explorer

_____

_____

_____

_____

FIGURE 3-81

5 Viewing a Computer on a Network

Instructions: In the spaces provided, list the steps to view the shared folders on the Charlie-potter computer in the Sales domain on the Microsoft Windows network.

1. _____ double click my network _____
2. _____ point to entire network _____
3. _____ double click _____
4. _____ point to entire content _____
5. _____ then double click point to microsoft windows network _____
6. _____ double click + point to Sail mail icon _____

   double click Sail mail icon

   double click the folders item

Use Help

1 Using Windows Help

Instructions: Use Windows Help and a computer to perform the following tasks.

1. If necessary, start Microsoft Windows 2000.
2. Answer the following questions about paths.
   a. What is a path? *windows 2000 uses paths command to search for executable files in the directory you specify*
   b. List three ways to open a document or run a program by specifying its path. *1) prune the the program i.e.* *2) start, run, typing the path 3) click start, point to programs, pointing to accessories, clicking command prompt, typing the path in the ms-dos window.*
   c. How do you specify a path? *type the drive letter followed by a colon : or a backslash \, types the name of the folders + subfolders that contain the file, sep. with a \, type the file n folder you want to open*
   d. Specify the path for a file named Nelson's Math Notes that is stored in the Nelson Files folder within the Office folder within the Program Files folder in drive C of your computer. _____
   C: \ Program Files Folder\nelson\Nelsons mathNOTES
3. Launch Windows Help. In the Windows 2000 window, click the Index tab, and then type `windows explorer` in the Type in the keyword to find text box. Answer the following questions about Windows Explorer.
   a. What method is recommended to copy a file or folder? *edit, copy, paste,*
   b. How do you select consecutive files or folders using Explorer? *Click the first item, press down + hold down the shift, + then click the last item*
   c. How do you select nonconsecutive files or folders using Explorer? *press + hold down CTRL + then click each item*
   d. While dragging to delete a file, how do you delete a file without first moving the file to the Recycle Bin? *right Click the file then delete*
4. You recently wrote a business letter to a friend explaining how to install Microsoft Windows 2000 Professional. You want to see what else you said in the letter, but you cannot remember the name of the file or where you stored the file on your computer. You decide to check Windows Help to determine the locations you could check to locate a misplaced file instead of using the Search command to find the file. List the first three locations suggested by Windows Help. Write those locations in the spaces provided.
   Location 1: *Start, search, files or folders*
   Location 2: *containing text*
   Location 3: *look in, click the drive, folder, or network you want to search.*
5. You and your brother each have a computer in your bedroom. A printer is attached to your computer and your brother, whose computer does not have a printer, would like to print some of his more colorful documents using the printer attached to your computer. You have heard that for a reasonable cost you can buy a network card and some cable and hook up the two computers on a network. Then, your brother can print documents stored on his computer on the printer connected to your computer. Using Windows Help, determine if you can share your printer. If so, what must you do in Windows 2000 to make this work? Print the Help pages that document your answer.
6. The Windows 2000 Professional operating system is installed on your computer and the computer is connected to a network. You read that Windows 2000 has tools designed for working with files stored on your computer and files stored on the network. You are unsure whether you should use My Briefcase or Offline Files to work with the files on your computer. Using Windows Help, learn about the difference between My Briefcase and Offline Files. Print the Help pages that explain My Briefcase and Offline Files.

1 File and Program Properties

Instructions: Use a computer to perform the following tasks and answer the questions.

1. If necessary, start Microsoft Windows 2000.
2. Double-click the My Computer icon. Maximize the My Computer window.
3. Double-click the Local Disk (C:) icon. Double-click the WINNT icon. If necessary, click Show Files.
4. Scroll until the Rhododendron icon is visible (Figure 3-82). If the Rhododendron icon is not available on your computer, find another Paint icon.

FIGURE 3-82

5. Right-click the Rhododendron icon. Click Properties on the shortcut menu.
6. Answer the following questions about the Rhododendron file:
   a. What type of file is Rhododendron? _Bitmap Image_
   b. What is the path for the location of the Rhododendron file? _C:\WINNT_
   c. What is the size (in bytes) of the Rhododendron file? _17,362_
   d. When was the file created? _March 7/05_
   e. When was the file last modified? _Dec 7/99_
   f. When was the file last accessed? _Oct 11/05_
7. Click the Cancel button in the Rhododendron Properties dialog box.
8. Scroll the right panel of the WINNT window until the notepad icon displays.

In the Lab

9. Right-click the notepad icon. Click Properties on the shortcut menu.
10. Answer the following questions:
    a. What type of file is notepad? _application_
    b. What is the path of the notepad file? _C:\WINNT_
    c. How big is the notepad file when stored on disk? _53,248 bytes_
    d. What is the file version of the notepad file? _5.0.2140.1_
    e. What is the file's description? _Notepad_
    f. Who is the copyright owner of notepad? _Copyright (c) Microsoft Corp 1981-1999_
11. Click the Cancel button in the Notepad Properties dialog box.
12. Close all open windows.

2 My Computer

Instructions: Use a computer to perform the following tasks.

1. If necessary, start Microsoft Windows 2000.
2. Double-click the My Computer icon. Maximize the My Computer window.
3. Double-click the Local Disk (C:) icon. Double-click the WINNT icon. If necessary, click Show Files.
4. Double-click the notepad icon in the WINNT window to launch the Notepad application program. Create the text document illustrated in Figure 3-83.

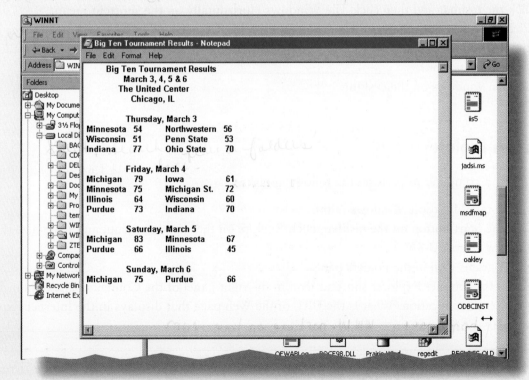

FIGURE 3-83

(continued)

In the Lab

My Computer *(continued)*

5. Perform the following steps to save the Notepad document in the My Documents folder using the name, Big Ten Tournament Results. Click File on the menu bar and then click Save As. When the Save As dialog box displays, type `Big Ten Tournament Results` in the File name text box. Click the My Documents button on the shortcut bar. Click the Save button in the Save As dialog box.

6. Click the Close button in the Notepad window. Click the Close button in the WINNT window.

7. Double-click the My Documents icon on the desktop. Is the Big Ten Tournament Results icon in the My Documents folder? _____ *Yes*

8. Double-click the Big Ten Tournament Results icon to open its window.

9. Right-click the taskbar and click Tile Windows Horizontally on the shortcut menu. Describe the desktop? *Big Ten file is on the top half of the Screen, My documents on the bottr*

10. Click the Big Ten Tournament Results - Notepad button on the taskbar. Using the DOWN ARROW key, move the insertion point to the end of the document. Press the ENTER key. Type `Tournament MVP: Robert Dodd` and then press the ENTER key.

11. Save the modified document. Print the modified document.

12. Close the Big Ten Tournament Results - Notepad window.

13. Click the My Documents icon on the taskbar.

14. Insert a formatted floppy disk in drive A of your computer.

15. Double-click the My Computer icon on the desktop. Double-click the 3½ Floppy (A:) icon. Are the two windows tiled on the desktop? _____ *Yes*

16. Right-click the taskbar and then click Tile Windows Horizontally on the shortcut menu.

17. Right-drag the Big Ten Tournament Results icon in the My Documents window to an open area of the 3½ Floppy (A:) window. Click Move Here on the shortcut menu. What window(s) contain(s) the Big Ten Tournament Results icon? _____

18. Close all open windows on the desktop.

3 Windows Explorer

Instructions: Use a computer to perform the following tasks.

1. If necessary, start Microsoft Windows 2000.

2. Right-click the Start button on the taskbar, click Explore on the shortcut menu, and maximize the Start Menu window (Figure 3-84).

3. Click the Programs icon in the Folders pane.

4. Double-click the Internet Explorer shortcut icon in the right panel of the Contents pane to launch the Internet Explorer application. What is the URL of the Web page that displays in the Internet Explorer window? *my home page, www.portage on line.com*

5. Click the URL in the Address bar in the Internet Explorer window to select it. Type `www.scsite.com` and then press the ENTER key.

In the Lab

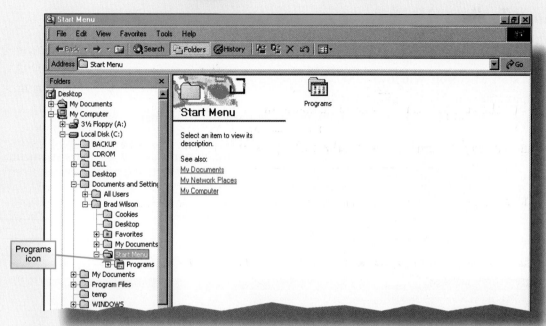

FIGURE 3-84

6. Right-click the Course Technology logo on the Web page, click Save Picture As on the shortcut menu, and click the Save button in the Save Picture dialog box to save the image in the My Pictures folder.

7. Click the Close button in the Microsoft Internet Explorer window.

8. Scroll the Folders pane to make the My Documents folder visible and click the plus sign to the left of the My Documents folder.

9. Click the My Pictures folder icon.

10. Right-click the logo icon and click Properties.
    What type of file is the logo file? ____*file folder*____
    When was the file last modified? _____
    What is the size of the file? ____191,237,755 bytes____

11. Click the Cancel button in the logo Properties dialog box.

12. Insert a formatted floppy disk in drive A of your computer.

13. Right-drag the logo icon onto the 3½ Floppy (A:) icon. Click Move Here on the shortcut menu. Click the 3½ Floppy (A:) icon in the Folders pane. Is the logo file stored on the floppy disk? _____

14. Click the Search button on the Standards Buttons toolbar and click the People hyperlink in the Search pane.

15. Type Steven Forsythe in the Name text box.

16. Click the Look in box arrow and then click Bigfoot Internet Directory Service in the Look in list.

17. Click the Find Now button. How many entries are listed for Steven Forsythe? _____
    What is the first e-mail address listed for Steven Forsythe? _____

18. Click the Close button in the Find People dialog box.

19. Click the Close button in the 3½ Floppy (A:) window.

In the Lab

4 Windows Toolbars

Instructions: Use a computer to perform the following tasks.

1. If necessary, start Microsoft Windows 2000.
2. Open and maximize the My Computer window.
3. Display the icons in the My Computer window using the Large Icons format.
4. Click View on the menu bar and then point to Toolbars (Figure 3-85).
5. If a check mark does not display to the left of the Address Bar command on the Toolbars submenu, click Address Bar. The Address bar displays in the My Computer window.
6. Click the Address box arrow.
7. Click the Local Disk (C:) icon in the Address list. How did the window change? _____

_____

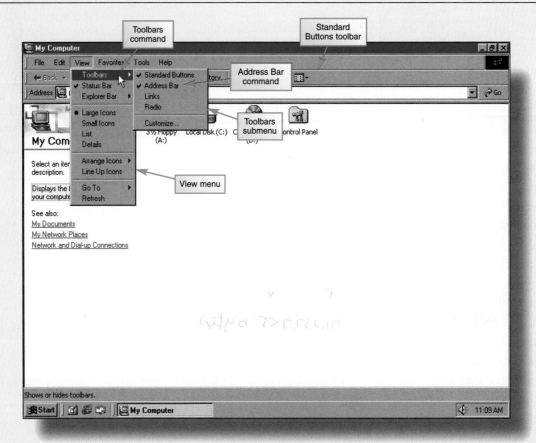

FIGURE 3-85

8. Double-click the WINNT icon. If necessary, click Show Files. What happened? _____

_____

9. In the WINNT window, if the Standard Buttons toolbar does not display, click View on the menu bar, point to Toolbars, and then click Standard Buttons on the Toolbars submenu.

In the Lab

10. Insert a formatted floppy disk in drive A of your computer.
11. If necessary, scroll down until the Coffee Bean icon displays in the window. If the Coffee Bean icon does not display on your computer, find another Paint icon. Click the Coffee Bean icon and then click the Copy To button on the Standard Buttons toolbar.
12. Click the plus sign to the left of the My Computer icon, click the 3½ Floppy (A:) icon, and then click the OK button.
13. Click the Address box arrow and then click the 3½ Floppy (A:) icon in the Address list.
14. The Coffee Bean icon displays in the 3½ Floppy (A:) window (Figure 3-86).

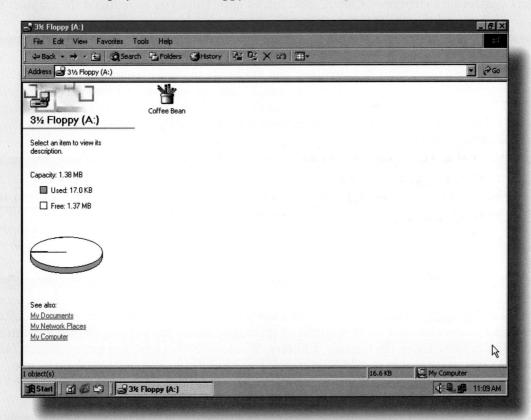

FIGURE 3-86

15. Click the Coffee Bean icon in the 3½ Floppy (A:) window to select the icon, click the Delete button on the Standard Buttons toolbar, and then click the Yes button in the Confirm File Delete dialog box.
16. In the 3½ Floppy (A:) window, return the toolbar status to what it was prior to Step 5.
17. Close the 3½ Floppy (A:) window.

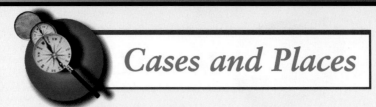

Cases and Places

The difficulty of these case studies varies:
◗ are the least difficult; ◗◗ are more difficult; and ◗◗◗ are the most difficult.

1 ◗ Your seven-year old brother cannot get enough of the graphics that display on computers. Lately, he has been hounding you to show him all the graphics images that are available on your computer. You have finally agreed to show him. Using techniques you learned in this project, display the icons for all the graphics image files that are stored on your computer (*Hint*: Graphics files on Windows 2000 computers contain file extensions of .bmp, .pcx, .tif, or .gif). Once you have found the graphics files, display all of them and then print the three you like best.

2 ◗ Your employer suspects that the computer you use has been used by someone else during off-hours for noncompany business. She has asked you to search your computer for all files that have been created or modified during the last 10 days. When you find the files, determine if any of them are Notepad files or Paint files that you did not create or modify. Summarize the number of them and the date on which they were created or modified in a brief report to your employer.

3 ◗◗ Backing up files is an important way to protect data and ensure it is not lost or destroyed accidentally. File backup on a personal computer can use a variety of devices and techniques. Using the Internet, a library, personal computer magazines, and other resources, determine the types of devices used to store backed up data, schedules, methods, and techniques for backing up data, and the consequences of not backing up data. Write a brief report of your findings.

4 ◗◗ A hard disk must be maintained to be used most efficiently. This maintenance includes deleting old files, defragmenting a disk so it is not wasteful of space, and from time to time, finding and attempting to correct disk failures. Using the Internet, a library, Windows 2000 Help, and other research facilities, determine the maintenance that should be performed on hard disks. This includes the type of maintenance, when it should be performed, how long it takes to perform the maintenance, and the risks of not performing the maintenance. Write a brief report on the information you obtain.

5 ◗◗ A file system is the overall structure in which files are named, stored, and organized. Windows 2000 supports three file systems: FAT, FAT32, and NTFS. You must choose a file system when you install Windows 2000, install a new hard disk, or format an existing hard disk or floppy disk. Before deciding which file system is right for you, you should research the three file systems to understand the benefits and limitations of each system. Write a brief report comparing the three file systems. Discuss the benefits and limitations of each system.

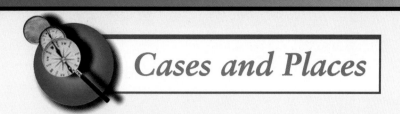

Cases and Places

6 ▶▶▶ In addition to using Windows 2000 on network computers, other networks (Novell NetWare, Banyan VINES, Artisoft LANtastic, and Artisoft POSConnect) are available. Using the Internet, magazines, newspapers, and other resources, obtain information about two of these networks. Prepare a report describing the purpose of each network, for whom the network is designed, costs of purchasing the network software, and additional interesting features of the software and network.

7 ▶▶▶ Visit a business in your area that uses a network. Interview the network administrator and several employees who use the network. Determine the type of network being used. Inquire about any installation problems, problems that currently exist, what problems the network solved, and ways to improve the network. Summarize your findings in a report.

8 ▶▶▶ Data stored on disk is one of a company's most valuable assets. If that data were to be stolen, lost, or compromised so it could not be accessed, the company could go out of business. Therefore, companies go to great lengths to protect their data. Visit a company or business in your area. Find out how it protects its data against viruses, unauthorized access, and even against such natural disasters as fire and floods. Prepare a brief report that describes the company's procedures. In your report, point out any areas where you find the company has not protected its data adequately.